Talking About Japan Updated *Q&A*

装幀 ● 菊地信義
装画 ● 野村俊夫

執筆 ● 井上恵一
　　　小沢絵里子
　　　佐近忠弘
　　　保坂美枝

翻訳 ● Patricia Mari Katayama
　　　Hisako Nozaki Ifshin
　　　Kirsten Rochelle McIvor
　　　Babel International
　　　David Thayne
　　　William R. Carter
　　　Giles Murray

編集 ● 翻訳情報センター

Published by Kodansha International Ltd.,
17-14 Otowa 1-chome, Bunkyo-ku, Tokyo 112-8652.

First Edition 2000
00 01 02 03 04　10 9 8 7 6 5 4 3 2 1

ISBN4-7700-2568-8

増補改訂第2版
英語で話す「日本」Q&A
Talking About Japan Updated *Q&A*

講談社インターナショナル［編］

まえがき

　この『英語で話す「日本」Q&A』は、1996年に創刊したバイリンガル・ブックスの第1弾として世に送り出したものです。日本に関する様々な分野の知識を、できるだけ簡潔に、かつ面白く紹介し、そしてそれをやさしい英語で表現したもので、外国の人たちと交流するとき身近に携えておきたい情報源としてご好評をいただき、4年の間に23刷を重ねることができました。

　しかし、今や、時は2000年となり、21世紀に向けて日本も刻々と変化を続けています。その変化の姿を反映させるために、ここに第2版をお届けすることになりました。改訂では、特に情報の基盤となる統計のデータを最新のものに改め、また、各分野にわたって情報を広げ、約1割のページ増となりました。

　講談社インターナショナルは35年にわたって、日本の文化を海外に紹介する出版物の刊行を続けています。今はインターネットに象徴されるように、各国の文化が国境をかるがると越えて交流する時代となり、わたくしたちに課せられた使命にもおのずと新しいテーマが加わってきました。その一つが日本人のバイリンガル化に対応する出版、このバイリンガル・ブックスの刊行でした。小社が今まで培ってきた英語出版と文化紹介のノーハウを駆使して、新しいテーマの本を次々とお届けしています。

　このシリーズが、日本の読者に役立つだけではなく、外国の人たちの日本語の勉強にもなり、日本に対する理解が促進されることも期待しています。

講談社インターナショナル株式会社

PREFACE

This book was originally issued in 1996 as the first in the Bilingual Books series. It has gained a reputation as a convenient source of information for communicating with those new to Japanese culture, covering various topics about Japan with compact and interesting explanations in simple English. The result has been 23 reprints in four years.

Now at the start of a new century in the year 2000, Japan is undergoing significant changes. And in order to reflect these changes, we decided to issue this revised version. This new version includes the latest statistical information that supports the narrative, and new information has also been added, increasing the overall volume of the book by about ten percent.

Kodansha International has introduced Japanese culture abroad through publications for some 35 years. With the Internet and other technology making it easier than ever for the cultures of the world to go beyond their borders, new facets have been added to our role. One such facet is the publication of this and other Bilingual Books that provide information in two languages. We will continue to use our expertise in English publications and introducing culture to issue many more such books in the future.

We hope that this series will be helpful for both Japanese readers as well as for those studying the Japanese language, while promoting an understanding of Japan.

Kodansha International Ltd.

目次

CONTENTS

 Land and Nature of Japan

Land of Japan

Geograohy of Japan

Climate of Japan

Natural Disaster in Japan

② 日本のルーツと歴史

日本の誕生

日本の国歌・国旗

日本語

日本の天皇

Origin and History of Japan

日本の歴史

明治から現代へ

③ 日本の政治と経済

日本の憲法

Japanese History

From Meiji the Present

3 Government and Economy

Constitution of Japan

4 Japanese Way of Life and Society

The Japanese at Work

Pensions

Health Care in Japan

Religions in Japan

5 Japanese Culture

Contemporary Culture

Traditional Culture of Japan

⑥ 日本人の衣食住

日本人の衣生活

日本人の食生活

6 Clothing, Cuisine and Housing in Japan

Clothing of the Japanese

Culinary Life of the Japanese

⑦ 生活と習慣

Life and Customs

1

日本の国土と自然

Land and Nature of Japan

Mt. Fuji ▶

日本の国土

Q 日本は地球上のどこにあるのですか?

中央に日本がある**世界地図**を想像してみてください。どの国でも,自分の国を地図の中心に据えています。日本の地図もそうです。

そこで,あなたがヨーロッパ人なら,日本を英語でFar East「極東」と称したように,イタリア半島の南端からアテネを経て,**北緯36度**に沿って東へ東へと進み,アジア大陸のイラン北部から中国大陸を横断し,そのはずれの海を渡れば**日本列島**の中央部にたどりつくと考えてください。

もし,あなたがアメリカに居るとすれば,サンフランシスコから太平洋を真西に進めば日本の東京にたどりつきます。緯度からすれば,ニューヨークは本州の北端の青森県,パリは北海道の北部にあたりますし,ロンドンは日本の**北端**よりも上の緯度の位置になります。

Land of Japan

• Where on the earth is Japan located?

Imagine a **world map** with Japan in the center. In any country, people make maps with their own country in the middle, and such is the case with the Japanese.

If you are in Europe, Japan is in the Far East, and you would get there by heading east starting from the southern tip of the Italian Peninsula. You would go through Athens, continue to make your way east along the **36 degree north latitude** to Iran, and then after traversing the Asian Continent across China and crossing the Sea of Japan, you will reach the center of the **Japanese islands**.

If you are in America, go due west from San Francisco and you will eventually reach Tōkyō. New York is on the same latitude as Aomori Prefecture, the northern part of Honshū (the main island) of Japan. Paris is on the same latitude as the northern part of Hokkaidō and London is located north of the **northernmost tip** of Japan.

Q 日本の大きさはどれくらいですか?

　　　日本の**陸地の面積**は約378,000km²です。日本は小さい国とよく言われますが，それでも，日本**列島**の北から南のはてまでとなると，約3,500kmはあり，その気候や風景の変化たるや他の国とは違った多彩な姿を持っています。

　　　しかし実を言うと，アメリカの州の1つであるカリフォルニア州よりも日本が小さいということは，あまり知られていません。カリフォルニア州は約411,000km²もあります。

Q 日本の現在の領土はいつ決まったのですか?

　　　1945年，日本は第2次世界大戦の敗戦国となり，この時点で，日清戦争 (1894年) 以前の領土

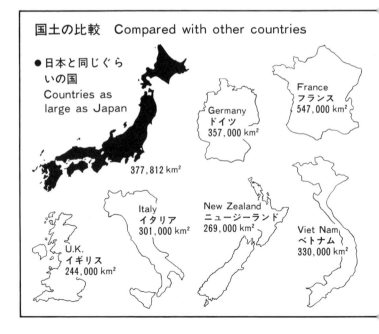

国土の比較　Compared with other countries

●日本と同じぐらいの国
Countries as large as Japan

377,812 km²

Germany
ドイツ
357,000 km²

France
フランス
547,000 km²

Italy
イタリア
301,000 km²

New Zealand
ニュージーランド
269,000 km²

Viet Nam
ベトナム
330,000 km²

U.K.
イギリス
244,000 km²

● How big is Japan?

Japan's **land area** is approximately 378,000 km². It is often said that Japan is a small country. However, the **archipelago** stretches some 3,500 km from the northernmost end to the southernmost, which means that climate and scenery vary greatly from region to region.

A fact that is not very well known is that Japan is smaller than California in the United States, which has a land area of about 411,000 km².

● When was Japan's present territory determined?

In 1945, when Japan was defeated in World War II, its land was reduced to its present size, the same size as it was prior to

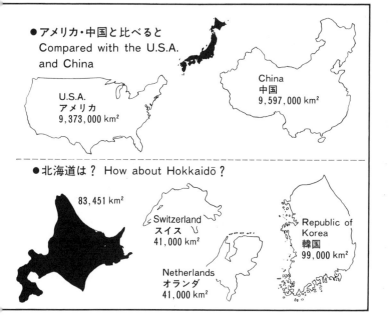

●アメリカ・中国と比べると
Compared with the U.S.A. and China

U.S.A.
アメリカ
9,373,000 km²

China
中国
9,597,000 km²

●北海道は？ How about Hokkaidō?

83,451 km²

Switzerland
スイス
41,000 km²

Netherlands
オランダ
41,000 km²

Republic of Korea
韓国
99,000 km²

に縮小させられ，現在は，北海道，本州，四国，
九州，沖縄と数千の小さな島々で成り立ってい
ます。

　沖縄は，1951年のサンフランシスコ講和条約
締結後も，そのままアメリカの施政権下に置か
れ，日本に復帰したのは1972年でした。

　終戦までに日本が領土としていたのは，現在
の領土のほかに，**樺太**，**千島列島**，韓国，台湾
がありますが，世界の目からは，日本が「**侵略**」
して保有したと解釈されました。

Kunashiri from a
height of 6,000
meters

　現在，千島列島の南部の歯舞諸島，色丹島，
国後島，択捉島は日本固有の**領土**であるという
主張のもとに，ロシアとの交渉が行われていま
す。

　沖縄県の八重山諸島の北，約160kmのところ
にある小島群の尖閣諸島は，沖縄県の石垣市
に属していますが，中国と台湾が**領土権**を主張
して問題になっています。

Ｑ 沖縄も昔から日本だったのですか？

The Shurei no Mon
of Shuri Castle in
Naha City

　明治維新（1868年）の時はまだ，沖縄は日本で
はなかったのです。沖縄の旧名の「琉球」という
のは中国人による命名で，15世紀初期から，琉
球王国という1つの国として存在していました。
しかし，国としての力は弱く，当時の中国の清
国と，日本の**薩摩藩**の両方に従属した形で存続
を保っていました。

　1872年に政府は琉球国王を琉球藩王として，
日本に組み込もうとします。そして，当時の清国
からの抗議がないまま，1879年になると，日本政
府は琉球を沖縄県にしてしまいました。

　沖縄に行くと，風土は日本でもあり，中国でも

the Sino-Japanese War in 1894. Today Japan consists of four main islands: Hokkaidō, Honshū, Shikoku, and Kyūshū, plus the Okinawa Islands, and thousands of other smaller islands.

Okinawa remained under American control even after the San Francisco Peace Treaty in 1951; it was returned to Japan in 1972.

Until the end of World War II, Japan owned **Sakhalin**, the **Kuril Islands**, Korea and Taiwan, which were regarded by the rest of the world as taken by **aggression**.

Currently, Japan claims the southern part of the Kuril Islands including the Habomai Islands, Shikotan, Kunashiri, and Etorofu as part of its **territory**, and negotiations with Russia are ongoing.

Another area in dispute is the Senkaku Islands, which are under the jurisdiction of Ishigaki City, 160 km north of the Yaeyama Islands in Okinawa Prefecture, for which not only Japan but also China and Taiwan claim **territorial rights**.

● Has Okinawa been a part of Japan from ancient times?

Okinawa was not a part of Japanese territory at the time of the **Meiji Restoration** (1868), the dawn of the modernization of Japan. Okinawa's former name, Ryūkyū, was given by the Chinese. The Ryūkyū Kingdom existed from the beginning of the 15th century, but since it was a weak country, it sought support from both the Ching Dynasty of China and the **Satsuma Clan** of Japan.

In 1872, the Japanese government tried to incorporate Ryūkyū into Japan and in 1879 they changed its name to Okinawa Prefecture without any protest from the Ching government.

Visitors may get the impression that Okinawa is both

あり，また東南アジアでもあり，という感じがします。しかし，琉球方言と言われる沖縄の言葉は，他の日本語の方言と異なって聞こえますが，同じ日本語であると考えられています。

日本の地形

Q 日本はどんな地形をしていますか？

日本は「山国」と言うことができます。アメリカのカリフォルニア州よりも小さいのに，日本の67％は山地で，平野はわずか13％しかありません。

その山地から流れ出る多くの川が，日本各地に大小の谷を作り，地形に様々な変化を与えています。そして河口に扇形の堆積平野を作っていますが，関東平野，大阪平野，濃尾平野などいくつかを除いて，いずれも狭い平野です。

Shoreline of Byōbugaura

日本の海岸線は非常に長く，その延長は約34,000kmあり，複雑な海岸線が，地域から地域へと移り変わる風景美を見せています。

Q 日本に島はいくつありますか。その中でいちばん大きい島は？

日本はおよそ6,800の島で成り立っています。その中には，人も住まないような島もあります。

本州，北海道，九州，四国も島といえば島ですが，日本人が"島"というときにはこの4つは含みません。"島"と呼ぶのは，これ以外のもっと小さな"島"なのです。

その中で最大の島と言うと，北海道の東の択捉島です。次がその隣の国後島，そして日本南

physically and spiritually a mixture of Japan, China and South-east Asia. The language, however, called the Ryūkyū dialect, is considered to be similar to Japanese, although it sounds different from the other Japanese dialects.

Geography of Japan

● What is the geography of Japan like?

Japan can be described as a **mountainous country**. Although it is a little smaller than California, 67% of its land surface is covered with mountains, and **plains** account for only 13%.

Rivers running from the mountains carve numerous **valleys and gorges**, and give a great deal of variety to the country's topographical features. At the **mouths of rivers**, **fan-shaped deltas** are formed, most of which are very small except for the Kantō, Ōsaka, and Nōbi plains.

The **coast line** of this island nation is extremely long, stretching for nearly 34,000 km. The complicated coastal line of Japan is indicative of the **scenic beauty** that varies from region to region.

● How many islands are there in Japan and which one is the largest?

Japan is made up of about 6,800 islands, some of which are not inhabited.

The areas of Honshū, Hokkaidō, Kyushū, and Shikoku can be called islands, but Japanese do not refer to them as so. When they say islands, they mean much smaller **isles** scattered around the main islands.

The largest of such islands is Etorofu, east of Hokkaidō, followed by the nearby Kunashiri. The next largest is Okinawa in

部の沖縄島, 本州中央部の北, **日本海**に浮かぶ
佐渡島と続きます。面積は下の表で比較してみ
てください。

Q 日本の湖はいくつありますか。その中でいちばん
大きい湖は？

Lake Biwa

実に多くの湖があり正確な数ははっきりしませ
んが, 面積が1km²以上の湖沼は100ぐらいあり
ます。その中で最大の湖は**琵琶湖**です。

この琵琶湖は世界的に有数の古い**淡水湖**で
す。約500万年前に今の三重県あたりで誕生し,
地殻変動で北へ動き, 現在の滋賀県の位置に達
したのは, 約120万年前だと言われています。

面積は約670km²ですが, カナダとアメリカ合

主な日本の山・川・湖・島
Main mountains, rivers, lakes and islands in Japan

■山　Five Major Mountains

山の名(Name)		所在地(Location)	高さ(Height)
富士山	Fuji-san	Yamanashi, Shizuoka	3,776 m
北岳	Kita-dake	Yamanashi	3,192 m
奥穂高岳	Okuhotaka-dake	Nagano, Gifu	3,190 m
間ノ岳	Aino-take	Yamanashi, Shizuoka	3,189 m
槍ヶ岳	Yariga-take	Nagano	3,180 m

■川　Five Major Rivers

川の名(Name)		所在地(Location)	長さ(Length)
信濃川	Shinano-gawa	Nagano, Niigata	367 km
利根川	Tone-gawa	Gumma, Ibaraki, Chiba, etc.	322 km
石狩川	Ishikari-gawa	Hokkaidō	268 km
天塩川	Teshio-gawa	Hokkaidō	256 km
北上川	Kitakami-gawa	Iwate, Miyagi	249 km

the south, and then Sado, located north of Honshū in the **Sea of Japan**. See the table below for a comparison of the island sizes.

● How many lakes are there in Japan? Which one is the largest?

It is hard to give an exact number, but as far as lakes larger than one square km are concerned, there are about 100 across the nation. The largest is **Lake Biwa**.

Lake Biwa is one of the oldest **freshwater lakes** in the world. It is believed that this lake dates back 5 million years. It moved north from its original location in Mie Prefecture to Shiga Prefecture because of **diastrophism** or **crust movement** that occurred 1.2 million years ago.

The area of the lake is about 670 km^2, which is far smaller

■湖　Five Major Lakes

湖の名前(Name)	所在地(Location)	面積(Area)
琵琶湖 Biwa-ko	Shiga	670 km^2
霞ヶ浦 Kasumiga-ura	Ibaraki	168 km^2
サロマ湖 Saroma-ko	Hokkaidō	152 km^2
猪苗代湖 Inawashiro-ko	Fukushima	103 km^2
中海　Nakaumi	Tottori, Shimane	86 km^2

■島　Five Major Islands

島の名前(Name)	所在地(Location)	面積(Area)
択捉島 Etorofu-tō	Hokkaidō	3,183 km^2
国後島 Kunashiri-tō	Hokkaidō	1,499 km^2
沖縄島 Okinawa-jima	Okinawa	1,202 km^2
佐渡島 Sadoga-shima	Niigata	854 km^2
奄美大島 Amami-ōshima	Kagoshima	712 km^2

衆国にまたがる2つの淡水湖スペリオル湖の
82,367km²，ヒューロン湖の59,570km²などに比
べれば，けた違いに小さな湖です。

Q 日本でいちばん高い山は？

もちろん富士山です。高さは3,776mで，チョ
モランマの8,848mをはじめとする世界の高峰か
ら見れば，大したことはありません。しかし，平
地から三角形にそびえ立つ姿の美しさは日本を
代表する景観です。

この**休火山**の頂上には，**直径**が800m，**深さ**
200mの火口があります。古くから**霊山**として信
仰の対象となっている山で，その端正な姿は多
くの俳句，短歌によまれています。

Snow-capped
Mt. Fuji

富士山の**裾野**には富士山から流れ出た**溶岩
流**でせき止められて生じた富士五湖があり，四
季を通じて多くの観光客が訪れています。

多くの有名な画家が富士山の絵に挑戦して
いますが，その中でも，江戸時代の**浮世絵師**，
葛飾北斎が，富士山を**いろいろな角度から**，い
ろいろな時間，季節の中で描いた「富嶽三十六
景」は特に有名です。

しかし，富士山には深刻な悩みがあります。
それは西側の大沢と呼ばれる崖が大きく崩壊を
続けており，美しい富士山の形が変わってきて
いることです。

than some of the larger lakes in the world such as Lake Superior (82,367 km²) and Lake Huron (59,570 km²), which span the area between Canada and the United States.

● What is the highest mountain in Japan?

It is the famous Mt. Fuji, which is 3,776 meters high. It can in no way be compared with the world's highest peaks such as Mt. Everest (Chomolungma, 8,848 meters) in terms of height. However, it has become emblematic of Japan with the striking beauty of its nearly perfect conical profile and wide-flowing skirt.

At the peak of this **dormant volcano** there is a crater, 800 meters **across** and 200 meters **deep**. From ancient times, Mt. Fuji has been an object of worship as a **sacred mountain**, and its perfection has long been celebrated in traditional verses such as *haiku* and *tanka*.

The five Fuji lakes at the **foot** of the mountain were formed from **runoff** from Mt. Fuji and serve as popular tourist spots throughout the four seasons.

Many renowned artists have taken up the challenge to depict Mt. Fuji. Among them, Katsushika Hokusai, an **ukiyo-e woodblock print artist** of the Edo period (1603–1867), won great acclaim for his *Fugaku Sanjū-rokkei* (36 scenes of Mt. Fuji), in which he painted Mt. Fuji **from various perspectives** at various hours of the day in each season.

However, Mt. Fuji is facing a serious problem. Landslides on the western side, known as Ōsawa, are changing the picture-perfect shape of the mountain.

Q 日本には火山はいくつありますか？

日本には80くらいの**活火山**があります。世界の活火山800ほどのうち，約10％が日本に集中していることになります。その日本には，北から南まで7つの**火山帯**が走っており，それぞれがいくつかの活発な火山を抱えているのです。

Mt. Fugen

近年の最大の**爆発**の一つは長崎県島原の雲仙・普賢岳（ふげんだけ）の噴火です。1990年に約200年ぶりに噴火し，**火砕流**によって43人もの命が失われ，島原市の一部が**溶岩**で覆われ，多数の人が避難生活を送りました。

Mt. Usu's eruption

2000年3月には、北海道の洞爺湖近くの有珠山が、約23年ぶりに活発な活動を始めました。しかし、前兆の地震から噴火が正確に予知され、噴火の前に周辺の住民は**避難をする**ことができたので、人命への被害は免れました。

Q 富士山は今度はいつ噴火しそうですか？

残された最初の記録によれば，富士山は，781年を最初として，1083年までに13回，約30年ごとに噴火を繰り返していました。

ところが，その次の14回目の爆発までは，428年間も間があき，1511年から1707年の間に3回噴火があっただけです。**火山活動**は観測されておらず，富士山は休眠中です。しかし，富士山も**噴火**の可能性がゼロということではないそうです。

地震と同じように，火山がいつ爆発するかを**予知する**ことは困難ですが，日本の火山**観測体制**はハワイと並んで世界でも優秀で，事前の活動の観測から，比較的早く警報を出すことができるようになってきています。

● How many volcanoes are there in Japan?

There are about 80 **active volcanoes**. It is said that about 10% of the world's 800 active volcanoes are concentrated in Japan. Seven **volcanic belts** run across the country, each of which has several active volcanoes.

One of the recent major **eruptions** was that of Mt. Fugen in Shimabara, Nagasaki Prefecture. This volcano erupted in 1990 for the first time in 200 years. Its **pyroclastic flow** killed 43 people, and **lava** discharged from its crater covered part of Shimabara city. Many people were forced to evacuate from their homes.

In March 2000, volcanic activity at Mt. Usu near Tōyako Lake in Hokkaidō began for the first time in 23 years. But tremors made it possible to accurately predict eruptions and **evacuate** people living nearby, avoiding any danger to human life.

● When is Mt. Fuji likely to erupt?

The first recorded eruption of Mt. Fuji was in 781, and it is said to have erupted 13 times, roughly once every 30 years, till 1083.

An interval of 428 years elapsed before the 14th eruption, and only three eruptions were recorded between 1511 and 1707. Since then, no **volcanic activity** has been observed, which indicates that Mt. Fuji is in a dormant state. However, there still is the possibility of an **eruption**, no matter how slim.

As is the case with **earthquakes**, it is difficult to **predict** volcanic eruptions; but Japan's excellent **observation system**, equal to that of Hawaii, provides relatively early warning about volcanic activity.

Q 日本でいちばん長い川はどれですか?

　　日本でいちばん長い川は**信濃川**です。長野県東部から新潟県の中央部を流れて,最後は新潟市で**日本海に注ぎこみます**。

　　信濃川は**水源から河口まで**367kmで,ミシシッピー川の3,780km,ダニューブ川の2,860km,ライン川の1,320kmに比べると比較になりません。しかし,国の規模にしては比較的長い川です。

　　第2位は関東平野を流れる利根川で322km,第3位は北海道の石狩川で268kmです。

　　日本は山国で海岸線からすぐに山地が続きますので,日本の川の多くが急流です。

Tone River

日本の気候

Q 日本はどんな気候の国ですか?

　　最大の特徴は,春,夏,秋,冬の移り変わりが非常に**はっきりしている**ことです。

　　一般に,3月,4月,5月が春,6月,7月,8月が夏,9月,10月,11月が秋,12月,1月,2月が冬とされています。

　　冬と夏との気温差は30度を超します。夏は高温である上に**湿度が高いので,**からっとした**大陸性の気候**に慣れた人は不快さを感じるでしょう。春と秋の気温は日本のほとんどどこでも快適な温度ですが,**天気が安定しません**。

　　夏の初めには北海道を除いて**梅雨**があり,6

● What is the longest river in Japan?

Japan's longest river is the **Shinano River**, which starts in the eastern part of Nagano Prefecture, runs through central Niigata, and **flows into the Sea of Japan** in Niigata City.

The Shinano, 367 km **from source to mouth**, may not be considered long when compared with famous rivers of the world such as the Mississippi (3,780 km), the Danube (2,860 km), and the Rhine (1,320 km), but it is relatively long for the size of the country.

The second largest river, the Tone River, flows for 322 km through the Kantō Plain. The Ishikari River in Hokkaidō is the third longest, stretching for 268 km.

Japan is a mountainous country and so most of the country's rivers flow rapidly down from the high mountains.

Climate of Japan

● What is the climate of Japan like?

The climate of most of Japan is characterized by four **distinct** seasons.

The spring months generally are from March to May, summer months are from June to August, autumn from September to November, and winter from December to February.

The difference between winter temperatures and summer temperatures is more than 30 degrees celsius. Summer months, with high temperatures and **high humidity**, may be uncomfortable for those who are used to a **dry continental climate**. In spring and autumn, almost all parts of Japan enjoy comfortable temperatures, but **the weather is very changeable**.

In the beginning of summer, all areas except Hokkaidō have

月から7月の半ばまで, 雨の多い日が続きます。

　秋も比較的に雨が多く, また, 夏の終わりから秋の初めにかけては, 北太平洋の西部で発生する**台風**にも見舞われ, 大きな被害が出ることがあります。

　また, 山地が日本列島を日本海側と太平洋側に分けていて, 冬は日本海側に**多くの雪**が降ることも日本の特徴です。

Q 日本で雪が多いのはどこですか？

Removing snow from the roof of a house

　亜熱帯の沖縄県は別として, 日本は雪が降る地域が多い国です。これは, 大陸から吹きつける冬の**季節風**が, 日本全国を背骨のように走る山岳地帯にさえぎられて, 北海道から本州の中部にかけての日本海側に雪を降らせるのです。

　新潟県と福島県の県境や北陸地方の山間部では, 3mを超える積雪をみることは普通です。地球上でも最も積雪の多い地方の1つ, 新潟県の山岳部では, 昔8mを超えたという記録があるそうです。

Q 日本でいちばんいい季節はいつですか？

　10世紀に清少納言という女性作家が『枕草子』という随筆で, それぞれの季節に趣があると書いています。それには「春は**曙(夜明け)**がよく, 夏は夜が, 秋は**夕暮れ**が, そして冬は早朝が, それぞれいい」と書かれています。

　このように季節それぞれに魅力がありますが, 一般的には春と秋, 特に5月初めの新緑のころと, 紅葉の10月から11月の半ばがいちばんいい季節だと感じる日本人が多いと思います。気候が安定していて, 旅行などには最高のシーズンだからです。

a **rainy season**, which usually lasts from early June to mid-July.

Autumn is also a time of substantial precipitation. From the end of summer to the beginning of autumn, **typhoons** generated in the western part of the North Pacific Ocean hit the country, sometimes causing extensive damage.

Mountain ranges, running almost the full length of Japan, divide the archipelago into the Japan Sea side and the Pacific side. The Japan Sea side has **heavy snowfall** in winter.

● Which part of Japan has the most snow?

Except for **semitropical** Okinawa, most parts of Japan have snow in winter. Northwesterly **seasonal winds** off the Asian continent, blocked by rugged mountains, bring heavy snows to the Japan Sea coast from Hokkaidō to the central part of Honshū.

On the border between Niigata Prefecture and Fukushima Prefecture, and in the mountains of the Hokuriku region, snowfall of over three meters is not unusual. The heaviest snowfall on record is eight meters in the mountains of Niigata Prefecture, one of the snowiest regions on earth.

● What is the most comfortable season in Japan?

Each season has its own **charm**, as Sei Shōnagon, a female author in the 10th century, wrote in her anthology of essays titled *Makura no Sōshi*. She wrote that **dawn** is best in spring, night is best in summer, **twilight** is best in autumn, and early morning is best in winter.

But the majority of Japanese would say that the best seasons are spring and autumn, especially early May when trees are covered in fresh green, and between October and mid-November when the leaves change colors. With the climate stable, these are the best times of the year to travel.

日本の自然災害

Q 日本に地震が多いのはなぜですか？

　　　　　日本列島は北米プレートとユーラシアプレートの上にのっていますが、このプレートの下に、太平洋プレートとフィリピン海プレートがもぐりこんできています。そのために非常に地震が多いのです。

　　　　　そして、日本の地層には、**活断層**と言われるものが随所に走っています。

　　　　　活断層は、過去数十万年の間に何度も動いた**形跡**があり、今後もその可能性があると判断できる断層のことです。その活動は、約1,000年に1度ぐらいの周期だとも言われています。1995年1月の阪神・淡路大震災は、この活断層による地震でした。

Q 近年、どこで大地震が起こりましたか？

　　　　　1995年1月17日午前5時46分に、大地震が兵庫県南部を襲いました。阪神・淡路大震災と名付けられた地震です。これまでの日本の大地震は、**海溝**近くのプレート境界面で起きることが多かったのですが、この地震は、神戸市の真下の活断層がずれて発生したものです。

Great Hanshin-Awaji
Earthquake;
collapsed express-
way

　　　　　阪神・淡路大震災は6,000人をこえる死者・行方不明者、4万人をこえる負傷者、家屋の損壊は20万戸にものぼる、史上最悪の大震災となりました。震源はマグニチュード7.2を記録しました。

　　　　　古くは1923年に9万人の死者と10万人の負傷者を出した、マグニチュード7.9の関東大震災が有名です。

Natural Disasters in Japan

• Why does Japan have a lot of earthquakes?

The **Japanese archipelago** is situated along the North American Plate and the Eurasian Plate. Squeezed in under these plates are the Pacific Plate and the Philippines Sea Plate, which makes the landforms unstable, causing a lot of earthquakes in and around the area.

There are many **active faults** in the strata that form the land of Japan.

An active fault is a fault that has shown **traces** of activity during the past several hundred thousand years, and is likely to start moving in the future. The cycle of its activity is said to be once every thousand years. The Great Hanshin-Awaji Earthquake in January 1995 was caused by such an active fault.

• Where did the latest large earthquake occur?

At 5:46 AM on January 17, 1995, a major earthquake hit the southern part of Hyōgo Prefecture. The earthquake would come to be known as the "Great Hanshin-Awaji Earthquake." Major earthquakes in Japan have often occurred on surfaces bordering plates near **undersea trenches**, but this particular earthquake was generated by the movement of an active fault that runs under the city of Kōbe.

The Great Hanshin-Awaji Earthquake became one of the most devastating earthquakes in history, with a death toll exceeding 6,000. More than 40,000 people were injured and 200,000 houses collapsed. The recorded magnitude was 7.2 on the Japanese scale.

In 1923, there was a 7.9 temblor called the "Great Kantō Earthquake of 1923" that killed 90,000 and injured 100,000.

Q これから大地震が起こりそうなところは どこですか?

明確な予知は, 現在の**科学技術**をもってしても不可能ですが, 過去のデータから危険と推定される所はいくつかあります。

静岡県の**駿河湾**を震源域と想定している「東海地震」は, 極端にいえば, 明日起こっても不思議ではないという説もあります。そのために, この地域は常時, 観測されています。

東北地方の**三陸沖**も大地震の発生が心配されています。日本の下に太平洋プレートがもぐりこんできているところだからです。海に面しているこの地域の地震では**津波**の心配もあるので, 要注意です。

Coast of Sanriku

活断層は**全国各地**にありますが, 特に, 中部地方, 近畿地方に多いようです。東京では北西部から東の方に向けて, 比較的に大きい活断層があります。いずれも地震の可能性があると言えるでしょう。

Q 英語になっているtsunamiとは何ですか?

津波は, おもに地震によって一気に変化した**海底**の地形の影響で押し寄せる高い波のことをいいます。歴史的に見れば, 日本のほとんどの**海岸**が, これまで津波に襲われた過去を持っています。ことに, 東北地方の三陸海岸に被害が目立ちます。

Damage from tsunami

この原因は, 三陸海岸は**リアス式海岸**で, 小さな湾は岸壁の奥に食い込んだようにして存在していますので, 岸に達するときには津波の高さが大きくなっているからです。

1993年の北海道南西沖地震では, 奥尻島に

● Are there any areas likely to have major earthquakes in the near future?

There are several areas considered dangerous based on data accumulated over a long period of time, although precise prediction of earthquakes is not yet possible with today's **scientific technology**.

Some specialists say that a major earthquake could occur at any moment in **Suruga Bay**, Shizuoka Prefecture, located in the Tōkai region. This area is being constantly monitored.

Off the coast of Sanriku in the Tōhoku region, where the Pacific Plate is in the process of squeezing itself under the Japanese islands, is another area of concern. There is also the possibility of tsunami, or **tidal wave**, should an earthquake hit this region which faces the sea.

Active fault lines run **throughout the country**, but a large portion are found in the Chūbu and Kinki regions. Tōkyō also has a relatively large active fault running from its northwestern part toward the east. Wherever there is an active fault, earthquakes are possible.

● What is a tsunami?

A tsunami is a high tidal wave generated by a shift in the **ocean floor**, which is in most cases caused by earthquakes. Most parts of the Japanese **seacoast** have experienced a tsunami. The Sanriku coast in the Tōhoku region has been especially hard hit.

The reason, scientists assume, is the formation of a **ria coastline**, consisting of a multitude of narrow and complicated bays, which may make the tsunami wave exceptionally high.

Immediately after an earthquake off the southwestern coast

最大20mもの高さの津波が襲来し、**死者・不明者**が230人という被害をだしました。

Q 台風は1年にどれくらい来るのですか?

The eye of a typhoon

　大ざっぱに言って、台風は平均して年4回、日本を襲っています。台風は北太平洋の西部で発生しますが、その数は、過去の平均では27個ぐらいです。そのすべてが日本に向かってくるわけではありません。台風を移動させる上層の風の流れが、発生した季節によって異なるからです。

　冬や春に発生する台風は、**貿易風**に乗って西に進み、日本には来ません。ところが、夏や秋に発生した台風は、太平洋**高気圧**の西縁をめぐって北に向かい、日本を襲うことが多くなるのです。

Q 台風とハリケーンはどこが違うのでしょう?

　台風は、北太平洋西部で発生する**熱帯低気圧**で、**最大風速**が秒速17.2m以上の暴風雨のことをいいます。台風の語源は「大きな風」を意味する中国語の "taifung" だと言われています。

　ハリケーンは、北大西洋とインド洋に**発生する**熱帯低気圧で、最大風速が秒速32.7m以上の**暴風雨**です。

　発生場所と最大風速のとらえ方の違いこそあれ、その性質は台風もハリケーンも基本的には同じものです。

of Hokkaidō in 1993, a major tsunami with a peak height of 20 meters hit the coast of Okushiri Island. The number of **dead and missing** totaled 230.

● How often does Japan have typhoons?

Roughly speaking, about four typhoons hit the country annually. The average number of typhoons born in the western part of the North Pacific Ocean is 27 per year. Not all of them head for Japan because of the influences of seasonal upper layer winds that move typhoons.

Typhoons in spring and winter go west on the **trade winds** and never land in Japan, but those in summer and autumn go around the west end of the **high pressure system** in the Pacific Ocean, and in many cases move in the direction of Japan.

● What is the difference between typhoons and hurricanes?

A typhoon is a **tropical cyclone** that develops in the western part of the North Pacific Ocean, and refers to a rainstorm with a **maximum wind speed** of over 17.2 meters per second. The origin of the word *typhoon* is said to have come from the Chinese word *taifung*, which means big wind.

A hurricane is a tropical cyclone that **develops** in the North Atlantic Ocean or the Indian Ocean, and is defined as a **rainstorm** with a maximum wind speed of over 32.7 meters per second.

The nature of typhoons and hurricanes is basically the same, although they differ in **the place they are born** and the way their wind speed is defined.

日本のルーツと歴史

Origin and History of Japan

Haniwa, clay images placed ▶ in ancient burial mounds

日本の誕生

Q 日本という国はいつごろ誕生したのですか?

日本では2月11日が「**建国記念の日**」とされています。これは『古事記』や『日本書紀』という古文書に書かれた**神話伝承**に基づくものですが,学問上,史実かどうかということには疑問が残ります。

日本には5世紀以前の**文献**はなく,中国の資料によるほうがわかりやすいようです。中国の『後漢書』には,57年に「日本の奴国(なこく)の王が使節をよこした」と,そして『魏志倭人伝』には「邪馬台国(やまたいこく)に卑弥呼(ひみこ)という女王がいて,30ほどの国をまとめていた」という記述があります。

The Account of the Wa People

『日本書紀』では,この卑弥呼が**神功皇后**(じんぐう)であるとしていますが,現在の古代歴史学では否定されており,邪馬台国が滅びた後,7世紀ご

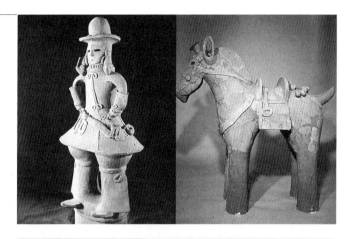

Birth of Japan

• When did Japan emerge as a nation?

In Japan, February 11th is **National Foundation Day**. This date is based on **legends** chronicled in the ancient *Kojiki* and *Nihon shoki* texts, but from an academic perspective, there is doubt over the historical accuracy.

Since Japan has no **written records** earlier than the fifth century, we can probably learn more from Chinese texts. According to the Chinese text *Gokanjo* (History of the Later Han Dynasty), in the year 57 A.D. the king of the Japanese kingdom of Na dispatched a mission (to China), while "The Account of the Wa People" in the *Wei zhi* (The Wei Chronicle) contains a reference to a queen named Himiko in the land of Yamatai, who ruled over about 30 countries.

Although the *Nihon shoki* regards Himiko as **Empress Jingū**, historians dispute this claim. It could be that following the decline of Yamatai rule, by the seventh century the country

ろまでに，1つの**国としてのまとまり**ができ，これ
が**大和政権**の始まりと考えられます。

Q 日本をニホン，あるいはニッポンと呼ぶように なったのはいつごろからですか？

Kojiki

『日本書紀』や『古事記』によると，古い時代の
日本のことを「豊葦原瑞穂国」とか，「葦原中国」
と呼んでいます。しかし，中国や韓国では**古代
日本**を「倭」と称していました。日本ではこれを
「ヤマト」と言っていました。

ところが，しばらく中国との交渉が途絶えてい
た後，7世紀の初め，中国の『旧唐書』という書
物に，次の文句が登場します。「日本国は倭国
の別種なり。その国，日の辺に在るを以ての故に，
日本を以て名と為す……倭国自らその名の**雅な
らざる**を悪み，改めて日本と為す」

「日本」の**登場**です。『日本書紀』は8世紀の編集で
すので，それまでの資料に使われていた「倭国」が，
「日本」に書き換えられていったに違いありません。

Q 日本は「ニホン」か「ニッポン」，どちらが 正しい言い方ですか？

1934年，**文部省**の臨時国語審議会が「ニッポ
ン」を**正式の呼び方**としています。それまでもバ
ラバラだったわけです。しかし，この決定は**法律
として制定されたわけではなく**，今でもどちらの
言い方も通用しています。

切手には Nippon と印刷されていますし，日
本が海外に派遣するスポーツ団のユニホームな
ども Nippon が多いので，公式には「ニッポ
ン」が認められているといっていいでしょう。

was unified into one **polity**, which then served as the basis for **Yamato rule**.

● How did Japan come to be called *Nihon* or *Nippon*?

In the *Nihon shoki* and the *Kojiki*, **ancient Japan** is referred to as "Toyoashiharamizuho no kuni" and "Ashiharanakatsu kuni." However, in China and Korea, ancient Japan was called "Wa" (*Wo* in Chinese), while Japan referred to itself as "Yamato."

However, the following passage appeared in the Chinese *Jiu Tang shu* at the beginning of the seventh century, following a break in Japan's relationship with China: "Nihon-koku" (*Ribenguo* in Chinese) is distinct from "Wa-koku" (*Woguo* in Chinese). This country is named "Nihon" because it exists near the sun.... It has been renamed "Nihon" since the people of "Wa-koku" disliked the **inelegance** of their name.

Thus was the **dawn** of *Nihon*. As the *Nihon shoki* was compiled in the eighth century, references to "Wa-koku" in existing materials were most likely replaced with "Nihon."

● Is it correct to refer to Japan as "Nihon" or "Nippon"?

In 1934, the **Ministry of Education**'s Provisional Deliberation Council on the Japanese Language designated *Nippon* as the **official name**. Until this time, usage was random. However, the use of *Nippon* **was not decreed by law**, and even today, both names are commonly used.

Since postage stamps are marked *Nippon* and Japanese athletes sent overseas often wear uniforms emblazoned *Nippon*, it can be said that *Nippon* is regarded as the official name for Japan.

Q 日本人はどこから来たのですか？

日本人は人種的に純粋であると信じている人がいますが，現在の研究では，日本人はその身体的な特徴から，いくつかの**種族**の混合だと言われています。

とすると，どんな人種が混合したのかということになりますが，東南アジアから海を渡ってきた種族（縄文タイプ），朝鮮半島を経由してきたツングース系の種族（弥生タイプ），そしてアイヌ系の種族などが，長い間に混じり合って日本人を作っていったものと考えられます。

Q アイヌ民族はいつごろから日本にいたのですか？

Traditional ceremony of the Ainu

今から約1000年ほど前，樺太（からふと），千島列島，北海道および本州の北部に広がる擦文（さつもん）文化圏を作っていた民族がアイヌだと言われています。アイヌのほうが**先住民族**なのです。

アイヌは狩猟，漁猟，植物の採集など，自然に依存した生活をしていましたが，15世紀ごろから，アイヌ人たちが「和人」と呼んだ日本人が北海道に**侵入**を始め，住んでいた広大な自然環境を奪われていきます。

激しい衝突が繰り返された結果，18世紀末には，北海道のアイヌは完全に日本の**支配下**に入ってしまうことになりました。

その後，明治政府になってからは，内地人との**同化**政策がとられ，アイヌ民族としての存在は脅かされていきました。アイヌ文化，アイヌ語は消滅の危機にさらされてきましたが，1997年にアイヌ文化振興法が制定され，国としてアイヌ文化を復興し，保持していくことになりました。

● Where did the Japanese people come from?

Although there are people who believe in the racial purity of the Japanese, current studies hold that the physical features of the Japanese people reveal their derivation from a mixture of several **ethnic groups**.

So, what racial groups comprise this mixture? We can say that the Japanese stock was created over a long period of time by the gradual mixture of the *Jōmon* strain, an ethnic group from South-east Asia that crossed the sea to Japan, the *Yayoi* strain, Tungusic people arriving through the Korean peninsula, and the Ainu ethnic group.

● How long have the Ainu people inhabited Japan?

It is commonly held that about 1,000 years ago the Ainu ethnic group established the "Satsumon culture," which encompassed a region spanning Sakhalin, the Kuril Islands, Hokkaidō, and northern Honshū. The Ainu are the **aboriginal people** of Japan.

The Ainu were long dependent upon nature, making a livelihood from hunting, fishing, and gathering. However, beginning in the 15th century, with **invasions** by the Japanese whom the Ainu called *Wajin*, the Ainu's vast natural lands were gradually taken from them.

By around the 18th century, a series of vicious clashes led to the complete **subjugation** of the Ainu people by the Japanese.

Following the establishment of the Meiji government, policies encouraging **assimilation** with mainstream Japanese were implemented, threatening the existence of the Ainu as an ethnic group. The Ainu culture and language once faced extinction, but the government passed the Ainu Culture Promotion Law in 1997 to promote and protect the Ainu culture.

日本の国歌・国旗

Q 君が代はいつ制定されたのですか？

　　1893年（明治26年），文部省から，**初等教育に**おいて祝日の儀式に際して歌うべき歌として公布されています。

　　実は，**日本国歌**の必要を説いたのはイギリス人軍楽隊長のフェントンという人で，歌詞には『古今和歌集』『和漢朗詠集』の中にある読み人知らずのこの歌が選ばれました。

　　そして何度かメロディーが検討された末，1880年に雅楽家の林広守の旋律が採用され，ドイツ人音楽教師エッケルトが編曲し，今の君が代が完成しています。

　　しかしその後の，日清戦争，日露戦争，満州事変，そして太平洋戦争などという不幸な歴史の中で，軍国主義化した国の国歌となった君が代には，戦後，風当たりが強くなりました。**軍国主義，天皇制**の象徴として君が代を拒否する人たちが続出したのです。

　　不思議なことですが，事実上，君が代は日本の国歌として歌われていながら，法律で規定されているわけではありませんでした。やっと1999年8月，**日の丸を国旗**，君が代を国歌とする**国旗・国歌法**が成立しました。しかし，この法律に対しては，新しい国歌を作るべきだという強い反対の声があります。

Japan's National Anthem and National Flag

● **When was *Kimigayo* established as the national anthem?**

In 1893 (26th year of Meiji), the Ministry of Education decreed that *Kimigayo* would be incorporated into **primary education** as the anthem to be sung at ceremonies honoring national holidays.

Actually, the person who stressed the need for establishing a **Japanese national anthem** was a British military bandleader named Fenton. The words for the song came from a poem in the *Kokinwakashū* and the *Wakanrōeishū*.

After much deliberation over the selection of a melody, a tune by the *gagaku* (ancient court music) composer Hayashi Hiromori was adopted in 1880, and then arranged by the German music educator Franz Eckert to constitute today's *Kimigayo*.

However, during the adverse course of history that followed, including the Sino-Japanese War, the Russo-Japanese War, the Manchurian Incident and the Pacific War, the national anthem took on militarist overtones, which exposed it to a wave of criticism in the postwar period. An increasing number of people came to dismiss *Kimigayo* as a symbol of **militarism** and the **emperor system**.

Strangely enough, while *Kimigayo* was sung as the de facto national anthem, it was not legally decreed as such for many years. Finally, with the passing of the **National Flag and Anthem Law** in August 1999, the **Rising Sun** became the **national flag** and *Kimigayo* the national anthem. But despite the new law, the calls for a different national anthem are as strong as ever.

Q 君が代の歌詞はどんな意味ですか?

歌詞はこうなっています。

君が代は
千代に八千代に
さざれ石の
巌<ruby>いわお</ruby>となりて
苔のむすまで

「君」という言葉は,「主人, 家の長, 友人, 愛人」の意味で, **現代語**でも, 親しい相手あるいは目下の人に対して,「君」と呼び掛けたりします。しかし, 軍国主義の時代にはこの「君」は「天皇」に直接結びついていました。

歌詞全体の意味は, 簡単に言えば,「いつまでも元気で!」「末長く!」といった意味ですから, これから問題になるとすれば, 歌詞が**文語**だし, メロディーも8ビートに慣れた若者たちには, いかにも悠長に聞こえてしまうということでしょう。

日本の国歌と国旗 ─────

● 君が代 Kimigayo

Words : Anonymous
Music : Hayashi Hiromori

● What do the words to *Kimigayo* mean?

These are the **lyrics** to *Kimigayo*:

Thousands of years of happy reign be thine;
Rule on, my Lord, till what are pebbles now
By age united to mighty rocks shall grow
Whose venerable sides the moss doth line.

Kimi can mean lord, household head, friend, or lover. In **modern Japanese** *kimi* is used to address a close companion or a subordinate. But during the militarist period, *kimi* also was directly associated with the Emperor.

The overall meaning of the words, simply stated, is somewhat similar to "To your good health! And long life!" The problem then would probably lie in the fact that the lyrics are **antiquated**, and the melody too slow for young people accustomed to eight-beat melodies.

National Anthem and Flag

● 日の丸 Hinomaru

The vertical to horizontal ratio is set at 2 : 3, the disc is to be placed at the exact center, and the diameter of the disc is to equal three-fifths of the vertical measurement of the flag.

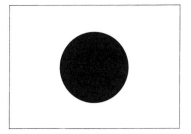

Q 日本の国旗，日の丸はいつ制定されたのですか？

Hinomaru

　君が代と同様に，日の丸（日章旗）を日本の国旗とする……という法的な規定はありませんでしたが，1999年8月の国旗・国歌法によって正式に国旗になりました。

　白地に赤い円を描いた現在のデザインは，1854年，徳川幕府が日本の船の船印として取り入れたものです。これは日本の船を外国の船と区別するためのもので，必ずしも日本の国旗というわけではなかったのです。

　明治時代になり，1870年には太政官布告でこの船印の規格を制定していますが，その後，いつのまにか国旗として定着してしまいました。

　日の丸も，軍国主義の名の下に誤った道をたどった日本を象徴することになりましたので，太平洋戦争後，君が代と同様，日の丸を拒否する人たちもいます。

Q 日本の国の花は何ですか？

Chrysanthemum

　法律で定められた**国花**はありません。しかし**皇室の紋章**であるキクか，または，国民に愛好されているサクラが日本の国の花と言われています。

　国花には中国のウメのように法律で制定されたものもありますが，フランスのユリやアイリス，イギリスのバラやスイセンといったように自然にきまったものが多いようです。

Q 日本の国鳥は何ですか？

　一応，**キジ**が日本の**国鳥**ということになってい

● When was the national flag adopted?

As with the national anthem, there were no laws designating the Rising Sun as the national flag until the National Flag and Anthem Law made it official in August 1999.

The current design—**a red disc in the center of a white field**—was originally adopted by the Tokugawa government in 1854 to be used on flags for Japan's ships. This was done in order to distinguish Japanese ships from foreign ships, and was not necessarily intended to stand as Japan's national flag.

During the Meiji period, in the year 1870, a proclamation issued by the *Dajōkan* (Grand Council of State) adopted this as the standard flag for ships, and over time this became accepted as the national flag.

As the Rising Sun has come to symbolize a Japan that once traveled an erroneous militarist path, there are now in the postwar period a number of people who, as with *Kimigayo*, reject the Rising Sun.

● What is the national flower of Japan?

There is no legally designated **national flower**. However, the chrysanthemum, the **crest of the imperial family**, and the beloved cherry blossom are commonly regarded as the national flowers of Japan.

While there are national flowers like China's plum blossom that have been designated by law, there are also many such as France's lily and iris, or Britain's rose and daffodil, that have come to be accepted informally.

● What is the national bird of Japan?

The **pheasant** is now regarded as the **national bird** of Japan.

Green pheasant

ますが, これは1947年, 日本鳥学会の第81回例会で選ばれたものです。

キジが選ばれたのは, 緑色のキジは日本固有の種であり, また, 日本の**民話**の中にもたくさん登場し, 日本の**風土**に根づいている鳥であるからでしょう。

日本語

Q 日本語はどこから来たのですか?

日本語がいちばん似ている言語は朝鮮語です。確かに主語・目的語・述語の並び方などの**共通点**があります。しかし, まだ, **同系の言語**であるという証明はされていません。

日本語はウラル・アルタイ語族の1つではないか, 南方系のマライ・ポリネシア語族ではないか, チベット・インドの諸語と関係があるのではないか, タミル語と同系ではないかとか, 実にいろいろな説があります。

起源はわかりませんが, 言語としては, 中国との文化的な交流の中から, 中国語の語彙を多数, 日本語の中に受け入れ, さらに漢字の中国字音から平仮名, 片仮名を作りだすなどして, 漢字と仮名で構成される日本語が作られていきました。

Q 日本語の特徴はどこにありますか?

まず発音の特徴ですが, 基本的に1つの音は, 「ん (n)」を除いて, 母音だけ, あるいは**子音＋母音**で表されます。

It originally was designated as such in 1947 at the 81st Meeting of the National Bird Society of Japan.

The Japanese pheasant, or *kiji*, was most likely selected because this green pheasant is unique to Japan, and furthermore because it appears often in Japanese **folk tales** and so has become an integral part of the Japanese **cultural landscape**.

Japanese Language

● What are the origins of the Japanese language?

The closest language to Japanese is Korean. There are definite **commonalities** in the arrangement of the subject, direct object, and predicate. However, there is no determining evidence that they belong to the **same linguistic family**.

There are many theories about the origins of the Japanese language: one of the Ural-Altaic languages; one of the southern, Malayo-Polynesian languages; a relative to the Indo-Tibetan languages; or one of the Tamil languages.

While its origins remain uncertain, the Japanese language has incorporated many Chinese words. The *hiragana* and *katakana* syllabaries were created based on the Chinese readings for the characters, resulting in a language that incorporated both Chinese characters and *kana* syllabaries.

● What are the distinguishing features of Japanese?

First of all, regarding its pronunciation, Japanese consists primarily of syllables which, with the exception of ん ("n"), are made up of single vowels and **consonant-vowel** pairs.

時計→ to-ke-i
私→ wa-ta-ku-shi
元気→ gen-ki

　アクセントは英語のような**強弱アクセント**ではなく，**高低アクセント**で，横浜［ヨコハマ］の［ヨ］は低く［コハマ］は少し高く発音します。

　しかし，アクセントは日本全国同じというわけではなく，西日本と東日本で，また地域で異なる語がたくさんあります。

　日本語の語彙は，和語（大和言葉）と言われる日本固有の語と，漢語から取り入れた語，そして現代では，外国語から取り入れたカタカナ語から成り立っています。
　文章は，基本的に

　　1) 主語＋補語＋述語動詞
　　　彼は＋大学生＋です。
　　2) 主語＋目的語＋述語動詞
　　　私は＋アイスクリームを＋食べた。

という形をしていますが，述語が文末に来ること，修飾語は必ず被修飾語の前に来ることを守れば，**語順**は比較的自由です。
　英語などに比べて特徴があるのは，韓国語と同様に，敬語が高度に発達していることです。また，会話では男性語と女性語の区別が明瞭であることも特徴です。

tokei (a clock, a watch) → *to-ke-i*
watakushi (I, my, me) → *wa-ta-ku-shi*
genki (vigor, cheerful) → *gen-ki*

Japanese has no **strong stress accent** like that of English but rather has a **high-low pitch accent**, such that when pronouncing the word Yokohama, the "Yo" sound is relatively low, while "kohama" is pronounced at a slightly higher pitch.

However, this accent system is not applied uniformly throughout Japan, as seen in the regional variations between eastern and western Japan. There are also many words that vary by region as well.

The Japanese vocabulary consists of native words, *wago* or *yamato kotoba*, words adopted from Chinese, and in the modern period, *katakana* words that express foreign loan words.

The basic sentence structure is as follows:

(1) Subject + Complement + Predicate
   *He + university student + is.
(2) Subject + Object + Predicate
   *I + ice cream + ate.

As long as the predicate comes at the end of the sentence, and the modifier always precedes the subordinate modifier, the **arrangement of words** is relatively free.

Like Korean, but in contrast to English, Japanese has highly developed polite forms. Another feature is that spoken Japanese has distinctive male and female patterns of speech.

Q 平仮名，片仮名はどうして できたのですか？

　　日本語には3つの文字の形があります。漢字，平仮名，片仮名です。漢字は中国から取り入れられた**象形文字**です。

　　仮名は，漢字が持っている意味を捨てて，その読み方（発音）を簡単な形にして表したものということができます。実例を上げてみましょう。

以(i) → レ乙 → ～レ → い
加(ka) → 加 → カワ → か
礼(rei) → 礼 → 礼 → れ

　　漢字が平仮名に変えられていく姿がわかると思います。

　　8世紀の中ごろ編集された万葉集には，和歌が4,500首ほど収録されていますが，すべて，漢字に当てた音で表されています。

　　その後，次第に上記の例のように漢字が簡略されていき，9世紀の終わりには，現在のような平仮名の字体が出来上がりました。

　　片仮名は平仮名がさらに単純化されたもので，平仮名と並行して作られ，9世紀の初頭にはすでに使われている文献があります。

　　そして，平仮名は書簡文や物語文などに，また片仮名は漢文の難しい文字の読みや**注釈**に使われていきます。

Q 漢字はいくつ覚えればいいのですか？

　　漢字の字の種類は，約5万もあると言われています。その中から多くの漢字が日本語に取り

● How did the *hiragana* and *katakana* syllabaries originate?

There are three traditional characters in the Japanese language: *kanji*, *hiragana*, and *katakana*. *Kanji* are **ideograms** brought from China.

We might say that *kana* do not convey the meaning of *kanji*, but rather stand for simplified sounds. Let's take a look at the following examples.

以(i) → レ人 → ～ゝ → い
加(ka) → 力口 → 力ヽ → か
礼(rei) → ネし → iし → れ

You can see in this diagram the process by which *kanji* are transformed into *hiragana*.

The *Manyōshū*, which was compiled in the mid-eighth century, contains about 4,500 *waka* poems; yet most are written with *kanji* with randomly assigned sounds.

Over time, *kanji* were simplified, and by the end of the ninth century, they had evolved into the current *hiragana* syllabary.

Katakana, which are even more simple than *hiragana*, developed alongside the *hiragana* syllabary, and was already used in written works by the beginning of the ninth century.

Hiragana came to be used in correspondence and narratives, while *katakana* was used for **annotations** and as phonetic symbols for difficult *kanji*.

● How many *kanji* must one learn?

There are said to be some 50,000 *kanji*, most of which have been adopted into Japanese. There are also *kanji*, such as 峠

入れられ，また，峠，裃など，日本で作られた漢
字も出てきました。

しかし，日常生活でたくさんの漢字が必要な
わけではありませんので，現在では1,945字が一
般的に使用する「**常用漢字**」の目安として選定さ
れています。

Q 漢字，平仮名，片仮名は どのように使いますか？

多くの名詞は漢字で書かれており，動詞と形
容詞の多くは漢字と平仮名混じりで書かれます。
助詞や助動詞は平仮名，**外来語**は片仮名で書
かれます。

例えば，「私は動物園でパンダを見た」という
文では，名詞の「私」「動物園」，動詞の「見た」
の「見」は，通例，漢字で書きます。

全部を平仮名，片仮名で書いても，意味がわ
かることは多いのですが，日本語にはたくさん
の**同音異義語**がありますので，意味の理解のた
めには，**表意文字**である漢字を入れるほうがいい
とされています。

Q 日本語の文は縦書き，横書き， どっちが多いんですか？

日本に残された歴史的な文献はすべてが縦
に書かれています。昔は日本語は縦書きだけだ
ったのです。

しかし，西洋の文献が流入してきて，アルファ
ベット，アラビア数字，**数学の公式**などを取り入れ
るとなると，どうも**縦書き**では具合が悪いのです。

幸い，漢字と仮名は個々に意味と働きを持っ

tōge (mountain pass) and 裃 *kamishimo* (old ceremonial dress), which were created in Japan.

However, many *kanji* are not necessarily used in daily life, and today, 1,945 characters have been designated as *jōyō kanji*, or "***kanji* in common use**."

● How are *kanji*, *hiragana*, and *katakana* used?

Many nouns are written in *kanji*, verbs and adjectives are written mostly in *kanji-hiragana* combination, particles and auxiliary verbs in *hiragana*, and **loan words** in *katakana*.

For example, in the sentence "*Watashi wa dōbutsuen de panda o mita*" (I saw a panda at the zoo), *watashi* (I = noun), *dōbutsuen* (zoo = noun), *mi* of *mita* (part of the verb 'saw') are usually written in *kanji*.

Sentences written entirely in *hiragana* and *katakana* can be understood, but since there are thousands of **homonyms** in Japanese, it was decided that *kanji*, which are **ideographic**, should be included for clarification purposes.

● Is Japanese text more commonly written vertically or horizontally?

All extant historical documents in Japan are written vertically. Long ago, Japanese was only written vertically.

However, with the introduction of Western writing materials and the need to accommodate the alphabet, arabic numerals, and **mathematical formulas**, the **vertical style** seemed ill-suited.

Fortunately, since each individual *kanji* and *kana* has its

ているものですから，縦に並べても，横に並べても意味は通じますから，数字や横文字を多用しなければならない自然科学関係の文は，次第に**横書き**になっていきます。今では学校の教科書も，国語・古文などを除いて，ほとんどが横書きになっています。

　店頭に並ぶ一般の出版物の多くは縦組みですが，若い人たちは，横に読むこと，横に書くことには全く抵抗はなく，横書きがますます増えています。

日本の天皇

Q だれが日本の最初の天皇になったのですか？

　『古事記』や『日本書紀』という日本の古代歴史を記録した本によりますと，日本の初代の天皇は神武（じんむ）天皇となっています。紀元前660年のこととされています。

Prince Shōtoku

　しかし，事実として証明されたことではなく，『古事記』『日本書紀』共に8世紀になってから編纂されたものですから，神話として作られたもの**という説が有力です**。

　実在した可能性があるのは，第10代の崇神（すじん）天皇からと言われますが，記録が残っているのは，592年から628年まで在位した第33代推古天皇からです。この時代，**皇太子**として聖徳太子が登場しています。

Q 天皇のルーツはどこにありますか？

　日本民族がどこから来たのかもわかりませんし，日本誕生自体がナゾなのですから，天皇の

own meaning and function, they could be arranged vertically or horizontally without losing their meaning. Science-related text, which required the use of numbers and foreign words, gradually came to be written in the **horizontal style**. Today, most school textbooks—with the exception of subjects such as Japanese or classical literature—are set in horizontal text.

Most general books sold in stores are set in vertical text. However, as young people today find no difficulty reading or writing Japanese in horizontal lines, this style will become increasingly common in the future

The Emperor of Japan

● Who was the first emperor of Japan?

According to the ancient historical chronicles, the *Kojiki* and the *Nihon shoki*, Japan's first emperor was supposedly Emperor Jimmu, who lived around 660 B.C.

However, this has not been proved to be true; **it is widely held that** the *Kojiki* and *Nihon shoki* are based on legend, as both were compiled after the eighth century.

Although it is often said that the tenth emperor, Sujin, was possibly the first historical emperor, it is not until the 33rd empress, Suiko, who reigned from 592–628, that actual records can be found. It was during this period that Prince Shōtoku emerged as the **imperial prince**.

● What are the origins of the imperial line?

Just as it is unclear where the Japanese people came from and how Japan as a nation emerged, the origins of the imperial

ルーツもわかっていません。邪馬台国の卑弥呼がその祖先であるという説，邪馬台国と対抗していたと言われる狗奴国の末裔であるという説，大和地方の**豪族**の1つの祖先であるという説………いろいろです。

しかし，いずれにしてもいくつかの国が勢力を競い合っていた中で，**大和朝廷**と言われるまでの存在になったどこかの勢力の子孫であるというわけです。

Q 日本にはこれまで何人の天皇がいましたか？

もちろん歴史的事実はわかりませんが，『日本書紀』『古事記』に書かれた神武天皇から数えると，平成の天皇は125代ということになります。

Q 平成の天皇はどういう人ですか？

Emperor and
Empress of Japan
©JAMP

1945年の太平洋戦争の敗戦により，天皇の地位は大きく変わります。新憲法によって，これまでの国の「元首」から，国の「象徴」と言われる存在となりました。この大きな変動のさなかに居たのは，現天皇の父の昭和天皇です。

太平洋戦争終結時には天皇は11歳でした。そして，アメリカ軍の駐留の下に，日本に**民主主義**が取り入れられた中で，これまでの帝王教育とは異なり，英語の教師としてアメリカからエリザベス・バイニング夫人を招くなど，新しい教育を受けられています。

Elizabeth Vining

皇族以外の人を皇太子妃に迎えたことも**異例**でしょう。しかも，軽井沢のテニスコートで見そめたというのですから，ほほえましいではありま

line are also unknown. There are many hypotheses: Himiko of the Yamatai polity is the direct ancestor of the emperor; the emperor is descended from Yamatai's rival polity, Kunakoku; or the emperor was descended from a **powerful clan** from the Yamato region.

Yet, despite the different theories, what seems to be true is that the imperial line descended from a regime that would eventually lay claim to the **Yamato Court** following a power struggle among a number of polities.

● How many Japanese emperors have there been?

Of course it is impossible to know with historical accuracy, but if we begin with Emperor Jimmu chronicled in the *Nihon shoki* and *Kojiki*, the current emperor would be the 125th reigning monarch.

● What is the current emperor like?

With the defeat of Japan in the Pacific War in 1945, the status of the emperor underwent a drastic change. According to the new constitution, the emperor was transformed from the head of state to a symbol of the state. The person who stood at the middle of this profound transformation was the Shōwa emperor, father of the current emperor, Akihito.

The emperor was 11 years old at the end of the Pacific War. And, while **democracy** was being introduced to Japan under the occupation by American forces, in contrast to past emperors, he was given a new education, which included his tutelage in English under an American instructor, Elizabeth Vining, sent from the United States.

It was also a **break from tradition** when a person outside the royal family became the crown princess, and it is even more heartwarming to know that the crown prince fell in love with

せんか。

1989年，昭和天皇の跡を継いで天皇となりますが，**平和主義に徹した**おだやかな人柄ということができます。

Q 元号はどうやって決めるのですか？

昔は，天皇の崩御による新天皇即位の場合だけでなく，生前の退位や，天変地異などの災厄を避ける祈願のため，また，幕府の将軍の交代の時などに年号が改められました。

しかし，明治に**年号**が改まったときに，天皇の在位は**即位**から崩御までと定められました。太平洋戦争後の1947年5月3日から施行された日本国憲法で，天皇は「国の象徴」という存在になりましたが，在位についてはその定めに従っています。ただし元号は，これまでは天皇の決定によるものでしたが，現在では，**内閣**が元号を定めることになっています。

新天皇の即位が決まると，内閣は**有識者**に新年号案の提出を求め，その案の中から決定をします。「平成」という年号は，初めてこの新しい方法で定められたものです。

Q 天皇はどんな仕事をしているのですか？

1947年の日本国憲法の**施行**によって，天皇の存在は戦前と全く異なりました。明治維新以降に強化された天皇の**統治権**と**神権**はなくなり，「日本国の象徴」という存在になります。そして，天皇の仕事は，憲法に定められた「内閣の承認のもとに行う**国事行為**」に限られることになりま

his future bride on a tennis court in Karuizawa.

In 1989, the crown prince succeeded the Shōwa emperor to become the current Heisei emperor. He can be described as a man of a gentle disposition who **stands firmly for peace**.

● How are era names determined?

Long ago, era names were changed not only upon the accession of a new emperor, following the death of his predecessor, but the name could also be changed during the reign of an emperor for such reasons as to ward off natural disasters or upon the succession of a new shōgun to the *bakufu* government.

However, when the new **era name** for the Meiji period was established, it was determined that the emperor's reign would begin from the time of **accession** and continue until his death. In the Japanese Constitution that was promulgated on May 3, 1947 following the end of the Pacific War, the emperor was made a "symbol of the state," but the provisions regarding imperial rule were left unchanged. Until this time, era names had been decreed by the emperor; however, it is the **cabinet** that today determines era names.

When the accession of a new emperor is determined, the cabinet seeks from various **opinion leaders** proposals for a new era name, and selects one from among the proposals. The era name "Heisei" was the first selected under this new system.

● What sort of work does the current emperor engage in?

Owing to a **decree** in the 1947 Japanese Constitution, the emperor's role was completely transformed. The **sovereignty** and **divinity** of the emperor, which was strengthened following the Meiji Restoration, was abolished, and the emperor became the "symbol of the Japanese state." And, as stipulated in the Constitution, the emperor's role was confined to serving in "**state**

した。具体的には，**総理大臣・最高裁判所長官**
の任命，**国会**の開会・解散の告示，法典の公布
などです。

　また，国民体育大会などの国民的行事への出
席，海外からの各国元首との親善的な応接，外
国への**親善訪問**など，政治的な影響を及ぼさな
い範囲で，積極的に国民と外国との融和に努力
をしているのも，仕事ということができるでしょう。

Q 女性も天皇になれるのですか？

　記録に残る歴代の天皇の中に，女性が10人
ほどいます。いちばん古くは推古天皇(592–628)，
いちばん新しくは後桜町天皇 (1762–70) です。
　天皇は**世襲制**で，男系の男子が継ぐという形
で継承順位が決まっていきますが，先代の天皇
が没した後，即位の条件をみたした皇位継承者
がなかった場合，先代天皇の**皇后**，**皇女**，ある
いは**皇太子妃**が即位したことがあったようです。
しかし現在の**皇室典範**では，皇位を継承でき
るのは男系の皇族に限られています。
　2000年の2月現在，天皇には皇太子と秋篠宮
という2人の子息が健在です。しかし，皇太子に
はまだ子供がなく，秋篠宮の子供は2人とも女児
ですから，現在は**皇位継承**の順位は，皇太子，
秋篠宮，今上天皇の弟である常陸宮，昭和天皇
の弟である三笠宮の順となります。しかし，そ
のどなたもが男児を遺さなかった場合、法律の
改正をすれば，皇后あるいは皇女の皇位継承
も可能になると考えられています。

functions approved by the cabinet." Specifically, these functions include ceremonies marking the appointment of the **prime minister** and **chief judge of the Supreme Court**, the opening and closing of **Diet** sessions, and the promulgation of new laws.

It can also be added that another function is to actively strive to harmonize relations between Japan and other countries through nonpolitical means such as by attending state ceremonies and national athletic meets, welcoming foreign heads of state, and paying **goodwill visits** to foreign countries.

● Can a woman become emperor?

Recorded imperial chronologies note ten women emperors. The first was the Empress Suiko (592–628), and the most recent was the Empress Go-Sakuramachi (1762–70).

Although the imperial line is determined by a **hereditary system** whereby paternal male heirs succeed to the throne, in a few cases, when the death of a reigning emperor left no heirs who could satisfy the requirements for imperial succession, the **empress**, **imperial princess**, or the **crown princess** succeeded to the throne. But under the current **Imperial Household Law** only males in the imerial family are allowed to succeed to the throne.

As of February 2000, the Emperor's two sons, the Crown Prince and Prince Akishino, are in good health. However, since the Crown Prince does not yet have any children and Prince Akishino's two children are both girls, the line of **succession to the throne** would be in the order of the Crown Prince, followed by Prince Akishino, Prince Hitachi (the brother of the Heisei Emperor, and Prince Mikasa (the brother of the Shōwa Emperor). However, in the event that there is no son, it may open the possibility for a change in the law to allow an empress or princess to succeed.

Q 現在，皇族と言われるのはどんな方ですか？

　　　天皇家の一員として，結婚をして「〜宮」という称号を持つことができるのは，天皇の直系の子供に限られます。

　　　従って，2000年2月現在，**皇族**と言われる方々は次の通りです。天皇・皇后，皇太后，皇太子・皇太子妃，秋篠宮(あきしののみや)・秋篠宮妃とその子供，紀宮(のりのみや)。天皇のご兄弟である常陸宮(ひたちのみや)・常陸宮妃。昭和天皇のご兄弟である三笠宮(みかさのみや)・三笠宮妃，亡くなられた高松宮(たかまつのみや)のお妃。三笠宮の子息である寛仁親王(ともひと)・妃とその子供，桂宮，高円宮(かつらのみや たかまどのみや)・高円宮妃とその子供。

　　　皇室は「**皇室典範**」という法律で身分や権利・義務などを規定されておりますが，一般国民と同様に法律が適用されます。唯一異なるのは**戸籍**がないということです。

　　　そして名前に必要な**名字**がありません。皇太子は，単に徳仁(なるひと)，皇太子妃となった小和田雅子さんは，単に雅子なのです。**宮家の名前**が与えられたとき，それが姓の役割をします。

日本の歴史

Q 邪馬台国はホントにあったんですか？

　　　中国の歴史書「魏志倭人伝(ぎ し わ じんでん)」に，日本は2世紀後半には非常に国が乱れ，多くの国々が争っていたが，邪馬台国が卑弥呼を女王に立てた

● At present, who is considered to be part of the imperial family?

The only people who as members of the imperial family can marry and hold the title -*miya* (prince or princess), are the children of the Emperor.

Accordingly, as of February 2000, those considered to be members of the **imperial family** are: the Emperor and Empress; the Empress Dowager; the Crown Prince and Princess; Prince and Princess Akishino, their children; Princess Nori; the brother of the Heisei Emperor (Prince and Princess Hitachi); the brothers of the Shōwa Emperor (Prince and Princess Mikasa) and the wife of the late Prince Takamatsu; the children of Prince Mikasa (Prince and Princess Tomohito); their children, Prince Katsura, Prince and Princess Takamado and their children.

The status, rights, and responsibilities of the imperial family are stipulated under the **Imperial Household Law**, but imperial family members are subject to the same laws governing regular citizens. The only difference is that they do not have **family registers**.

Also, there is no required **surname** for the imperial family. The name of the Crown Prince is simply Naruhito; Owada Masako, who became the Crown Princess, is simply called Masako. When an **imperial family name** is accorded, this serves as the surname.

Japanese History

● Did the country of Yamatai really exist?

According to "The Account of the Wa People" in the Chinese historical text *Wei zhi* (The Wei Chronicle), Japan in the latter half of the second century was undergoing much strife,

ところ大乱が治まった，とあります。

邪馬台国が存在したのはまちがいないのですが，その所在地については，昔から**論争**の種になっています。

学説は大きくわけると2つあります。1つは邪馬台国は九州にあったとする説，もう1つは奈良県付近にあったとする説で，今でも論争が続いています。

Q 古墳時代とはどんな時代ですか？

Haniwa

古墳とは当時の支配者（豪族）の**墓**で，形は各種あるのですが，いずれも小山のように土を盛りあげ，その表面には埴輪とよぶ土製の人物や馬などを飾り，内部には遺体のほかに，武器・鏡・装身具などの**副葬品**をおさめる石室があります。

こうした古墳がさかんにつくられた4世紀から7世紀末を古墳時代といいます。この時代，次第に大和国家としての**統一**が出来上がっていきます。

7世紀はじめには聖徳太子（574–622）が，「冠位十二階制」や「憲法十七条」を制定して，国家としての基盤を作りました。

Nintoku
Mausoleum

またこの時代は，中国，朝鮮からの**渡来人**が手工業や農業，土木技術の新技術を伝えた時代です。

Q 奈良時代とはどんな時代ですか？

奈良時代は，8世紀の大部分，710年から794年の間，現在の奈良に都が置かれていた時代

with most of the countries at war, but the countries were unified with the accession of Himiko as Queen of Yamatai.

While there is no doubt that Yamatai did exist, for a long time there has been much **debate** over the actual location of this country.

There are two major theories. One holds that Yamatai was located in Kyūshū, while the other claims that Yamatai was located near Nara Prefecture; the debate continues to this day.

● What was the Kofun period like?

"Kofun" is the name for the **tombs** of the rulers (*gōzoku*) of the period. While they came in various shapes, all were built of mounded earth, with clay sculptures (*haniwa*) of people and horses adorning the exterior of the tomb, and **funerary goods** such as weapons, mirrors, and personal ornaments enclosed with the body inside the interior stone chamber.

The Kofun period refers to the period from the fourth century to the seventh century when these tombs were actively built. It is during this period that gradual **unification** under the Yamato polity took place.

In the beginning of the seventh century, Prince Shōtoku (574–622) laid the foundations for the state by instituting the *Kan'i Jūnikai* (twelve grades of cap rank), a system of courtly ranks, and the Seventeen Article Constitution.

This was also the period when Chinese and Korean **immigrants** came to Japan and conveyed new technology in handicrafts, farming, and construction.

● What was the Nara period like?

The Nara period spans most of the eighth century, from 710 to 794, marking the years when the present-day city of Nara

The Great Buddha
of Tōdaiji Temple

です。この都を平城京と呼びます。

　奈良時代には**中央集権**となり，律令制度が敷かれます。

　6世紀半ばに日本に伝わった仏教はこの時代に政府に保護されて，大いに栄えました。現存する銅製の仏像では世界最大の，東大寺の大仏が作られたのもこの時代です。

　また，中国の唐に何度も人を派遣するなど海外との交流も盛んな時代で，唐の文化を中心に，朝鮮の文化やインド，ペルシアの文化の影響も見られる時代です。

Q 平安時代とはどんな時代ですか？

　現在の京都に都が移されたのは8世紀末のことで，ののち1000年以上，ずっと日本の都でしたが，そのうちの12世紀末までの約400年間を平安時代といいます。

　奈良時代に続いて，天皇の下で**貴族**が実権を握って政治を行っていきますが，同時に各地域の**豪族**が次第に**私有地**を拡大し，周辺との争

日本の歴史の主な時代

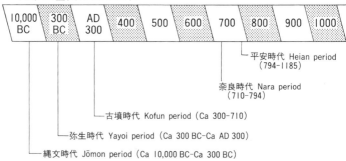

| 10,000 BC | 300 BC | AD 300 | 400 | 500 | 600 | 700 | 800 | 900 | 1000 |

　平安時代 Heian period
　（794-1185）

　奈良時代 Nara period
　（710-794）

　古墳時代 Kofun period（Ca 300-710）

　弥生時代 Yayoi period（Ca 300 BC-Ca AD 300）

　縄文時代 Jōmon period（Ca 10,000 BC-Ca 300 BC）

was the seat of the capital. This capital was called Heijōkyō.

The Nara period saw the **centralization of power** and the implementation of the *ritsuryō* (legal codes) system of government.

Buddhism flourished in the middle of the sixth century in Japan under the protection of the state. It was during this period that the world's largest existing bronze sculpture of Buddha—the Great Buddha of Tōdaiji temple—was built.

Foreign interaction thrived during this period, with a number of embassies dispatched to Tang China. China exerted a great influence on the culture, and was in turn influenced by the cultures of Korea, India and Persia.

● What was the Heian period like?

At the end of the eighth century, the capital was moved to present-day Kyōto, which remained Japan's capital for over 1,000 years. The Heian period designates a span of roughly 400 years until the 12th century.

Continuing from the Nara period, **aristocrats** under the emperor held actual power and controlled the government; but at the same time, **powerful clans** from a variety of regions

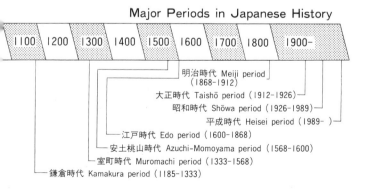

Major Periods in Japanese History

| 1100 | 1200 | 1300 | 1400 | 1500 | 1600 | 1700 | 1800 | 1900– |

明治時代 Meiji period (1868–1912)
大正時代 Taishō period (1912–1926)
昭和時代 Shōwa period (1926–1989)
平成時代 Heisei period (1989–)
江戸時代 Edo period (1600–1868)
安土桃山時代 Azuchi-Momoyama period (1568–1600)
室町時代 Muromachi period (1333–1568)
鎌倉時代 Kamakura period (1185–1333)

いから身を守るために武装して団結します。そして，ついに平氏とよばれる一族が政治の全権を握ります。やがて来る武士の時代の**さきがけ**です。

　文化の面では，唐の文化の**模倣**と**吸収**から脱して，日本の独特の風土や日本人の感性による文化へと移行しました。仮名の発達と仮名文の普及により，世界的に有名な紫式部の『源氏物語』，清少納言の『枕草子』などが生まれたのもこの時代です。

Ｑ 鎌倉時代とはどんな時代ですか？

　平安時代末期に政治の実権を握っていた平氏も，1185年，ついに源氏に滅ぼされます。

Minamoto no Yori-tomo

　平氏を滅ぼした源頼朝（みなもとのよりとも）は，鎌倉（神奈川県）に拠点を定め，**守護**と**地頭**を任命して諸国に置き，勢力を固めました。そして，源頼朝は1192年に征夷（せいい）大将軍となり，鎌倉幕府が成立しました。武家政治の始まりです。幕府は武士の長である将軍が政務をとった**軍事政権**です。天皇は単なる**名目的な存在**でした。

　しかし，頼朝が亡くなった後，未亡人の北条政子の一族，北条氏（ほうじょう）が権力を握り，1333年，後醍醐天皇が鎌倉幕府を倒し，天皇政治を復活するまで続きます。

　文化の面では，武士らしい，力強く，剛毅で，

expanded their **private landholdings** and became unified and militarized in order to protect themselves from war with neighboring regions. Eventually, the Taira clan was able to grasp full political control. It was a **harbinger** of the age of the warrior that was soon to follow.

In the cultural sphere, Japan was able to move away from its reliance on **imitating** and **assimilating** Tang culture and proceeded to forge a culture that incorporated a distinct Japanese spirit and sensitivity. Due to the development and spread of *hiragana* and *katakana*, world-renowned literary works such as the *Tale of Genji* by Murasaki Shikibu and *Makura no Sōshi* by Sei Shōnagon were created during this period.

● What was the Kamakura period like?

The Taira family, which had grasped political power toward the end of the Heian period, was overthrown by the Minamoto family in 1185.

After Minamoto no Yoritomo defeated the Taira family, he set up his base in Kamakura (Kanagawa Prefecture), and by assigning **constables** and **stewards** throughout the country he was able to solidify his power. In 1192, Minamoto no Yoritomo was given the title *seii tai shōgun* (barbarian-subduing generalissimo) and established a *bakufu* (shogunate) government at Kamakura. This was the beginning of warrior clan politics. *Bakufu* was the name for a **military regime** in which the head of the warriors, the shōgun, controlled political affairs. The emperor was simply a **figurehead**.

After Masako Hōjō was left a widow at Yoritomo's death, her family, the Hōjō clan, took over and remained in power until Emperor Go-Daigo defeated the Kamakura *bakufu* government in 1333 and effected a restoration of imperial rule.

In the cultural sphere, the period gave birth to a number of

そして写実的な**仏像彫刻**に名作が生まれました。

仏教は庶民の信仰を集めるようになり，法然が浄土宗，日蓮が日蓮宗を興すなどしました。禅宗もこの時代に栄えました。

鎌倉時代の出来事として忘れてならないのは，**蒙古の来襲**です。1274年，1284年の2度にわたって，フビライ・ハンの大軍が九州の博多に押し寄せましたが，いずれの時も，運良く大あらしとなり，蒙古の艦隊は退却していきました。

Q 室町時代とはどんな時代ですか？

室町時代は2つに分けられます。南北朝時代と戦国時代です。

Emperor Go-Daigo

南北朝時代は，1333年に足利尊氏の力で鎌倉幕府を倒し，政治を京都の朝廷に取り戻した後醍醐天皇と，これに背いて，光明天皇をかついで，1336年に京都北部の室町に幕府を開いた足利尊氏とが対立していた時代です。

後醍醐天皇の没後は，足利一族による鎌倉幕府が全国支配に乗り出しますが，幕府の力は弱く，諸国には自ら武力を持った守護大名の勢力が高まってきました。1467年，将軍家の相続問題から，10年におよぶ応仁の乱が起こり，幕府の権威は失われ，**群雄割拠**の戦国時代となります。

戦国時代は，1467年の応仁の乱以後，1573年に織田信長が幕府を滅ぼすまでの約100年間です。

室町時代には，全般的には，農業生産が向上

famous realistic **Buddhist sculptures** noted for being powerful, bold, and warrior-like.

As Buddhism assimilated the faith of the commoners, Hōnen established Jōdoshū and Nichiren established Nichiren-shū. Zenshū also prospered during this period.

One of the more unforgettable narratives of the Kamakura period was of the **Mongolian invasions**. In the years 1274 and 1284, the forces of Kublai Khan attempted to invade Kyūshū at Hakata, but both times the Mongolian troops were defeated with the help of large storms at sea.

● What was the Muromachi period like?

The Muromachi period can be divided into two periods: the Northern and Southern Courts period and the Warring States period.

The Northern and Southern Courts period was a time of conflict between Emperor Go-Daigo, who had overthrown the Kamakura *bakufu* in 1333 and restored political power to the palace in Kyōto, and Ashikaga Takauji, who set up a *bakufu* government in Muromachi in northern Kyōto under the Emperor Kōmyō in 1336.

After the death of Emperor Go-Daigo, the Ashikaga clan of the Muromachi *bakufu* set out to rule the entire country, but the power of the *bakufu* weakened while the power of the Shugo *daimyō* throughout the country increased. In 1467, problems of succession in shōgun families marked the Ōnin War that lasted ten years. And as the *bakufu* lost power, the country entered the Warring States period of **fighting and disorder**.

The Warring States period is the 100-year period beginning with the Ōnin War in 1467 and continuing until Oda Nobunaga's defeat of the *bakufu* in 1573.

Overall, the Muromachi period saw the rise of agricultural

Francisco Xavier
（神戸市立博物館）

し，商業も発展し，都市が栄えました。

　文化面でも**水墨画**，能，狂言，**茶の湯**，生け花などがこの時代に広まりました。**キリスト教**もまた，1549年のフランシスコ・ザビエルの来日によって，日本に伝えられました。

Q 安土桃山時代とはどんな時代ですか？

Oda Nobunaga
（長興寺）

　戦国時代にライバルを次々と倒していったのが織田信長でした。しかし彼は，**全国統一**を目前にして**家臣**の明智光秀（あけちみつひで）に殺されてしまいます。その後を引き継いだのが，やはり家臣だった豊臣秀吉でした。安土桃山時代はこの織田信長と豊臣秀吉が政権を握っていた時代です。1568年（1573年説もある）から約30年という短期間ですが，日本の**封建社会**を発展させた点で重要な時代です。

Toyotomi Hideyoshi

　注目すべき2つの政策は**検地**と**刀狩り**です。農地面積や収穫高などを調べ，年貢の量と責任者を決める検地，そして，農民から一切の武器を取りあげる刀狩りは，農民の身分を固定化し，武士の支配的地位を決定づけました。

　文化は桃山文化と呼ばれ，仏教の影響が弱まり，自由で豪華な様相を呈しました。高くそびえる天守閣を持つ城郭建築や金箔にきらめく**障壁画**がその典型です。

Q 江戸時代とはどんな時代ですか？

　豊臣家を滅ぼし，1603年，徳川家康が江戸

production, the growth of commercial activity, and the development of cities.

Culturally, this period witnessed the birth of **ink painting**, *nō* and *kyōgen* theater, the **tea ceremony**, and Japanese flower arrangement. And with the arrival of Francisco Xavier in 1549, **Christianity** was brought to Japan.

● What was the Azuchi-Momoyama period like?

During the Warring States period, Oda Nobunaga went on to defeat one rival after another. However, just before he could achieve **unification of the country**, he was killed by his own **vassal**, Akechi Mitsuhide. The person who succeeded him was another of his subjects, Toyotomi Hideyoshi. Azuchi-Momoyama covers the period when political control was held by Oda Nobunaga and Toyotomi Hideyoshi. The short, roughly 30-year span beginning in 1568 (some say 1573) was a crucial period in terms of the development of Japan's **feudal society**.

The two policies which deserve attention are the **cadastral survey** and the **sword hunt**. The cadastral survey, which appraised the area and productivity of agricultural land, and the sword hunt, which confiscated all weaponry held by peasants, served to establish the domination of the warrior class and entrench the status of the peasant.

In terms of culture, this period gave rise to what is known as the *Momoyama* culture, which saw the weakening of Buddhist influence and the emergence of a free and sumptuous style. Typifying this culture were the building of castles with soaring towers and the creation of wall and **screen paintings** glittering with gold leaf.

● What was the Edo period like?

The Edo period is the 260-year span following Tokugawa

Tokugawa Ieyasu

（東京）に幕府を開いて全国を支配した260年余が江戸時代です。

幕府の**最高権力者**，将軍から1万石以上の領地を得た者が大名で，その**領地**と支配機構を藩と言います。幕府は藩を通して全国の領土と民衆を支配します。この支配体制が幕藩制です。

武士をいちばん上の階級とする士農工商の制度で身分差別を強め，対外的には，**鎖国政策**をとり，キリスト教を禁じた時代でもあります。

しかし，国内の作物の栽培は進み，漁業も発達し，商人が力をつけて，**貨幣経済**が発展しました。

文化の面では，17世紀末〜18世紀初めに元禄文化が花開きます。町民が担い手で，**人形浄瑠璃**や歌舞伎が人気を博し，松尾芭蕉が俳句を大成しました。浮世絵が創始され，歌麿，北斎，広重ら多くの浮世絵師が出ました。

明治から現代へ

Q 明治時代はどうやって誕生したのですか？

1853年，ペリー率いるアメリカ軍艦が浦賀沖に現れ開国を迫るや，国内は開国か**尊皇攘夷**か

Ieyasu's defeat of the Toyotomi family and the establishment of a *bakufu* government in Edo (now Tōkyō) in 1603.

The *daimyō* ranged from the *shōgun*, who sat at the **apex of power**, to lords controlling land worth over 10,000 *koku* (a unit of measure based on rice production), and their **domains** and the power structure imposed on them were known as *han*. The *bakufu* controlled the land and the people of the nation through these *han* units. This system of government is known as the *bakuhan* system.

This period also saw the reinforcement of a status system known as *shi-nō-kō-shō* (warrior-peasant-artisan-merchant), which placed the warrior in the top social class, and externally, the establishment of a **policy of national seclusion** and the prohibition of Christianity.

However, during this period, advances were made in domestic agricultural production as well as in fishing industries, which strengthened the merchant class and gave rise to a **monetary economy**.

Culturally, this period saw the flourishing in the latter 17th and early 18th centuries of what is known as the Genroku culture. Fostered by the townspeople, arts such as the **puppet theater** and *kabuki* gained popularity, while Matsuo Bashō produced masterpieces in the *haiku* poetic form. The art of *ukiyo-e* prints which was fostered by Utamaro, Hokusai, Hiroshige and many other artists, also began during this period.

From Meiji to the Present

● What gave birth to the Meiji period?

In 1853, Commodore Perry and his squadron of American ships appeared in Uraga Bay to press for the opening of the

Commodore Perry

を巡って大混乱に陥りました。

　倒幕の主力となった薩摩藩（鹿児島県）と長州藩（山口県）も，当初は尊皇攘夷でしたが，欧米の力を知るに至って**開国**へと方向転換します。

The last shōgun, Tokugawa Yoshi-nobu

　一方，民衆は**物価上昇**に苦しみ，富裕な商店を襲う打ち壊しや一揆が各地で続発，ここからも幕藩制の根底が揺るぎました。ついに15代将軍，徳川慶喜は，1867年，政権を朝廷に返します。そして天皇中心の政府を樹立する王政復古の大号令が出され，長い**封建制度**は終わりを告げます。明治時代の誕生です。

Q 明治時代とはどんな時代ですか？

Emperor Meiji

　徳川氏から**朝廷**へと政権が移行し，幕府と藩による政治から国家統一へと向かうことになりました。経済は資本主義制度へと移行して，近代日本の制度ができた時代です。

　1889年，明治憲法（大日本帝国憲法）が施行されて，国の政治形態の基本ができますが，「天皇は神聖にして侵すべからず」という条項があり，天皇は神格化され，日本は次第に**国家主義**で統一されていきます。

　これに反対して，人民の自由と権利を伸ばすことを主張する**自由民権運動**が起こりますが，結

country, leaving in their wake a domestic crisis over whether to open up or "**revere the emperor and expel the barbarians**."

Even Satsuma (now Kagoshima Prefecture) and Chōshū provinces (now Yamaguchi Prefecture), which eventually overthrew the *bakufu*, initially supported the move to "revere the emperor and expel the barbarians," but eventually, with their growing knowledge of the Western power, they decided to switch their allegiance toward the drive to **open up the country**.

On the one hand, the masses were suffering under **inflation**, and riots and attacks on shops of wealthy merchants occurred in various regions, weakening the foundations of the *bakuhan* system. This led in 1867 to the relinquishing of power by the 15th Tokugawa shōgun, Yoshinobu, to the imperial court. A decree was made which established a government centered around the emperor, bringing to a close the long-lasting **feudal system**. This is how the Meiji period came into being.

● What was the Meiji period like?

This period saw the transfer of power from Tokugawa to the **imperial court**, and the transition from a system of government based on the *bakufu* and *han* domains to a unified state. This was also the period that witnessed the transition to a capitalist economy and the establishment of a modern Japanese state system.

In 1889, the Meiji Constitution (the Constitution of Imperial Japan) was promulgated, laying the foundation for the political structure of the state. It contained a clause maintaining the divinity of the emperor, proclaiming that the country "must not violate the sanctity of the emperor," and thus Japan gradually became unified under the force of **nationalism**.

In protest against nationalism, **human rights movements** arose to assert and extend the rights and freedom of citizens.

局は，**国家主義の名のもとに**，国益が優先され，朝鮮半島，中国大陸への進出をします。

そして，これに反対する諸外国との軋轢（あつれき）も強まり，明治時代だけで，**日清戦争**（1894–1895），**日露戦争**（1904–1905）に突入し，1910年には韓国を日本に**併合する**という事態になっていきました。

Q 大正時代とはどんな時代ですか？

Emperor Taishō

この時代は1912年から26年までの14年間という短い期間ですが，明治時代の藩閥・官僚政治による国家権力の増大に反発して，憲法にのっとった政治を守ること，誰でもが**選挙権**を持つことができる**普通選挙**を求める運動などが繰り広げられます。

米騒動や**労働争議**も起こり，民本主義，自由主義，社会主義の運動が高まった時代です。この運動を「大正デモクラシー」と呼んでいます。

しかしこの運動も，結局，高まる国家主義の動きに抗することはできず，日本は次第に軍国主義の国になっていきます。

Q 太平洋戦争敗戦までの昭和時代はどんな時代ですか？

昭和を簡単に説明するのは困難です。太平洋戦争の敗戦の1945年の前と，その後1989年まで続いた時期とでは，根本的な違いがあるからです。

日露戦争後，日本は**満州**における権益の確保政策を続け，大陸に駐留する**関東軍**は満州占領を進めて，1932年には「満州建国宣言」を

But in the end, **under the banner of nationalism**, Japan let state interests take precedence and advanced into the Korean peninsula and the Chinese continent.

Friction increased with countries that opposed Japan's advances, and in the Meiji period alone, Japan entered into the **Sino-Japanese War** (1894–5) and the **Russo-Japanese War** (1904–5), and went on to **annex** Korea in 1910.

● What was the Taishō period like?

This was a short 14-year period from 1912 to 1926, which saw opposition to growing state power in the hands of the *han* bureaucratic clique from the Meiji period. There was a spread of popular movements which demanded that government abide by the constitution and called for **common elections** which extended **voting rights** to all citizens.

This was a period when **rice riots** and **labor disputes** occurred, and democratic and socialist movements were heightened. Such movements are referred to as Taishō Democracy.

However, even these movements in the end could not stem rising nationalism, and Japan would increasingly turn into a militarist state.

● What was the Shōwa period like before the end of World War II?

It is difficult to explain in brief the Shōwa period because of the fundamental difference between the pre-World War II period before Japan's defeat in 1945 and the postwar period which lasted until 1989.

After the Russo-Japanese War, Japan continued its policy of extending power in **Manchuria**, and the **Kwantung Army** stationed on the continent furthered its occupation of Manchuria, and in

Hiroshima reduced to rubble by the atomic bomb explosion

します。

これに異議をとなえる**国際連盟**は調査団を送りますが，日本は国際連盟を脱退してしまいます。

さらに1937年，深夜演習中の日本軍と中国軍が衝突するという**盧溝橋事件**を契機に中国との間に戦争となり，ついには，東南アジア一帯にも日本が介入するにおよび，1941年12月8日の真珠湾攻撃を開始の合図に，日本はアメリカその他の国々との**全面戦争**に突入しました。

結果は，1945年8月，敗戦。

Q 敗戦後の昭和時代はどんな時代ですか？

敗戦の結果，日本は**連合軍**の占領下におかれることになり，新しい日本国憲法の制定，農地改革，教育改革，財閥の解体，日本の伝統的な家制度の廃止などの改革が進められました。

Emperor Shōwa and General MacArthur

新憲法では，国民が国の主権者であることが明記され，天皇は国の象徴とされました。のちに**自衛隊**が誕生しますが，**憲法第9条**には軍備の放棄がうたわれました。農地改革では**小作制度**が廃止され，地主が所有していた農地の多くは農民に開放されました。教育改革では**男女共学**になり，小学校6年間，中学校3年間の義務教育が定められました。また，家制度の廃止で，子供を**家への従属**から解放し，核家族の誕生，女性の自由な恋愛などへの道が開かれていきました。

1951年6月に日本は，**共産圏を除く48か国と**

1932 issued the "Declaration of the Founding of Manchukuo."

In protest, the **League of Nations** sent an **investigative commission** to Manchuria, while Japan withdrew from the League.

In 1937, propelled by the **Marco Polo Bridge Incident** when Japanese forces on night training clashed with Chinese troops, Japan entered into a war with China, and soon it intervened in all of Southeast Asia. Japan's attack on Pearl Harbor on December 8, 1941 signaled its thrust into **full-scale war** with the United States and other countries.

In the end, Japan was defeated in August 1945.

• What was the Shōwa period like after the end of World War II?

After Japan was defeated, the country was placed under the **allied forces**, while reforms that included the creation of a new constitution, agrarian and educational reforms, dissolution of *zaibatsu*, and abolition of the Japanese traditional family system were carried out.

The new Constitution ruled that sovereignty lies with the citizens and that the emperor serves as a symbol of the nation. **Article 9 of the Constitution** forbids Japan from possessing arms, although a **self-defense force** was later formed. Under agrarian reform, the **tenant farmer system** was abolished and the farms held by landlords were distributed to the farmers. With educational reform, a **coeducational system** was instigated and six years of elementary school and three years of junior high school were made compulsory. The abolition of the family system freed children from the old **clan bondage**, nuclear families became the norm, and women obtained the freedom to choose marriage partners.

In June 1951, Japan signed the San Francisco Peace Treaty

Signing ceremony
of the San Francisco
Peace Treaty

の間にサンフランシスコ講和条約が締結され，占領体制は終わり，同時に，アメリカとの間に**日米安全保障条約**を締結しました。

戦後の経済復興には困難が伴いましたが，アメリカの支援，1ドルが360円という安定した**為替相場**，また，1950年に起こった朝鮮戦争の際の軍事需要などによる景気で，日本の経済力は強まり，1955年から60年にかけて，日本の国民総生産は，毎年9％以上の伸びを見せました。

高度な工業技術によって船舶，テレビ，自動車など，多くの製品の主要な生産国になり，1970年代，1980年代には輸出が増大しました。それに対して海外から輸出規制の圧力が高まりましたが，日本の貿易収支はとりわけアメリカに対して，大幅な黒字を続けました。

政治は，**自民党**がほぼ独占的に権力を握り続けましたが，経済の**高度成長**はいろいろなひずみも生じ，様々な公害や環境破壊などを生んできました。

文化的には，あらゆる面でアメリカ，ヨーロッパの**流行**が取り入れられ，特に若者を中心に一気に西欧化したのもこの時代です。

そして好景気にあおられて，1986年，いわゆるバブル経済が始まります。異常な地価の高騰に日本中が浮かれる中，1989年1月，昭和天皇が亡くなられ，時代は平成**に移る**ことになりました。

Q 平成時代はどんな時代ですか？

昭和の終わりに発生したバブル経済は，1991年に入ると一気にしぼみはじめます。地価は下がり，株価も急速に下がり，特に，バブル時代に

with 48 countries, none of which were from the **Communist bloc**, thus leading to the end of allied occupation. At this same time, Japan also concluded the **United States-Japan Security Treaty**.

Japan's postwar economic rehabilitation has involved difficulties, but the Japanese economy became stronger with America's support, a stable **exchange rate** of 360 yen to the dollar, and the prosperity resulting from the war boom during the Korean War in the 1950s. The GNP of Japan grew nine percent every year from 1955 to 1960.

Due to a high level of engineering skill, Japan became a major exporter of various products such as ships, TVs, and automobiles, and in the 1970s and 1980s Japanese exports rose sharply. Pressure from abroad to exercise self-restraint in exports mounted, but Japan's trade surplus kept rising, especially with the United States.

As for politics, the **Liberal-Democratic Party** has maintained a monopolistic grip on power, but the **high growth rate** has brought about various problems such as pollution and destruction of the environment.

And culturally, this was a period when all sorts of **fads** from America and Europe were introduced, and almost overnight the country became westernized.

Powered by the strong economy, the economic "bubble" began to form in 1986. Land prices rose to exorbitant levels and, with the country in a state of euphoria, the Emperor Shōwa passed away in January 1989, **making room for** the new Heisei period.

● What is Japan like in the Heisei period?

The "bubble" economy that formed at the end of the Shōwa period suddenly collapsed in 1991. Land prices fell, stock prices collapsed and, most notably, banks that had extended financing

不動産向け融資を拡大し続けた銀行は，膨大な**不良債権**を抱え込むことになりました。経営が破綻した銀行も出て，預金者に大きな不安を与えることになりましたので，政府は60兆円もの資金を導入して，金融システムを保護する策をとりました。しかし，製造業は**不景気**の風をまともに受けてリストラを余儀なくされ，**倒産**も相継ぎ，失業者が世に溢れだしました。アメリカ，イギリスでは年々**失業率**が減っているのに対して，日本では次第に上昇して，2000年2月には失業率が4％前後にまで上がりました。

　自民党の政治の**腐敗**，政治改革への取り組みの**怠慢**に対する一般市民の憤りで，1993年には，日本新党の細川護熙を首相にした**連立政権**が誕生したものの，1996年には自民党が勢力を盛り返し，再び権力の座につきました。その自民党の政権下，2000年になっても景気が回復する気配はなく，日本はいよいよ21世紀を迎えることになりました。

Ex-premier,
Hosokawa Morihiro

for real estate during the bubble found themselves with huge amounts of **non-collectable loans**. After a few banks went bankrupt, resulting in a great deal of uncertainty among depositors, the government stepped in to protect the banking system with 60 trillion yen. But the manufacturing sector took the **depression** head on and was forced to restructure to survive. A string of **bankruptcies** occurred and the unemployment rate rose. While the **unemployment rate** for the United States and England shrunk year by year, Japan's unemployed increased, and in February 2000 the rate reached around four percent.

Due to the anger of the general population with **corruption** in the Liberal-Democratic Party and a **negligent attitude** toward government reform, a new **coalition party** under the New-Japan Party of Hosokawa Morihiro took over, but the Liberal-Democratic Party recovered and returned to power in 1996. Again under the Liberal-Democratic Party, the economy has shown little sign of recovery as Japan faces the 21st century.

日本の政治と経済

Government and Economy

The Diet Building ▶

日本の憲法

Q 日本の現憲法は，いつ，どのようにして
作られたのですか？

1945年8月の太平洋戦争後，日本を占領下
に置いた**連合国総司令部（GHQ）**から憲法改正
の勧告を受けて，日本政府は翌1946年1月に**改
正案**を作成しました。その内容は旧大日本帝国
憲法の影を濃厚に残したもので，国民の権利は
拡張されましたが，国の主権は天皇にあるまま
としていました。

そこで連合国最高司令官マッカーサーはこれ
を拒否し，2月13日に別の憲法試案，いわゆる
マッカーサー草案を提示し，日本政府にこの検
討を求めました。

日本政府はこの草案をもとに3月6日に新憲
法をまとめ，1947年5月3日に，現在の日本国憲
法が施行されることになったのです。

日本の**保守層**の中には，この憲法は自分たち

Constitution of Japan

• When and how was the Japanese Constitution made?

As suggested by the **general headquarters of the allied forces** occupying Japan after World War II, the Japanese government completed a **draft of the revision** of the Meiji Constitution in January 1946. In this draft, with no major changes from the original constitution, sovereignty rested with the emperor, although the people's rights were extended significantly.

General MacArthur rejected this draft and presented the so-called "MacArthur draft" on February 13 for the Japanese government's consideration.

The government drew up a new constitution based on the MacArthur draft on March 6, and it came into force on May 3, 1947.

Some **conservatives** in Japan have criticized this new con-

で手に入れたものというよりも「与えられた憲法」
だとして，批判の声を上げる人もいます。

Q 日本国憲法はどんな特色を持っていますか？

日本国憲法は、**前文**および11章103条から出
来ています。憲法の特色を表す基本的な理念と
して、**国民主権、基本的人権の尊重、平和主義**の
3つがあげられます。

国民主権とは、国の全ての権力は国民の意志
に基づくとする考えで、選挙により国民に選ばれ
た国会議員が、国民の**代わり**として行動するの
をたてまえとしています。

このため、それまで絶対的な権力者とされた
天皇の地位は国と国民の統合の象徴へと大き
く変わりました。

基本的人権の尊重は、個人個人の生命や自
由を大切にし、最大限に保障するべきだとする
考え方です。憲法ではこの基本的人権を「**侵す
ことのできない永久の権利**」であると規定してい
ます。また、これを徹底して保障するために、裁
判所に法律の**妥当性**を審査する権利も与えられ
ています。

平和主義はこれら3原則のなかでも他の国に
ない特色的な理念で、平和国家として歩む姿勢
として、国と国との問題の解決方法に戦争とい
う手段はとらないこと、そのために**戦力**を持たな
いことを明記しています。

stitution because it was something given to the people, rather than something they acquired by themselves.

● What are some of the special characteristics of the Constitution of Japan?

The Constitution of Japan has a **preface** and 11 chapters containing a total of 103 articles. Three basic concepts that characterize the Constitution are (1) **sovereignty of the people**, (2) **respect for fundamental human right**s, and (3) **opposition to war**.

Sovereignty of the people, or "popular sovereignty," is the concept that all government powers are based upon the will of the people. It is associated with the principle that members of parliament will be chosen by the people through elections and will act as their **representatives**.

Thus, the position of the emperor, who had previously been considered the absolute holder of power, was greatly changed to make him a symbol of the unity of the people.

Respect for fundamental human rights is the concept that each individual's life and freedom are very important and should be protected as much as possible. The Constitution states that fundamental human rights are "**eternal rights which cannot be violated**." To protect these rights and to be sure that they are thoroughly respected, courts are given the right to study and pass judgment on the **appropriateness** of all laws.

Among these three principles, "opposition to war" is a distinctive concept that is not so clearly expressed in the constitutions of most other countries. The Japanese Constitution clearly states that Japan, in its stance of behaving as a peaceful nation, will not use war as a way to resolve problems between countries and will thus not maintain **war-making capabilities**.

Q いつも問題になる憲法第2章第9条とはどんな内容ですか？

第9条の全文を挙げてみましょう。

「日本国民は，**正義と秩序**を基調とする国際平和を誠実に希求し，国権の発動たる戦争と，武力による威嚇又は武力の行使は，国際紛争を解決する手段としては，永久にこれを**放棄する**。

前項の目的を達するため，陸海空軍その他の戦力は，これを保持しない。国の**交戦権**は，これを認めない。」

素直に読めば，いかなる軍備も持たないと読むことができます。しかし，この条項には自衛権は含まれない，とする日本の保守勢力の主張に支えられて，1954年に**自衛隊**が誕生しました。

Q 憲法はどのようにしたら改定できるのですか？

憲法を**改正**するためには，**衆議院，参議院**，それぞれ総議員の3分の2以上の賛成で発議され，それを**国民投票**にかけて，過半数の賛成を必要とします。現憲法は占領下に押しつけられたものと考える人もいたり，近代国家として自分の国を守る軍隊を持つことは当然で，PKOに協力するための海外派兵を可能とするためにも，9条を改正すべきなどの声がありますが，1947年の現憲法の**施行**以来，現在まで一度も憲法改正のための国民投票が行われたことはありません。

● What is the content of Article 9, Chapter 2 of the Constitution, which is said to be the most controversial?

Article 9, Chapter 2 of the Japanese Constitution translates as follows:

"Aspiring sincerely to an international peace based on **justice and order**, the Japanese people forever **renounce** war as a sovereign right of the nation and the threat or use of force as a means of settling international disputes.

"In order to accomplish the aim of the preceding paragraph, land, sea, and air forces, as well as other war potential, will never be maintained. The **right of belligerency** of the state will not be recognized."

The article, when interpreted straightforwardly, means that Japan can never possess any type of military forces. However, the **Self-Defense Force** came into existence in 1954, supported by conservatives who insisted that the right of self-defense is not implied in the article.

● How can the Constitution be amended?

Amendments to the Constitution first require the approval of more than two thirds of the members of the **House of Representatives** and the **House of Councilors**, and then the approval of the majority of the people of Japan by a **national referendum**. Some people feel that the present Constitution was forced on Japan during the postwar occupation, and one can hear voices to the effect that Article 9 should be revised because it should be taken for granted that a modern state should have a military organization to protect its own land, or in order to allow the sending abroad of military personnel to cooperate with peace-keeping operations (PKO) of the United Nations. However, since the **promulgation** of the present Constitution in 1947, no

政治の仕組み

Q 日本の議会はどういう構成になっていますか？

The House of
Representatives

　日本の**議会**は Diet と表現され，衆議院と参議院の2院で構成されています。

　両院とも国民を代表する議員で構成されています。国民の意思を代表するのが衆議院，衆議院の判断の不備や行き過ぎを是正する役目をするのが参議院です。

Q 議員は何人いて，どうやって
　　選ぶのですか？

Streetside
campaigning for
an election

　2000年2月現在，衆議院は500人，参議院は252人が定員となっています。

　衆議院に関しては，大激論の末，1994年に選挙法が改正され，小選挙区比例代表制が採択されてこの数字になっています。

　衆議院の選挙制度は2つの投票方法によっています。500人の内300人は**小選挙区制**，つまり全国を300に分けた区域の中からそれぞれ1名が選ばれます。

　そして残りの200人には**比例代表制**が適用されます。この制度では，全国を11のブロックに分けて**選挙区**とし，投票は**候補者**ではなく，政党に対して行います。政党に対する投票で各政党が全国で得た数に比例して，議席を配分します。

　有権者は小選挙区で候補者を1人，比例選挙区で政党を1つ選んで**投票**することになります。

national referendum for its amendment has been conducted.

Government System

• What is the parliamentary system of Japan like?

The parliament of Japan is called the **Diet**, and is made up of the House of Representatives and the House of Councilors.

Both houses consist of elected members representing the nation. The House of Representatives mainly represents the people's opinions, and the House of Councilors checks the power and judgment of the House of Representatives.

• How many members of the Diet are there and how are they elected?

As of February 2000, the House of Representatives has 500 members and the House of Councilors has 252.

The number in the House of Representatives reflects the most recent revision of the election law, which, after heated discussions, was enacted in 1994.

The election system for the House of Representatives consists of two voting methods. Of the 500 seats, 300 are elected according to the "**small electoral district system**," in which one candidate is elected for each of the 300 districts of the country.

And the "**proportional representation system**" is applied to the remaining 200 seats. With this system, the country is divided into 11 large **electoral districts**, and votes are cast for political parties instead of **candidates**. The seats for members of the Diet are allocated to each party in proportion to the number of votes gained nationwide.

Therefore, a **voter** casts a **ballot** for one candidate in the small electoral district, and a ballot for one party in the larger

　　　参議院は，100人を比例代表制で選び，残り
の152人を都道府県を単位とした選挙区から選
出します。

　　　任期は，衆議院議員が4年，参議院議員は6年
です。参議院議員は，3年ごとに半数が改選さ
れます。

Q 日本の政治の仕組みはどうなっていますか？

The Supreme Court

　　　日本の政治体制は多くの民主国家同様，**立
法**，**司法**，**行政**で成り立っています。それぞれの
権力分野は独立しています。国会が立法権を，
内閣が行政権を，裁判所が司法権を持っていま
す。

　　　そして，実際の政治は国会が内閣を組織する
という「**議院内閣制**」によって行われています。**首
相**は議会の議決で選任され，**大臣**は首相が選
任します。

　　　しかし，アメリカのような他の民主主義国家と
違って，大臣は議員の中から選任されることが
多いので，立法府と行政府の境界線が**あいまい
になる**という現実があります。

Q 首相はどのようにして選ばれるのですか？

　　　日本の首相は国会の議決で決まりますが，だ
れでも首相に立候補できるかというと，そういう
わけにはいきません。

　　　日本の政治は政党政治です。そして首相の
資格は国会議員であること，および**文民**である

proportional electoral district.

A hundred members of the House of Councilors are elected according to the "proportional representation system" and the remaining 152 members are elected from electoral districts based on prefectural units.

Terms of office are four years for members of the House of Representatives and six years for members of the House of Councilors. Half of the members of the House of Councilors are elected every three years.

● What is the government system of Japan like?

The Japanese government, as in many democratic countries, is composed of a **legislative branch**, an **administrative branch**, and a **judiciary branch**. Each of the branches is independent from the others in terms of power. The Diet is vested with legislative powers, the cabinet with administrative powers, and the court with judiciary powers.

The execution of administrative powers is based on the "**parliamentary cabinet system**" in which the cabinet is organized by the Diet. The **prime minister** is designated by the Diet and the **state ministers** are chosen by the prime minister.

However, unlike in some democratic countries such as the United States, the majority of state ministers are chosen from among members of the Diet. This fact can **obscure** the line between the legislature and the administration.

● How is the prime minister elected?

The Japanese prime minister is chosen by the Diet, but not everyone can run for prime minister.

Because of the nature of the Japanese government, which is party-based, a candidate for prime minister must be a member

ことが条件です。日本では正式の軍隊はありません。ので, 誰もが文民ですが……

　政党は勢力拡張をねらい, それぞれに, また連立して自分たちの党の党首, リーダーを首相の座に推します。

　そのために政党間の権力闘争が激しく渦巻き, 国民の利益よりも自分たちの利益に走ることになりかねません。いつも**金権政治**の駆け引きになる恐れがあるのです。日本で政治が遠いものに感じられるのは, この首相の選び方にあるのかもしれません。

Q 日本にはどんな政党がありますか?

　1990年代に入ってから政界の**再編成**が進んでおり, 自由民主党の分裂, 社会党の衰退, 公明党の変身など, 大変流動的な状態が続き, 1993年以降, **連立内閣**が続いています。

　一応, 2000年の4月の段階で, 衆参国会に議席を持つ政党は, 次の通りです。
　　自由民主党
　　民主党
　　社会民主党
　　自由党
　　保守党
　　さきがけ
　　日本共産党
　　公明党

of the Diet. And he or she must be a **civilian**. (Actually, all Japanese are civilians since there is no formal military in Japan.)

Political parties, independent and coalition alike, recommend the presidents or leaders of their parties for the position of prime minister, in hopes of increasing their power.

The fight for power among parties is so heated that emphasis is often placed on their self-interest rather than on the interests of the people. There is always a fear of **money politics** being the name of the game. The fact that most people in Japan feel somewhat isolated from actual politics may stem from the way the prime minister is chosen.

• What political parties are there in Japan?

Since the beginning of the 1990s there have been a series of **realignments** in Japan's political world. The breakup of the Liberal-Democratic Party, the decline of the Social Democratic Party, and transformations of the Kōmeitō have meant a continuing situation of great fluidity in which all cabinets since 1993 have been **coalition cabinets**.

The parties which have seats in the Diet as of April 2000 are:

> The Liberal-Democratic Party
> The Democratic Party of Japan
> The Social Democratic Party
> The Liberal Party
> The Conservative Party
> Sakigake
> The Japanese Communist Party
> Kōmeitō

Q 大臣は何人いるのですか？

　　　　大臣の選任は内閣総理大臣の権限ですが，
次の決まりがあります。
1) 内閣総理大臣以外の国務大臣は，総員20人
　　以内。(2001年1月以降は14人以内。)

2)　文民でなくてはならない。
3)　過半数が**国会議員**でなくてはならない。

　　　　上記の決まりですが，これまでの例としていつ
も目一杯の人数がなり，しかも国会議員以外の
人が大臣になるのは，毎回，せいぜい1人か2人
というのが慣例です。
　　　　国会議員のだれもが大臣になりたがるのは本
音で，「大臣病」という言葉があるほどです。

　　　　行政改革によって，2001年から省庁の数は1
つの府，11の省庁に再編され，大臣の数は14名
以内と定められています。

Q 日本の「官僚」はどうして優秀と言われるのですか？

　　　　首相が代われば各省庁の大臣も代わります
が，通常，官僚は**終身雇用**でそれぞれの省庁に
雇われていますから，自ずとその道の専門家と
なっていきます。

　　　　中央官庁に入って官僚として活躍するために
は，国家公務員上級試験に合格していなければ
ならず，合格者の多くは有名大学出身であるこ
とも，官僚は優秀であると言われる理由となっ

● How many ministers are there in the cabinet?

The prime minister has the power to choose state ministers with the following qualifications:

1) The number of state ministers excluding the prime minister must be fewer than 20 (fewer than 14 beginning in January 2001).

2) State ministers must be civilians.

3) The majority of the state ministers are to be chosen from **Diet members**.

So far, the maximum allowable number of ministers have always been chosen and the vast majority have been members of the Diet, with only one or two at a time selected from outside the Diet.

Virtually every member of the Diet has an ambition to become a state minister, and there is even a term called "minister disease."

Administrative reforms specify that, beginning in 2001, there will be one cabinet office and 11 ministries and agencies, while the number of state minister positions will number no more than 14.

● Why are Japanese bureaucrats said to be so competent?

In comparison with ministers, who change their job every time the prime minister changes, bureaucrats normally work for one ministry or agency on a **lifetime employment** basis, which means they have enough time to develop their expertise in certain areas.

To work as a bureaucrat in one of the central ministries or agencies, one must pass the State Higher Civil Service Examinations. The fact that the majority of those who pass the examinations are graduates of well-known universities con-

ています。

　問題は，各省庁の役人がそれぞれ自分たちの職務に忠実なあまり「縄張り意識」に陥ることです。その結果「縦割り行政」となり，各省庁間の密接な結びつきを失っています。このような**お役所主義**では，1か所で決めればいいことを，あちらこちらの省庁の許可が必要になるということになります。そこで，効率よく柔軟性のある「**行政改革**」が日本の将来の大きな課題の1つです。

Ｑ 首都東京は，いつ，どのようにして 決められたのですか？

The Tōkyō Metro-
politan Government
Office

　1867年，明治維新で徳川幕府が倒され，1868年の明治政府の誕生と共に，それまで徳川幕府の**城下町**であった江戸を，引き続き新政府の拠点とすることにし，名前を江戸から東京と改めたものです。「東の京」ということからの命名です。

　しかし，政治，経済，文化の主要な機能が東京都に集中しすぎていることから，行政機関，国会などを東京都から地方に移そうという案も出ています。候補地には東北（宮城，福島，茨城，栃木），東海（静岡，愛知，岐阜），近畿（三重，滋賀，京都，奈良）の3つの地域が挙がっています。

tributes to the reputation bureaucrats have of being very capable individuals.

The problem is that some officials are so dedicated to their duties that they fall into the pit of being territorial about their jobs. This results in what is called "vertically-split administration," which inhibits close-knit relations between the various ministries and agencies. With this type of **red tape**, it is common that something that could just as well be decided at a single office is sent around from one office or ministry to another to get a series of stamps of approval, even if it should not really be necessary to do so. It is Japan's task for the future to implement **administrative reform** while encouraging efficiency and flexibility.

● When and how was Tōkyō designated as the capital of Japan?

Through the Meiji Restoration, the Tokugawa shogunate (feudal government) turned its power over to the emperor in 1867, and in 1868 a new government was formed around the Emperor Meiji. Edo, the **castle town** of the feudal government, was designated as the headquarters of the new government and its name was changed to Tōkyō, which literally means "eastern capital."

However, because Japan's most important political, economic and cultural functions are today thought to be overly concentrated in Tōkyō, suggestions have been made to move the Diet and various administrative organs of government away from Tōkyō. The three regions proposed are Tōhoku (specifically Miyagi, Fukushima, Ibaragi, and Tochigi prefectures), Tōkai (Shizuoka, Aichi, and Gifu prefectures), and Kinki (Mie, Shiga, Kyōto, and Nara prefectures).

Q 日本の地方行政はどのように行われていますか?

　　日本は憲法で**地方自治**が保障されています。従って，都道府県の知事，区長，市長，村長や議会の議員を選挙で選び，それぞれの地域の行政を任せます。

　　しかし，地方公共団体の事務の大半は，国から委託された行政事務であり，また，財政面では，地方の税金だけでは地域の**公共事業**の遂行は困難ですので，国への依存度が非常に高いのが現実です。一般に，地方自治体の財源の70%は国からの交付金によるものと言われています。その中で東京都だけは国からの**交付金**をもらっておらず，都独自の収入を得るために，銀行に対して外形標準課税をするなどの工夫をしています。

Q 都，道，府，県はどう違うのですか?

　　歴史的な経過による呼び方の違いだけで，**地方自治法**上は全く同じです。

　　都は東京都だけに用いられ，道は北海道だけに用いられます。府がつけられるのは2つあって，大阪府と京都府です。県は43あります。

● How is the local government of Japan conducted?

The Constitution of Japan guarantees **local autonomy**. Governors, ward chiefs, city mayors, village mayors and members of their assemblies are directly elected by residents.

However, the municipalities are heavily dependent on the state, because their major job is business entrusted by the state, and **public works** in those municipalities cannot be implemented without financial assistance from the state. It is said that, on average, 70% of the financial resources of local governments comes from subsidies from the central government. The government of Tōkyō Prefecture is the only local government that does not receive national **subsidies**. One method that Tōkyō Prefecture has devised to raise revenues to meet its expenditures is to exact a tax (standardized in outward form) from banks operating within the prefecture.

● How are *to, dō, fu,* and *ken* different?

The difference is simply a matter of their historical backgrounds; they are all defined in the same manner under the **local autonomy law**.

To is used exclusively for Tōkyō, as in Tōkyō-to (Tōkyō Prefecture, sometimes called Tōkyō Metropolis), and *dō* is used only for Hokkaidō. There are two prefectures with *fu* attached to them, which are Ōsaka-fu and Kyōto-fu, and there are 43 *ken*, usually translated as prefecture.

経済・産業・貿易

Q 日本経済が強かった理由は何ですか？

　　　日本の経済が伸びた理由は，東西冷戦のおかげと言われます。アメリカとソ連を始め，冷戦の影におびえる各国が，**軍備**に予算をとられている間に，平和憲法の下で，日本は経済のみに集中できたのです。

　　　貿易依存度という指標があります。貿易額（輸入額＋輸出額）を**国民所得**で割ったもので，その貿易の活発さを表します。

　　　日本の貿易依存度は，1955年では10％でしたが，1970年には20％を超えています。1985年以降も22–23％を維持していました。

　　　世界各国の中で，このように伸びたのは日本だけで，強力な工業生産力と輸出力がこれを支えました。1980年代半ばの日本の急速な経済発展は，世界に脅威を与えてきました。

　　　国民総生産も，1960年には日本は世界の国民総生産の2.8％を占めていただけですが，1980年には10.1％という急激な伸びを示したのです。

　　　日本経済は1980年後半まで順調な伸びを示します。その後，いわゆるバブル経済という，かつてない土地と株価の**急上昇**が，3年にわたって日本を襲います。

　　　しかし，1991年には，株価と土地の**急落**と共にバブルははじけて，日本は深刻な**景気後退**に見舞われ始めました。

Economy, Industry and Trade

• What is the reason for Japan's economic strength?

A contributing factor to the growth of Japan's economy is said to have been the Cold War threat. While many countries such as the United States and the former Soviet Union allotted a tremendous amount of money to their **armaments** after World War II, Japan under its peace constitution was able to concentrate its efforts on the economy.

One of the indices that measure the vitality of a country's trade economy is the so-called "degree of dependence on foreign trade." This is the ratio of the total amount of trade (imports and exports) to the **national income**.

Japan's degree of dependence on foreign trade was 10% in 1955, and exceeded 20% in 1970. It has been steady at 22% to 23% after 1985.

Among all the countries in the world, Japan was once unexcelled in economic growth, supported by competitive industrial production and strong exports. Japan's rapid growth until the mid-80s greatly amazed the world.

As far as the **Gross National Product** is concerned, Japan's GNP was only 2.8% of the world's GNP in 1960, but it grew rapidly to 10.1% in 1980.

Japan's economy showed steady growth till the late 80s. Then a period of unprecedented asset and stock price **inflation**, called the "bubble economy," swept across the nation for about three years.

In 1991, when the "bubble" burst with the **plunge** of stock and land prices, Japan's economy started into a serious **recession**.

Q 日本経済の伸びは不景気で止まったのでしょうか?

　次の表は日本, アメリカ, EUの1995〜98年の実質経済成長率です。1990年代後半にも不況が続く姿がこの数字に表れています。

	1995	1996	1997	1998
日本	2.5	3.9	0.8	△2.6
アメリカ	3.1	3.4	3.9	3.5
EU	3.2	1.8	2.7	2.8

（OECD, "Economic Outlook" (1998)による。1998年は予測）

　バブル経済の崩壊後の1990年代, 日本経済はずっと低迷を続けてきました。1995年には, 1ドル約80円という円高を記録したり, 世界からは, 米(コメ)も含めてあらゆる分野での**輸入規制**の撤廃を迫られるなどして, 日本は国際的な競争力を失ってきてしまいました。

Looking for a job at a job placement office

　それでも96年までは経済成長率はプラスでしたが, 97年, 98年にはついにマイナス成長を記録しました。倒産する企業, また, **リストラ**でなんとかこの不況を切り抜けようとする企業も相継ぎ, 失業者が大幅に増えました。これまではパートタイムの労働者, 年齢の若い労働者の失業が中心でしたが, 90年代末には, すべての年齢層に失業者が増えました。

　しかし, 2000年に入って日本経済は最悪の状態を脱しました。特に99年の2月に**ゼロ金利政**

● Has the growth of Japan's economy stopped because of the recession?

The chart below shows the economic growth rate of Japan, the United States and the European Union between 1995 and 1998. It indicates how seriously Japan was affected by the recession, even in the late 1990s.

	1995	1996	1997	1998
Japan	2.5	3.9	0.8	△2.6
United States	3.1	3.4	3.9	3.5
EU	3.2	1.8	2.7	2.8

(OECD, *Economic Outlook*, 1998. The numbers for 1998 are estimated.)

During the 1990s, the years following the collapse of the "bubble economy," the Japanese economy continued to experience a long recession. In 1995 the exchange value of the yen reached an all-time high of around 80 yen to a dollar. It was a time when Japanese exports were losing international competitive power, and also a time when Japan was being pressured by the rest of the world to eliminate **import restrictions** on a variety of products, including rice.

Nevertheless, until 1996 there was a positive annual economic growth rate. The growth rate turned negative, however, in 1997 and 1998. Many enterprises went bankrupt, and many did what they could to try to survive the recession through **restructuring**. Much greater numbers of people became unemployed. Previously, unemployment had been seen mainly among part-time and very young workers, but by the end of the 1990s there were many more unemployed among all age groups.

By the year 2000, the Japanese economy had left the worst of this situation behind. A recovery of stock prices was seen, espe-

策がとられて以降は，株価の回復が見られています。政府の景気対策の効果も現れ，経済成長率はプラスになってきました。

Q 対米黒字が減らないのは どうしてですか？

日本の**貿易黒字**は長い間，米国から非難を受けています。1970年代は，繊維製品，カラーテレビ，工業機械，1980年代は自動車，半導体，VTR などが日本優位で，対米黒字が減らないとアメリカからの非難を受けてきました。1990年代には，日本の経済構造自体に問題あり，という主張も出てきました。

1993年7月に設置された日米新経済協議のもとに，経常黒字縮小とアメリカの**財政赤字**削減を目指す「マクロ経済政策」，個別の製品を取り上げる「分野別の協議」，そして，日米だけでなく「地球的協力分野」の3つの観点から協議が進められました。しかし，90年代後半も，自動車，半導体，鉄鋼について**貿易摩擦**が続きました。

Q 日本が外国にいちばん強い製品は 何ですか？

この答えは日本の製品の輸出依存度を見てみると明解です。輸出依存度というのは，生産数量に対する輸出数量の割合です。

1998年の数字です。

1位	磁器ディスク装置	76.8%
2位	集積回路	75.7%
3位	複写機	72.1%

cially after the adoption of a **zero interest rate policy** in February 1999. As one sign of the effectiveness of government policies to revive the economy, the growth rate again began to improve.

● Why hasn't Japan's trade surplus against the United States been reduced?

Japan's **trade surplus** has long been criticized by the United States. In the 1970s, textile products, color TV sets, and industrial machinery were the targets, while in the 80s, the targets of criticism were automobiles, semiconductors and VTRs. In the 90s, the criticism turned to Japan's economic structure itself, saying it has been the major cause of the trade surplus problem.

Negotiations took place between the two countries based on the United States-Japan Framework Talks on Bilateral Trade launched in July 1993. The talks have focused on the following three areas: reduction of Japan's trade surplus as well as the United States' **financial deficit**, negotiations concerning each product, and global cooperation. However, even in the latter half of the 1990s **trade frictions** continued with regard to automobiles, semiconductors, and steel.

● What Japanese products are most dominant abroad?

The answer to this question lies in the "degree of dependence on exports," which means the ratio of exports to the amount of production of Japanese products.

The following are the figures for 1998:

1. magnetic disk equipment   76.8%
2. integrated circuits   75.7%
3. copy machines   72.1%

Shipping of cars

4位	二輪自動車	60.8%
5位	カラーテレビ	60.1%
6位	工作機械	53.8%
7位	ファクシミリ	46.6%
8位	乗用自動車	45.7%

（通商白書, 1999）

　上記の製品は，世界の市場に広く受け入れられており，製品の質が圧倒的によく，価格の上でも競争に負けません。

Q 日本は何をいちばんたくさん輸入していますか？

　1998年の輸入依存度を見るとすぐに分かります。次の表は**国内消費**のうち，主に輸入に頼っている品の順位です。

LNG tanker

1位	鉄鉱石	100.0%
1位	ボーキサイト	100.0%
3位	銅鉱石	99.9%
4位	原油	99.7%
5位	石炭	97.1%
6位	天然ガス	96.5%
7位	亜鉛鉱	87.7%
8位	塩	85.5%

（通商白書, 1999）

　この数字と，前の質問の「日本が外国に対していちばん強い製品は何ですか？」の輸出依存度の数字を見ていますと，日本の経済がいわゆる**加工貿易**で，エネルギーや工業原料の多くを輸入し，加工して製品を輸出することによって成り立っているという姿が浮き彫りになってきます。

4.	motorcycles	60.8%
5.	color TVs	60.1%
6.	machine tools	53.8%
7.	fax machines	46.6%
8.	automobiles	45.7%

(MITI White Paper, 1999)

The above products have been widely accepted in the world market because of their high quality and competitive prices.

● What does Japan import most?

The "degree of dependence on imports" in 1998 provides the answer to the question. The following is the ranking of items where **domestic consumption** is mainly dependent on imports.

1.	iron ore	100.0%
1.	bauxite	100.0%
3.	copper ore	99.9%
4.	crude oil	99.7%
5.	coal	97.1%
6.	natural gas	96.5%
7.	zinc ore	87.7%
8.	salt	85.5%

(MITI White Paper, 1999)

Compare the figures shown above with those of the degree of dependence on exports in answer to the previous question. This brings out the fact that Japan's trade consists of what is called "**added-profit trade**," in which it sustains itself by importing energy sources and raw materials, processing them into products, and exporting them to the world.

Q 日本は自給自足ができますか？

他の**先進国**と比べても，はるかに日本は輸入食料に依存しています。主要な国の輸入総額の中で，食料・飲料と燃料の輸入の割合を見てみましょう。

	食料・飲料	燃料
日本	13.2%	17.3%
アメリカ	4.6%	9.4%
ドイツ	8.8%	7.8%
フランス	8.9%	3.8%
イギリス	9.0%	8.2%
イタリア	10.1%	8.5%

（国際連合「貿易統計年鑑」，1996年）

日本は食料だけでなく，燃料や，何かを生産するためのエネルギー源も他の国に頼らねばなりません。いざ，耕地を増やして何か農作物を作ろうとしても，元の**農地**は**宅地**に売られて，耕作できる土地はほとんどなくなってしまっており，不可能なのです。

Q 日本の農業は，戦後，どのように変わってきたのですか？

Reaping rice

1960年には，農業に従事する人の人数は，総**就業人口**の26.8%でしたが，1996年には，なんと，4.9%にまで減っています。耕地面積も，22%も減少しています。

しかし，品種の改良と栽培技術の向上，**化学肥料**と農薬の大量使用，農作業の機械化によって，個々の作物の耕地単位当たりの収穫量は大幅に伸びました。

● Can Japan be self-sufficient?

Compared with other **developed countries**, Japan is far more dependent on imported foodstuffs. The following chart indicates the ratio of imported provisions, beverages and fuels to the total imports of major developed countries.

	Provisions & Beverages	Fuels
Japan	13.2%	17.3%
United States	4.6%	9.4%
Germany	8.8%	7.8%
France	8.9%	3.8%
United Kingdom	9.0%	8.2%
Italy	10.1%	8.5%

(*UN Yearbook of International Trade Statistics*, 1996)

Japan must depend on other countries in terms of not only foodstuffs but also fuel and sources of energy for production. Promoting farming by increasing arable land is almost impossible because a large part of former **agricultural land** has been used for **housing**, and there is very little land left to be cultivated.

● How has Japan's agriculture changed since World War II?

The number of people engaged in agriculture was 26.8% of the **working population** in 1960, but dropped to 4.9% by 1996. The arable land area was also reduced by 22%.

However, productivity showed substantial growth due to improvements in breeding, cultivation technology, utilization of **chemical fertilizers** and **insecticides**, and automation of production processes.

一方，政府は，戦後の農業の振興のために，食糧管理制度，牛肉や砂糖など各種の価格安定法などの保護政策をとってきましたが，そのため，**国際競争力**がなくなってしまいました。

現実に，生産効率が悪く，輸入価格に対抗できない農産物は淘汰され，日本の食用農産物の**自給率**は激減しているのです。

1965年まで自給率が100％近くあった野菜類でさえ，1996年には86％（概算）と言われます。果実は，1960年は100％であったものが，1996年は47％だそうです。小麦は7％，大豆はなんと3％だけです。もはや日本は食料の自給自足は不可能な国になっています。

Q 水産国ニッポンにとって，
今，何がいちばんの課題ですか？

Fish market

日本はアイスランドに次いで，1人当たりの魚介類の消費量が多い国ですが，**漁獲量**は，1989年以降，減り続けています。

かつては水産王国日本として，世界一の**漁業生産**を誇っていましたが，1989年には中国に抜かれました。

1996年度の漁業生産は約600万トンで，世界の生産量の6.3％を占めていますが，それでは国内消費をまかなえず，約4割を輸入に頼っています。

国際的な**200カイリ漁業専管水域**の設定により，日本が得意としていた**遠洋漁業**の道がせばめられた今，栽培漁業を振興する以外に道がありません。

The postwar government took measures to protect the farmer by enforcing the Food Law and price control laws for produce such as beef and sugar, which resulted in a loss of **international competitiveness** for Japanese farm produce.

Consequently, agricultural products with lower production efficiency have been weeded out in competition with imported products, and the **self-sufficiency rate** of Japan dropped dramatically.

The self-sufficiency rate of vegetables, which was 100% in 1965, dwindled to 86% by 1996. The rate for fruits was reduced to 47% by 1996 from 100% in 1960. Only 7% of flour and 3% of soybeans are produced domestically. This shows that it is virtually impossible for Japan to feed itself without imports.

● At present, what is the biggest problem for the fishery industry in Japan?

Japan consumes the second largest amount of seafood in the world after Iceland, but its **haul** has been on the decline since 1989.

Japan boasted the world's largest **fish catch** for many years until 1989, when China took over first place.

The yield in 1996 was approximately 6 million tons, which was 6.3% of the world yield, but that does not meet the needs of this fish-eating nation. About 40% of the fish consumed is imported.

With the **200-mile limit zone** restricting **deep-sea fishing**, which Japan specialized in, **cultivated fisheries** may be the only way for Japan's fishing industry to survive.

Ｑ 工業国ニッポンの21世紀の見通しは？

　　日本の工業は戦後，鉄鋼，アルミニウム精錬，石油化学，セメント，繊維などの基礎素材産業，および，金属工業，機械工業，化学工業などの重化学工業が，アメリカから**最新技術**およびオートメーション方式による**大量生産技術**が取り入れられたことにより，短期間に大きく発展します。

　　しかし，1973年，1979年の2度におよぶ**石油危機**のために，燃料費，原料費が高騰し，産業は**停滞**してしまいました。

　　そこで注目されたのが**高度の加工技術**を必要とする分野で，特に，エレクトロニクス技術を駆使した日本の製品群が，世界で圧倒的な強さを見せていきます。

　　しかし，1990年代に入ってから急速な円高となり，輸出をテコにして発展してきた日本の産業にストップがかかりました。日本製品の強さに対する欧米の反発もあって，これ以上，外国からの導入技術で**技術革新**をすることも難しくなってきました。

　　21世紀の日本が取るべき根本的な課題は，日本独自の基礎研究の中から新しくリーディング産業を作りだすことと言われています。

Ｑ 日本の物価は世界に比べて，まだ高いと言われているのですか？

　　日本の物価の高さは世界最高で，経済企画庁の1997年の調査によれば，東京の**生計費**はニューヨークの1.18倍，ロンドンの1.08倍，パリの

● What are the prospects for Japan as an industrialized nation in the 21st century?

Japan's post-war industries are categorized into two types: the basic material industries such as steel, aluminum refining, petrochemicals, cement, and fiber, and the heavy chemical industries such as metal, machinery, and chemicals. By introducing **state-of-the-art technology** and **mass-production systems** from the United States, these industries developed rapidly in a short period of time.

However, due to the **oil crises** in 1973 and 1979, fuel and raw material expenses soared, which triggered a **stagnation** in industrial growth.

Next, attention was turned to the electronics industry, which required a **high-level processing technology**. Japanese products demonstrated an overwhelming strength in the world market.

In the 1990s, when the yen rapidly appreciated, Japanese industries which had been propped up by exports ceased to grow at the same fast pace as before. Also, American and European antipathy toward strong Japanese products affected the situation, making **technological innovation** using imported technology more difficult.

It is said that the task facing the country in the 21st century is to create its own distinctive, leading industries from among fields in which basic research is now being done.

● Are prices in Japan higher than in other countries in the world?

Prices in Japan are among the highest in the world. A 1997 survey by the Economic Planning Agency indicates that **living expenses** in Tōkyō are 118% of those in New York, 108% of

1.23倍になっています。

　たとえばコーラ1缶の値段は東京で平均109円なのが，ニューヨークでは53円，ロンドンでは65円といった具合です。

　しかし，1990年代半ばに入り，円高による輸入品の価格の下落，景気低迷による商品価格の低下，**輸入規制緩和**による「価格破壊」などの理由により，消費者物価の上昇率は1％を割り，衣料，家具，通信費などは逆に下がりました。

Q 日本の労働組合はどんな組織になっていますか？

A May Day scene

　日本では**企業別組合**が，労働組合の基本的な単位となっています。つまり，ある企業の従業員になったら，その企業別組合の組合員になる，という形です。

　各会社の組合は，同種産業の企業が集まって作った一種の企業別組合の支配下に入っています。そして，その企業別組合が集まって作ったのが，現在の「日本労働組合総連合会」です。労働組合員の約60％を組織しています。

　他に，連合は労使協調路線だと批判して，共産党系の「全国労働組合総連合」（通称「全労連」）と，旧社会党左派系の「全国労働組合連絡協議会」（通称「全労協」）が組織されています。組織率は2つ合わせても9％ぐらいです。

　日本では**産業別組合**が育っていませんが，IMF・JC（全日本金属産業労働組合協議会）だけは，IMF（国際金属労働者連合）という国際的な組織に属していて，活発な活動をしています。

those in London, and 123% of those in Paris.

The average price of a can of Coca Cola, for example, is 109 yen, while in New York it is 53 yen and 65 yen in London.

However, the situation started to change in the mid-90s. The annual rise in the consumer price index fell below 1% as prices of items such as clothing, furniture and communications utilities went down. The reasons behind this change include the impact of the strong yen on prices of imported goods, the devaluation of merchandise due to the lingering economic recession, and price wars fueled by **deregulation of imports**.

• How are Japanese labor unions organized?

Most unions in Japan are **company unions**. In other words, when you are employed by a particular company, you become a member of that company's union.

Each company union is under the control of a type of industrial union composed of businesses in the same industry. In turn, industrial unions are part of the Japan Federation of Labor Unions, which organizes approximately 60% of unionized labor.

Other labor organizations include the Communist-run National Federation of Labor Unions, which maintains that the Japan Federation is too ready to compromise with business, and the National Labor Union Liaison Committee, which is affiliated with the left wing of the Socialist Party. Altogether these two organizations represent about 9% of union members.

Japan does not have **industrial unions** as such, but one organization, the IMF-JC (International Metal-workers Federation Japan Council) is affiliated to and actively involved in the International Metal-workers Federation, a worldwide organiza-

組合加入者の約20％を組織しています。

　しかし，雇用者数約5400万人の中で，労働組
合に組織されているのは，1998年の段階で約
1200万人です。組織率は年々落ちており，働く
人の組合離れは進む一方です。

Q 今，日本はどんな公害に悩んでいますか？

Disposal of
industrial waste

　日本の**公害**の多くは，狭い国土に過剰な人口
を抱えて，工場地と住宅地とが接近しているこ
とから発生しています。
　三重県の四日市市で起こった喘息のような呼
吸器疾患は，近隣の**石油コンビナート**の排煙に
よるものであることが証明されました。有名な水
銀汚染による水俣病や，カドミウム汚染によるイ
タイイタイ病も，近接する工場からの廃水が原
因でした。

　また，**ごみ焼却場**や**産業廃棄物処理施設**など
から発生する**ダイオキシン**には発がん性や免疫
毒性があり，近年，その対策が大きな問題とな
っています。

Red tide

　公害の発生源が特定できるものは，1967年の
「公害対策基本法」によって規制されています
が，特定の何が原因とは言えない公害にも私た
ちは悩まされています。
　大気中に放出された窒素酸化物や炭水化物
が強い太陽光線で化学変化して起こす「**光化学
スモッグ**」，工場や家庭の排水中の窒素やリン
などによって，海水中のプランクトンなどが過剰
な栄養を得て発生し，魚や貝など貴重な海の

tion. About 20% of union members come under the jurisdiction of this committee.

Of the 54 million people employed in Japan, however, in 1998 only 12 million belonged to unions. Union membership is declining each year, with fewer and fewer workers wanting to get involved.

● What kind of pollution is Japan facing now?

Pollution in Japan has worsened because of the overpopulation of this small country, where industrial and residential districts are located next to each other.

It has been proven that the asthma-like respiratory diseases observed in Yokkaichi City in Mie Prefecture were caused by smoke dispersed from the local **petroleum industrial complex**. Minamata disease in Kumamoto Prefecture, caused by mercury poisoning, and *itaiitai* disease in Toyama Prefecture, caused by cadmium poisoning, were both caused by **waste water** from neighboring plants.

Dioxin released into the environment by municipal **waste incinerators** and **industrial waste disposal facilities** is a cause of cancer and harms the body's immune system. In recent years much attention is being given to finding ways to minimize these problems.

In 1967, the Environmental Pollution Prevention Act went into effect, which regulates pollution from sources that can be determined, but pollution of which the cause is not known or is obscure is a matter of grave concern.

For example, **photochemical smog** is air pollution generated by nitrogen oxide and carbohydrates in the air which go through a chemical change in strong sunlight. Plankton in the sea, when mixed with excessive nitrogen and phosphorus contained in waste water from households and factories, is respon-

生命を奪う「**赤潮**」，大気中の酸性汚染物質を含んだ「**酸性雨**」，高速道路沿いの住居に被害を与える「**騒音**」……などなど，狭い日本の中で，日本人は公害と同居していると言ってもいいでしょう。

日本の税金

Q 日本人はどんな税金を納めていますか？

　　　税の内容は，自分の**所得**に課せられる「**直接税**」と，**消費**あるいは**支出**に課せられる「**間接税**」とに分けられます。

　　　直接税には，所得税，法人税，相続税，贈与税などが含まれます。所得には国税のほかに地方税も課せられます。

　　　間接税は商品の価格に加えられる5％の**一般消費税**に代表されます。負担するのは消費者ですが，国に収めるのは業者です。

　　　1999年度予算で，日本の税金の収入のうち，直接税は68％，間接税は32％です。他の国に比べて，日本とアメリカは直接税の比率が高く，イギリス・ドイツ・フランスなどでは，間接税が50％ぐらいを占めています。

　　　現在の税制では，21世紀の**高齢化社会**の**社会保障制度**の維持は不可能と言われ，間接税である消費税が引き上げられていく可能性が高くなっています。

Q 世界に比べて日本の税金は高いですか？

　　　日本の**国民所得**に対する租税負担率は，1998

sible for the unpredictable **red tide**, which kills precious sea life such as fish and shellfish. Sulfur oxide in the air creates **acid rain**, **noise pollution** affects residents near freeways, and so on. The Japanese live side by side with many types of pollution in their small land.

Taxes in Japan

● What kind of taxes do the Japanese pay?

Taxes in Japan are classified into two categories: direct taxes imposed on one's **income**, and indirect taxes imposed on one's **consumption** and **expenditures**.

Direct taxes include income tax, corporation tax, inheritance tax, and donation tax. Besides national taxes, local taxes are also imposed.

The 5% **consumption tax** is representative of indirect taxes which are levied on all goods. Purchasers pay the tax to merchants, and then it is the merchants' responsibility to pay the collected tax to the state.

Direct taxes account for 68% of the 1999 tax revenues of Japan, whereas indirect taxes account for 32%. In comparison with other countries, the ratio of direct taxes is higher in Japan and the United States; indirect taxes account for more than 50% in the United Kingdom, Germany and France.

It is feared that maintaining the **social security system** for the **aging society** in the 21st century will be impossible without raising the consumption tax.

● Are taxes in Japan high by world standards?

The tax burden ratio to the **national income** of Japan in 1998

年では，**国税**と**地方税**を併せて24.5％です。金額にすると，994,152円です（大蔵省「財政金融月報」552号）。1994年では負担率は23.2％でしたから少しずつ上がっています。

　世界でいちばん税金の負担率が高い国はイギリスで37％です。次に高いのがフランス，そしてドイツでそれぞれ33.5％，31％の負担です。一般的に，ヨーロッパ諸国は日本よりも税金の負担が大きいのですが，これらの国では間接税が半分ぐらいを占めています。

　日本では税金は高いという意識を持っている人が多くいますが，それは所得から取られる直接税率が高いからと言えます。

日本の警察と犯罪

Q 日本の警察にもFBIのような組織はありますか？

　日本の警察は**地方自治体**に属していて，全国的な捜査組織はありません。例えば，**東京警視庁**は基本的にそれが所属する自治体，つまり東京都だけで活動する権限が与えられています。警察官は各都道府県内で活動するように決められているのです。

Policewomen force

　従って，オウム真理教のサリン事件，弁護士一家殺害事件など，同一の犯罪者が日本全国で犯罪を犯した場合の捜査のためには，どこにでも行けるFBIのような組織がほしい，という声も出ました。

　国家公安委員会に所属する組織として**警察庁**がありますが，実際の捜査などには関わりません。警察に関する予算の確保，国の公安に関

was 24.5% with the **national taxes** and **local taxes** combined. The amount was ¥994,152 (from *No. 552 Monthly Financial Report* of the Ministry of Finance). The tax burden ratio in 1994 was 23.2%, and so there has been a gradual increase.

The United Kingdom, at 37%, is one of the countries with the highest tax burden ratio. In France and Germany the ratio is 33.5% and 31% respectively. European countries generally have higher tax burden ratios than Japan, but the majority of their taxes are indirect.

If one has the impression that Japanese taxes are very high, that is because the direct taxes, or visible taxes, from one's income are quite high.

The Police System and Crime in Japan

● Is there an organization like the FBI in Japan?

The Japanese police belong to **local municipalities**, and there is no police organization that conducts investigations nationwide. For example, *Keishichō*, or the **Tōkyō Metropolitan Police Department**, is basically given the authority to operate only in the area of the local government. Police officers work within their prefectures.

Some suggest that Japan needs an organization like the FBI which can go anywhere to investigate cases where crimes are committed by the same person or groups crossing prefectural borders, such as the incidents in which the Aum Shinrikyō religious sect was involved.

Even the **National Police Agency**, which is under the National Public Safety Commission, is not involved with actual investigations. The agency's job is to obtain the budget for the police,

Police box

する警察の運営，全国的な幹線道路の交通規制などが仕事です。全国規模で動くことができるのは，**過激派**などに対応する**公安調査庁**だけです。

しかし，各県の警察の連携で，**全国捜査**の効果を十分に挙げているのが日本の警察のすごさです。

Q 日本にはどんな犯罪が多いですか？

1998年の犯罪件数は203万3546件で，戦後最高の発生件数を記録しています。**検挙率**は38%で，ひところ上がっていた率が落ちてきています。検挙率は殺人，強盗，**放火**などの**凶悪犯罪**に関しては84.7%という高率です（警察白書，1998年）。犯罪の内容は次の通りです。

窃盗犯	88.0%
住居侵入，器物破損など	6.3%
詐欺，横領，賄賂など	2.9%
暴行，傷害など	2.1%
その他	0.7%

1990年代に入ってからの特徴としては拳銃による犯罪の増加です。拳銃は日本では所持を禁じられていますが，**暴力団**以外の一般市民の世界にも拳銃が流れ込んでおり，暴力団抗争以外の拳銃による殺人，拳銃強盗などが増えています。

manage operations for national public safety, administer traffic control of main roads throughout the country, etc. The only organization that can conduct nationwide investigation as a single entity is the **Public Security Investigation Agency**, which specializes in dealing with **extremists**.

However, the strength of the Japanese police is that they are able to conduct **nationwide investigations** effectively through cooperation among the prefectural police headquarters.

● What kind of crimes are the most common in Japan?

The number of reported crimes in 1998 was 2,033,546, which was the highest in postwar years. The **arrest rate** was 38%, which was a drop after an upward trend. For **felonies** such as murder, armed robbery and **arson**, the arrest rate was a high 84.7% (*White Paper of National Police Agency,* 1998). The crimes are classified as follows:

Theft	88.0%
Trespassing, property damage	6.3%
Fraud, embezzlement, bribery	2.9%
Violence, injury	2.1%
Others	0.7%

What characterizes crimes in the 1990s is the increase of crimes using guns, although guns are illegal in Japan. There have been an increasing number of cases where guns are used by people other than **gangsters**, in murders and armed robberies.

日本の防衛

Q 日本はこれまでどこの国と戦争をしてきましたか?

　　日本の歴史上,他国と戦ったのは,663年に日本軍が唐(今の中国)・新羅(今の韓国)の**連合軍**と戦った白村江の戦いが最初です。次は1274年と1281年,2度にわたって日本に攻めてきた蒙古(元)軍との文永・弘安の役です。

　　その後,豊臣秀吉が1592年,1596年の2度,朝鮮半島征服をねらって進攻しますが,1598年,秀吉の死で**撤退**しています。

The Sino-Japanese War

　　江戸時代は**鎖国**で,他国との接触を断っていますが,明治維新後,再び日本の朝鮮に対する侵略政策は顕著になります。これに反対して1894年,清国が朝鮮半島に出兵し,日本との間に日清戦争が起こりました。

　　戦争は翌年,日本の勝利に終わり,朝鮮独立,遼東半島・台湾・澎湖諸島の日本への**割譲**などが決まります。

The Russo-Japanese War

　　しかし,ロシア・ドイツ・フランス3国はこれに反対し,特にロシアは満州占領を強化して,着々と**南下政策**をとりましたので,1904年,ロシアとの戦争が始まります。結果は,翌年,日本の勝利。日本は朝鮮半島における優越権,南樺太の分譲などという成果を得ています。

　　その後,中国における**権益**の拡大をはかった日本は,中国との**全面戦争**に入り,ついには1941年,アメリカ,イギリス,オランダなどの連合国軍と太平洋戦争に突入します。

The Defense System of Japan

● What countries has Japan gone to war with?

The first war with a foreign country that appears in history was the Battle of Hakusukinoe in 663 in which Japan fought the **allied forces** of China and the Korean Kingdom of Silla. Next was the Battles of Bun'ei and Kōan with the Mongols in 1274 and 1281.

Toyotomi Hideyoshi made an attempt to conquer the Korean Peninsula in 1592 and 1596, but in 1598 his men had to **withdraw** because of his death.

During the Edo period, the government adopted a **national seclusion policy** and broke off all relations with foreign countries. However, after the Meiji Restoration, Japan's ambitions to invade the Korean Peninsula were rekindled, posing a threat to Chinese interest there. In 1894, the Qing Dynasty of China dispatched troops to the peninsula, which started the Sino-Japanese War.

Japan's victory the next year resulted in the independence of Korea from Chinese sovereignty and the **cession** of the Liaodong Peninsula, Taiwan and the P'enghu Islands to Japan.

However, Russia, Germany and France were strongly opposed, and so Russia bolstered its **strategy of advancing southward** to occupy parts of Manchuria. The Russo-Japanese War broke out in 1904. Japan once again won in the following year and increased its dominance in the Korean Peninsula, while also obtaining the southern part of Sakhalin Island.

Attempting to expand its **interests** in China, Japan wound up in an **all-out war** against China, and started the Pacific War in 1941 against allied forces, which included the United States, England, and the Netherlands.

1945年敗戦。他国との戦いが，近代国家になってからの100年たらずの間に，一気に増えているのが特徴的です。

Q 自衛隊って，軍隊ですか？

日本国憲法は，その第2章第9条で，**戦争の放棄**を宣言しています。しかしそれは，こちらから戦争をしかけて，武力で紛争を解決するようなことをしないことを言っているのであって，自分たちの国を守る権利を放棄したわけではない……という論理が大勢を占めました。

それが日本に**自衛隊**が存在することになった主な理由で，最初は1950年に，警察予備隊として誕生しました。1952年には保安隊と改称。そして1954年には自衛隊法が成立して，自衛隊に育ってしまったのです。

自衛隊は陸海空からなり，**戦闘機**もあり，**戦車**もあり，**地対空ミサイル**もありますが，実際は軍隊ではないのです！

Q 自衛隊の「戦力」は世界の中でどれくらいですか？

1997年に409億ドルであった日本の**防衛予算**について言えば，アメリカの2730億ドル，ロシア640億ドル，フランスの415億ドルに次いで，4位に登場です。続いて，中国，そしてイギリス，ドイツと続きます。（国際戦略研究所（イギリス）「ミリタリー・バランス1998–99」から）

The Self-Defense
Forces

しかしGNP（国内総生産）は非常に高いので，それに対する比率は，アメリカの3.6%，韓国の3.3%，サウジアラビアの12.4%に比べて，日本は1.0%です。

Japan lost the war in 1945. The number of wars greatly increased during the period of only 100 years after Japan became a modern country.

● Are the Self-Defense Forces a military organization?

No. The Constitution of Japan declares **permanent renouncement of war** in Article 9 of the Second Chapter. The postwar interpretation of this article was that Japan would never start a war or resort to military force to solve an international dispute, but that the country had not given up the right to defend itself.

This was the main reason why the **Self-Defense Forces** originated in 1950 as the National Police Reserve. This was reorganized as the National Safety Forces in 1952, developing in 1954 into the Self-Defense Forces with the enforcement of the Self-Defense Force Law.

Although the SDF, which consists of ground, maritime, and air self-defense forces, has **fighter planes**, **tanks** and **surface-to-air missiles**, it is not actually referred to as a military organization.

● How large is the war potential of the Self-Defense Forces compared with military organizations in other countries?

In terms of **defense budget**, which was $40.9 billion in 1997, Japan ranks fourth after the United States ($273 billion), Russia ($64 billion) and France ($41.5 billion). China, the United Kingdom, and Germany follow. (From *Military Balance 1998–1999* by the International Institute of Strategic Studies, London.)

However, since the gross national product of Japan is extremely high, the ratio of the defense budget to GNP is only 1.0% for Japan. This figure is 3.6% for the United States, 3.3% for South Korea, and 12.4% for Saudi Arabia.

4

日本の社会

Japanese Way of Life and Society

日本の人口と家族

Q 日本にはどれくらいの人が住んでいますか?

1998年10月段階の日本の**人口**は，1億2650万人です。この数は，中国，インド，アメリカ，インドネシア，ブラジル，ロシア，パキスタンに次いで世界8位の数字です。

しかし，国土面積が小さい日本の**人口密度**は，1km²あたり338人。1km²あたり29人というアメリカなんかとくらべれば日本はどこに行っても人ばかり……という外国人の皆さんの感想はもっともです。

Q 日本の人口は増えているんですか，
それとも減っているんですか?

1998年国連の人口動態統計によると，**人口の自然増加率**は1000人につき，日本は2.2人，イギリスは1.6人，フランスは3.4人，そして中国は11.1人，インドは18.4人です。

Japan's Population and Families

● What is the population of Japan?

As of October 1998, Japan had a **population** of 126.5 million, eighth largest in the world after China, India, the United States, Indonesia, Brazil, Russia and Pakistan.

Small in size, Japan has a high **population density** of 338 people per km². Compared with the United States, where population density stands at only 29 people per km², it may seem that there are too many people in Japan wherever one goes.

● Is Japan's population increasing or decreasing?

The United Nations' 1998 statistics of movement of population show that the **natural population increase** is 2.2 per 1,000 people in Japan, 1.6 in England, 3.4 in France, 11.1 in China, and 18.4 in India.

中国やインドの急激な人口増加は地球全体の問題ですが，**少子化**で増え方は少ないとはいえ，2000年を越えた今でも，日本の人口も少しづつ増えています。

しかし，厚生省の人口問題研究所の**推計**によれば，日本の人口は2007年に1億2778万人に達しますが，それをピークに増加率はマイナスに転じ，以降は減り始めると言われています。

2025年には1億2000万人，2050年には1億人，そして，2100年では，なんと，6740万人にまでなってしまうのだそうです。**核家族**，**少子化**の影響が21世紀に大きく現れてくるのです。

Q 日本人の平均寿命はどれくらいですか？

厚生省が発表した1998年の簡易生命表によ

日本の都市人口ランキング（1998年）
Population Ranking of Cities, 1998

（単位：1,000人 Unit：1,000 persons）

順位	市		人口	順位	市		人口
1	東京23区	Tōkyō 23 wards		18	浜松	Hamamatsu	561
			7,854	19	鹿児島	Kagoshima	542
2	横浜	Yokohama	3,325	20	船橋	Funabashi	539
3	大阪	Ōsaka	2,476	21	八王子	Hachiōji	500
4	名古屋	Nagoya	2,090	22	東大阪	Higashiōsaka	497
5	札幌	Sapporo	1,783	23	新潟	Niigata	485
6	神戸	Kōbe	1,448	24	尼崎	Amagasaki	471
7	京都	Kyōto	1,390	25	姫路	Himeji	471
8	福岡	Fukuoka	1,260	26	静岡	Shizuoka	471
9	川崎	Kawasaki	1,197	27	松山	Matsuyama	467
10	広島	Hiroshima	1,099	28	浦和	Urawa	467
11	北九州	Kitakyūshū	1,011	29	松戸	Matsudo	456
12	仙台	Sendai	965	30	川口	Kawaguchi	451
13	千葉	Chiba	852	31	大宮	Ōmiya	439
14	堺	Sakai	788	32	金沢	Kanazawa	437
15	熊本	Kumamoto	641	33	宇都宮	Utsunomiya	437
16	岡山	Okayama	612	34	横須賀	Yokosuka	433
17	相模原	Sagamihara	582	35	市川	Ichikawa	431

（「人口動態表」自治省 Ministry of Home Affairs, *Vital Statistics*）

The exploding population of India and China is a global problem, but Japan's population will also continue to grow into the 21st century, despite the **declining number of births**.

According to **estimates** by the National Institute of Population at the Ministry of Health and Welfare, Japan's population will peak in 2007 at 127.78 million before starting to decline.

By 2025, the population will drop to 120 million and then to 100 million by 2050. And by 2100, the population will fall to a mere 67.4 million. The emergence of the **nuclear family** and a **lower birth rate** will have an enormous effect in the 21st century.

● What is the average life span of the Japanese?

According to a 1998 survey by the Ministry of Health and

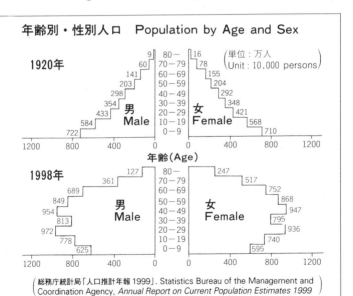

年齢別・性別人口　Population by Age and Sex

（総務庁統計局「人口推計年報 1999」. Statistics Bureau of the Management and Coordination Agency, *Annual Report on Current Population Estimates 1999*）

ると，男性の**平均寿命**は77.19歳，女性は83.82歳
になっています。

これは世界一の**寿命**だそうですが，約65年前
の1935年の平均寿命は，男性は46.92歳，女性
は49.63歳でした。男女ともに，65年の間に30歳
も寿命が延びているのです。

世界の**長寿**の国は，スウェーデン，ノルウェ
ー，アイスランドなど北欧に多いようです。日本
がこの国々と肩を並べたのは，社会的，経済的
に，成熟した証拠でもあります。

Q 日本の家族構成は平均して何人ですか？

1995年の総務庁統計局「家計調査報告」によ
れば，**日本の1世帯当たり**の人員数は，平均して
2.82人です。

1955年の調査では，1世帯平均，ほぼ5人で
したから，約40年の間に，急激に家庭の構成は
小さくなり，夫婦と子供を中心にした核家族に
なってしまいました。

少なくとも，夫婦2人が2人の子供を生んでい
かないと，人口は減少していくわけですから，平
均寿命が上がることで増えつづけている日本の
人口は，2007年からは減少していきます。

Q 昔と現代とでは，日本の家族はどのように違いますか？

武家の**家父長制**の延長で，明治時代でも，長
男が家の財産と戸主権を相続することが，**民法**
で定められていました。

しかし，第2次世界大戦後，このような家制度
は廃止されました。そして社会と産業構造の変
化に伴い，家制度の慣習を残していた農村部か
ら，次男や三男などはそのような制約の少ない

Welfare, the **average life span** of the Japanese is 77.19 years for males and 83.82 for females.

These latest figures represent the longest **life expectancy** in the world. Back in 1935, the average life span was 46.92 for males and 49.63 for females. It has increased by 30 years for both men and women over the past 65 years.

Other countries in the world which can boast of **longevity** are mostly in Nothern Europe such as Sweden, Norway, and Iceland. Japan joined these countries as it matured socially and economically.

● What is the average number of people per household?

According to the *1995 Household Survey Report* compiled by the Management and Coordination Agency, the average number of people **per Japanese household** is 2.82.

In 1955, the number was about five. During the past four decades, the family size has shrunk and the nuclear family, composed of only a couple and their children, has become the norm.

Estimates for the next century show that Japan's population, which is increasing owing to the longer average life expectancy, will begin to decrease from 2007 because of fewer children being born.

● How has the family changed over the years?

Because of the influence of feudal **patriarchalism**, **civil law** in the Meiji period determined that the eldest son would inherit the fortune and the patriarchal rights of the family.

However, the system was abolished after World War II. As the society and industry changed, almost all but the oldest children left the rural areas where the old system still remained and went to less conservative urban areas. Due to the less restric-

都会へと流出していきました。都会の自由な空気の中で，結婚は，恋愛結婚が見合い結婚を上回り，次第に夫婦を中心とした「核家族」になってきました。

日本人の特質

Q 日本人は集団で行動する，とよく言われるのはなぜですか?

社会の基本的な単位についての意識を，日本人は「家＝イエ」に置いています。ここで「イエ」というのは，「家族」の意味だけではなく，会社，学校，宗派など，運命を共にする「集団」も意味します。

封建的な家族制度や徒弟制度などはなくなりましたが，西洋の場合と違って日本の社会では「個」よりも「集団」が優先しています。終身雇用制度の会社がまだまだ多数を占めていますし，茶道や華道などの伝統的芸術には家元制度が残っています。

そのような集団の中では，集団への全面的な帰属が必要とされ，構成員はその集団に対する一体感をさえ抱くのです。その姿が外国人には，主体的な行動の欠如，個人的な責任感の希薄さ，と映るのだと思います。

しかし，集団がうまく機能すれば，構成員の存在意義も高まるわけで，「個」と「組織」のバランスを上手にとっているのが日本人，と言うこともできるでしょう。

tive atmosphere of cities, **arranged marriages** declined and the husband and wife have gradually become the center of the household.

Characteristics of the Japanese

● What is the reason for Japanese group behavior?

The basic unit of society in the Japanese mind lies in *ie*, which literally means "house," but also implies other groups that bind people together such as families, companies, schools, and religious sects.

Although the feudal family system and **apprenticeship** no longer exist, emphasis tends to be placed on groups more than individuals, unlike in the West. Many companies have **lifetime employment systems**, and the **hereditary system** still remains in many traditional art forms such as tea ceremony and flower arrangement.

In such a society, a strong sense of belonging to groups is basically required, and in many cases their members identify themselves with the organization. To some foreigners, there might seem to be a lack of independent behavior and sense of individual **responsibility**.

However, if the group functions well, the identity of the members increases, and so it can be said that the Japanese have a good balance between focus on the individual and on the group.

Q 日本人は「本音」と「建て前」を使い分けると
いうのは本当ですか？

　　　　　日本人は自分の意見を言わない, 2つの意見
を使い分ける, と外国人からは批判を受けます。
しかし,「本音」よりも「建て前」が優先されるこ
とによって秩序が保たれている日本の縦社会で
は, このほうが周囲にあつれきを起こさない, ま
た, 生き残りに必要だと考えられているのです。
　　　相手を傷つけることなく, 効果的に物事を解
決する方法としては, 建て前が用いられ, 自分
の意見を強硬に通そうとすることは避けようとす
る傾向にあるのです。

Q 日本人の精神に影響を与えている思想は何ですか？

　　　　　仏教と, **儒教**が, 日本人の精神形成に大きな
影響を与えています。
　　　仏教は, 人に生と死の観念を与え, **念仏**を通
して, 迷いや悩みを離れた**悟りの境地**に至るこ
とを教えています。

　　　儒教は, ご存知のとおり, **孔子**(紀元前552-
479)によって作られた**思想体系**で, 宗教ではあ
りません。その思想の中心には「**仁**」という言葉
があります。「仁」とは人を愛することですが, **キ
リスト教**や仏教のような博愛の精神ではなく, 親
や兄弟を愛することです。まず「仁」によって家
の中を治め, それを拡大して国家を治めようと
いう考え方です。

● Is it true that the Japanese differentiate between *honne* (true intention) and *tatemae* (enunciated principle) depending on the situation?

Some foreigners criticize the Japanese for not expressing their opinions or for having two differing opinions. However, in the Japanese **vertical society** where order is maintained by *tatemae* more than *honne*, this is considered necessary for keeping the peace and survival.

The tactics of *tatemae* (enunciated principle) are often used in order to solve problems efficiently without hurting anyone, while pushing one's opinions too hard tends to be avoided.

● What ideologies have influenced the spirit of the Japanese?

Buddhism and **Confucianism** have had a profound influence on the Japanese spirit and world view.

Buddhism teaches concepts of life and death and guides people through **chanting of the Buddhist invocation** to a **state of emancipation** (spiritual enlightenment) where there are no worries or uncertainty.

Confucianism is the **ideology** of **Confucius** (552–479 B.C.) of China and not a religion. One of the core concepts of Confucianism is *jin* (pronounced *ren* in Chinese), which basically means to love people, but this love is different from the love or philanthropy taught in **Christianity** or Buddhism. It means to love one's parents and brothers and sisters first. Governing a house with *jin* and later expanding it to the level of the state is encouraged.

日本の封建社会では，親や目上の人，ひいては国家元首を敬うという考え方は，支配者階級にとってはたいへん都合がいいものでした。このため近世では，武士が世襲的に支配していた封建社会を律する思想となり，明治時代になっても，儒教と西欧の近代的道徳とが結合した「教育勅語」が作られるなど，近代日本人の**道徳形成**にも重要な役割を演じ続けたのです。

その後，第2次世界大戦に敗戦した日本は，民主主義，平和主義を掲げて再出発することとなり，占領軍による民主主義的な諸改革は国民の思想にも大きな影響を与えました。それまでの国家や家族への奉仕を通じて個人の幸せを実現するというあり方から，個人の幸福がまず優先され，その総和として国家，国民が存在するという考え方への変化をもたらしたのです。

こうした個人主義的な思想は，その後の経済的な発展とあいまって，**物質至上主義，金銭万能思想**といった風潮ともなって現れています。

Q 日本人の性格にはどんな特質がありますか？

国際経営学者のロバート・マーチ氏は，「箱の中の日本人」という著書の中で，「日本ではグループ，会社，国家など，すべてが『箱』の中に入っていると考えると，日本人の**行動様式**が理解できる」と書いています。

つまり，せまい箱の中に入っているから——
・お互いに何を考えているのか分かるので，西洋人のように徹底的に討論しようとしない。
・箱の中で気持ちよく共存するために，自己主張をおさえ，習慣やしきたりを大切にする。

In the feudal era of Japan, the idea of respecting one's parents, elders, and the head of the state worked favorably for the ruling warrior class. The influence of Confucianism continued to dominate Japanese society into the Meiji period (1868–1912), when *Kyōiku Chokugo* (the Imperial Rescript on Education), incorporating modern Western morality with Confucianism, was compiled, which played a crucial role in **creating the moral values** of the Japanese.

After the defeat in World War II, Japan got a new start under policies of democracy and peace, and the democratic revolution had a great impact on the thinking of the general population. Up until that time, the philosophy of individual happiness obtained through serving the state and one's family, upon which the state and the populace existed, was changed to putting the happiness of the individual first.

This individualism combined with the forthcoming economic development and created a trend towards **materialism** and **money as a panacea**.

• What are some of the characteristics of the Japanese?

Business management professor Robert March, in his book titled *Reading the Japanese Mind*, explains an idea that is the key to understanding Japanese **behavior**. He points out that in Japan, groups, companies, and the state are all contained in what he calls "boxes."

It is easy for the Japanese in a box to understand what others in the same box are thinking, so unlike Westerners, they do not bother to discuss matters to an end.

In order to live comfortably while getting along with each other within a box, the Japanese do not assert themselves too much and make the most of conventional customs and practices.

・統制がとりやすいので，効率がよく，**上下関係**がはっきりして，また，安全な社会が生まれる——というのです。

　確かにこのように考えると「日本人はイエス・ノーが**はっきりしない**」「すぐ上司に相談する」などという外国人の非難に対して説明がつきますし，また**経済大国**になった理由や，犯罪の少ない安全な国である理由も分かってきます。

日本の教育

Q 日本の現在の教育制度は いつできたのですか？

　国民の誰もが教育を受けることができる近代的な**教育制度**が作られたのは，明治維新後の1872年です。江戸時代までは，庶民が教育を受けたのは寺小屋という施設でした。

　当初，**義務教育**期間は4年で，身分・性別・貧富を問わないという建て前になってはいましたが，学業に必要な経費は学生が負担するのが原則でした。

Terakoya in Edo period

　また，次第に**中央集権制**のもとでの教育となり，1903年には教科書が国定となりました。1907年には義務制も6年になります。

　そして，1945年の太平洋戦争の終結まで，国家主義の教育政策が強化されました。男女の教室も別にされていたのです。

　1947年，新しく**学校教育法**が成立します。これによって現在の**学校制度**ができ上がりました。小学校6年，中学校3年が義務制となりました。

He also mentions that in a "box" the entire system is easily controlled and thus efficient, and that there is a distinct **hierarchy** that makes for a safe society.

This theory provides a good response to foreigners who criticize Japanese as **being non-committal** when they have to say either yes or no and always having to ask their bosses what to do. It also helps explain why Japan has become an **economic giant** and also why the country has a surprisingly low crime rate.

Education in Japan

• When was Japan's current educational system established?

The original modern **educational system** was established in 1872. Before that, in the Edo period, *terakoya*—literal meaning "temple-shack"—was the place where ordinary people received an education.

At first the period of **compulsory education** was four years, and it was stated that everyone had an opportunity to study in the system regardless of one's social standing, sex, and whether one was rich or poor, as long as the students paid tuition and other necessary expenses.

The system developed under the **centralized government**, and nationally authorized textbooks came to be used in 1903. Compulsory education was extended to six years in 1907.

Until the end of World War II in 1945, education policy based on nationalism was emphasized. At the time, male and female students studied in different classrooms.

The new **School Education Law** was enacted in 1947, by which the current **school system** was formed. Under this system, six years of elementary school and three years of junior high school were

　　　　　その上が高校3年，大学4年となりますが，これ
　　　は義務制ではありません。

Q どういう学校がありますか?

　　　　　次のような学校の種類があります。（　）内は基
　　　本的な就学期間です。

　　　　　幼稚園（1–3年）
　　　　　小学校（6–12歳までの6年間）
　　　　　中学校（13–15歳までの3年間）
　　　　　高等学校（3年間）
　　　　　高等専門学校（5–5年6か月）
　　　　　短期大学（2年間）
　　　　　大学（4年間）
　　　　　専修学校（1年以上）
　　　　　専門学校（1年以上）
　　　　　特殊教育学校

　　　　　この中で小学校と中学校は義務教育です。
　　　高等専門学校は，工業，船舶に関する知識と技

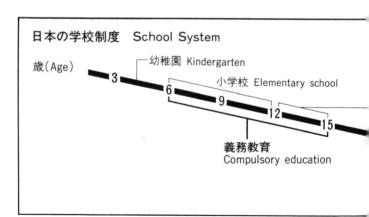

日本の学校制度　School System

歳（Age）
幼稚園 Kindergarten
小学校 Elementary school
3
6
9
12
15

義務教育
Compulsory education

made compulsory. Advanced education, offered but not compulsory, was three years of high school and four years of university.

● What are the schools like?

The following is a list of schools and length of study:

Kindergarten (1 to 3 years)
Elementary school (6 years, from 6 to 12)
Junior high school (3 years, from 13 to 15)
High school (3 years)
Technical college (5 to 5 1/2 years)
Junior college (2 years)
University (4 years)
Special training school (more than 1 year)
Vocational school (more than 1 year)
Special education school

Elementary and junior high schools are compulsory. The technical college is designed to provide technical training for

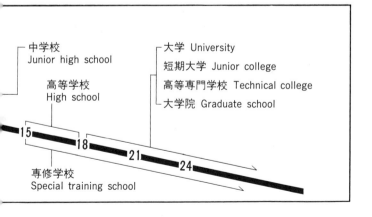

能の収得を目指したもので，中学を卒業すれば
受験資格ができます。

　専修学校は，料理，裁縫，簿記，建築設計な
ど様々な技術を学習する学校です。中学校卒
業者に対する高等課程，高校卒業以上の人に
対する専門課程に分かれています。

　特殊教育学校は，**身体が不自由な人**のための
学校です。

Q 日本にはどれくらい学校がありますか？

　公立，私立合計の数は下の通りです。

大学	604
短期大学	588
高等専門学校	62
高等学校	5,493
中学校	11,236
小学校	24,295
幼稚園	14,603
特殊教育学校	983
専修学校	3,573

（文部省「学校基本調査速報」1998年度）

　義務教育である小学校，中学校の数は，戦
後，急激に伸びた人口に追いつかず，1クラス
の生徒数が50人を超えたこともありました。しか
し，1980年代からは一貫して児童数の減少が続
いて，学級数の減少や定員割れ，**学校の統廃合**
なども増えてきています。

industrial purposes, including shipbuilding, for people with junior high school diplomas or higher academic education.

Special training schools teach courses such as cooking, sewing, bookkeeping and architectural design. These consist of the senior course for junior high school graduates and the professional course for people with a high school diploma or higher academic education.

Special education schools provide education for **people with physical disabilities**.

● How many schools are there in Japan?

The total number of schools, both public and private, is as follows:

Universities	604
Junior colleges	588
Technical colleges	62
High schools	5,493
Junior high schools	11,236
Elementary schools	24,295
Kindergartens	14,603
Specialized education schools	983
Specialized training schools	3,573

(Ministry of Education, Culture and Science, *School Survey Report,* 1998)

Because of the rapid population growth after World War II, the number of students in a typical elementary or junior high school class once exceeded 50. The number of children started to decline from the 1980s, and with fewer classes per grade and unfilled classrooms, **school closings and mergers** have been on the increase.

Q 高校，大学への進学率は どれくらいですか？

　　文部省の調査によれば，1998年の数字では48.2%です。1960年では10.3%ですから，約40年の間に大学に行く人は約5倍に増えています。

A successful
candidate

　　高校への進学率もアメリカと同様に非常に高くなっており，100%近くですから，高校も義務教育化すべきという声も出ているぐらいです。

　　高校卒業生の大学への進学率のトップはアメリカで，50%前後です。日本はそれに次いでいます。フランス，ドイツがこれに続き，さらにイギリスが続きます。

Q 日本の学校と，アメリカの学校の違いは どこにありますか？

　　アメリカでは医学部，法学部，商学部が大学院大学となっていることなど，大学の制度に違いがありますが，教育全体から見れば，現在の日本の学校の制度はアメリカと基本的には大きな違いはありません。

　　制度よりも，むしろ次のような違いを挙げなければならないでしょう。

　　例えば，アメリカには政府による「学習指導要領」などという画一的な教育方針の押しつけがないこと。公立の学校では，純粋な学問以外に実用的な技術の授業を選ぶことができること。

　　アメリカには政府による**教科書検定制度**もないし，**過剰な受験戦争**もありません。日本では有名な大学に入ろうとすると，**塾**に行ったりして厳

● What percentage of junior high school graduates go on to high schools, and what percentage of high school graduates go on to universities?

The percentage of high school graduates who go on to universities was 48.2% in 1998, according to a Ministry of Education study. The figure was 10.3% in 1960, which means about five times more students are entering universities than 40 years ago.

Nearly 100% of junior high school graduates go on to high school. Some say that high school should also be compulsory.

The percentage of American **high school graduates** going to universities is around 50%, which is the highest in the world. Japan ranks second followed by France, Germany, and the United Kingdom.

● What is the major difference between Japanese schools and American schools?

As a whole, the school systems of the two countries are not very different except that in the United States medical schools, law schools, and business schools are designed as graduate schools of universities.

Differences lie in other areas of the educational systems.

For example, American schools, unlike their Japanese counterparts, do not have a uniform "study guidance" system proposed by the government, and besides solely academic courses, they offer classes for acquiring practical skills.

Neither **textbook inspection systems** by the government nor **keen competition to enter colleges** exist in the United States. Going to a prestigious university in Japan usually means **cram**

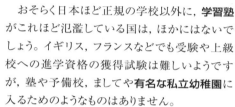

しい競争を勝ち抜かなければなりませんが，いったん大学に入ってしまうと比較的楽に卒業できてしまいます。入るのは簡単だが，ちゃんと勉強しないかぎり，そう簡単には卒業させてくれないアメリカの大学とは大きな違いです。

Q どうして予備校や学習塾が多いのですか？

College entrance examination

おそらく日本ほど正規の学校以外に，**学習塾**がこれほど氾濫している国は，ほかにはないでしょう。イギリス，フランスなどでも受験や上級校への進学資格の獲得試験は難しいようですが，塾や予備校，ましてや**有名な私立幼稚園**に入るためのようなものはありません。

日本の親の中には，有名な幼稚園，というのは有名大学までそのまま進学できるという意味ですが，そんな幼稚園に子供を入れたがる人もいます。

在学中の小学生から大学入試に再挑戦しようとする人まで，多くの生徒が入試に首尾よく合格しようと塾へでかけるのです。

理由ははっきりしています。学校の授業を聞いているだけでは，入学試験の問題を解くことができないのです。ある程度の訓練をしないと，受験戦争に勝ち残ることができないのです。

これもすべて，いい会社に就職するため，また早く昇進するためには，**有名な大学**を出ていなければならないという「**学歴社会**」が原因です。

近年，急速に進む少子化のため，予備校や学習塾もその**生き残り**に必死です。高い進学実績や独自のカリキュラムを武器に，安定した在校生をもつ塾がある一方で，定員を満たすために

Cramming school lessons

郵 便 は が き

1 1 2 - 8 7 9 0

料金受取人払

小石川局承認

3565

差出有効期間
平成14年3月
31日まで

東京都文京区音羽一丁目

十七番十四号

講談社

インターナショナル 行

愛読者カード係

|||i|||i||i"||i||i||i|i|i|i|i|i|i|i|i|i|i|i|i|i||||i|

★この本についてお気づきの点、ご感想などをお教えください。

本のタイトルを
お書きください

愛読者カード

ご愛読ありがとうございました。下の項目についてご意見をお聞かせ
頂きたく、ご記入のうえご投函くださいますようお願いいたします。

a　ご住所　　　　　　　　　　　　　　　〒□□□-□□□□

b　お名前　　　　　　　　　　　　　　　年齢　（　　　）歳

　　　　　　　　　　　　　　　　　　　性別　1 男性　　2 女性

c　ご職業　1 生徒・学生（小、中、高、大、その他）　2 会社員
　　　　　3 自営（商工、農林漁、サービス、その他）　4 公務員　5 教職員
　　　　　6 自由業（　　　　　　　　　　）7 無職（主婦、家事手伝い、その他）
　　　　　8 その他（　　　　　　　　　　）

d　本書をどこでお知りになりましたか。
　　1 新聞広告（新聞名　　　　　　　　　）2 雑誌広告（雑誌名　　　　　　　）
　　3 書評（書名　　　　　　　　　）4 実物を見て　5 人にすすめられて
　　6 その他（　　　　　　　　　　　　　　）

e　どんな本を対訳で読みたいか、お教えください。

f　どんな分野の英語学習書を読みたいか、お教えください。

御協力ありがとうございました。

schools and strong competition. But once you make it in, graduating is relatively easy. This is one big difference from universities in the United States where getting in is easy but graduating requires lots of work.

● Why are there so many preparatory schools and cram schools?

Japan is probably the country with the largest number of **preparatory schools** in the world. Although in some countries including France and the United Kingdom, entrance or qualifying examinations for advanced schools are very hard, no other countries have *juku*, or cram schools, even for entering **prestigious private kindergartens**.

Some Japanese parents are eager to send their children to such kindergartens which are affiliated with universities, which in most cases guarantees that the students can go on all the way to the universities, which are also considered prestigious.

Many students, ranging from elementary school pupils to those who make a second try to enter colleges, go to *juku* to prepare themselves to successfully pass entrance examinations.

The reason is clear. Just attending regular schools is not enough to survive in the examination war in terms of obtaining the knowledge necessary to be successful.

A society with a heavy emphasis on one's **academic career**, in which graduating from **first-rate universities** is among the first requirements to get quickly promoted, is behind all this obsession.

In recent years, the rapid decline in the number of children has made it necessary for preparatory and cram schools to **fight for survival**. Some schools maintain their numbers by boasting of high success rates and their own curriculums, but at other

学力低下を招く塾もあり，その明暗を分けています。

日本人と仕事

Q 日本の会社とアメリカの会社の違いは
どこにありますか？

　　　　基本的に次のような違いがあります。
1) 日本では基本的に**終身雇用**であることに対して，アメリカでは年次契約であること。

2) 昇進は，日本では基本的には年功序列であることに対して，アメリカでは実力主義であること。

3) 労働組合は，日本ではユニオンショップであるのに対して，アメリカでは産業別組合，職業別組合であること。

　　　　1990年代から経済成長にブレーキがかかっている日本では，終身雇用を続けていては生き残ることができないと考えている企業も多く，給与や昇給を決める際に，アメリカなどのように従業員の能力・実績を査定して，年俸制にする会社が増えつつあります。

Q 働き者で有名な日本の労働者は
どれくらい働いているのですか？

　　　　1997年の時点で，日本の製造業に従事する労働者の年間労働時間は1983時間で，アメリカの2005時間やイギリスの1934時間とほぼ等しくなっています。

schools fewer students means a **drop in academic levels**—and that is what decides the school's fate.

The Japanese at Work

- **What are the differences between Japanese and American companies?**

These are the basic differences:

1) In general, Japanese companies have a system of **lifetime employment**, while American companies employ workers on an annual contract basis.

2) Whereas in Japan employees are promoted according to length of service, in the United States promotion is mostly based on merit.

3) Japanese workers belong to company unions, while American workers belong to industrial unions.

The decline in the growth rate of the Japanese economy from the 1990s has caused many businesses to question whether they can survive while continuing to support a system of lifetime employment. An increasing number of companies are assessing the ability and work record of employees before they make decisions on salary and promotion, such as is done in the United States and elsewhere.

- **The Japanese are known for working long hours. Exactly how many hours do they spend at work?**

In 1997, Japanese workers in manufacturing labored 1,983 hours a year, not much different from the 2,005 hours for American workers and 1,934 hours for British workers.

　1993年に改正された「**労働基準法**」により、日本の企業における最長労働時間は、「1日8時間；週40時間」に規制されることになりました。それに基づいて多くの会社が**週5日制**になってきています。

　規模の小さい企業では、まだまだこの規制が守られていないのですが、日本の年間労働時間は、戦後50年余を過ぎてやっと欧米と肩を並べることになりました。

Q 休みはどれくらいありますか?

　1993年の労働基準法の改正で、休日に関しては、次のことが定められました。

・休日は少なくとも毎週1回
・年次**有給休暇**は、勤続6か月で、出勤率8割以上の者には10日

・勤続1年6か月以上の者には、勤続1年につき1日を、総日数20日まで加える

　この規定に従って、日本人の年間休日数は、祝祭日、有給休暇を合わせて約120日を越すようになりました。しかし、ドイツやフランスなどのように、年間150日を越えていて、だれもが夏には1カ月の長い休暇を楽しむといった状況にはまだまだほど遠いようです。

　特に、終身雇用で会社に忠実な日本人サラリーマンには、長期休暇を申し出ることは会社に迷惑とかけることになるのではないか、とためらってしまうという心理があるようです。もっとも現代の若い人は、その点を割り切ってきているようですし、会社自体が、会社ぐるみで長期に休日を設けるところも増えてきています。

Under the revised **Labor Standard Law** of 1993, however, the maximum number of hours employees may work was limited to eight per day, and 40 per week. Most companies are therefore moving toward a **five-day work week**.

This law is still often not upheld by small businesses, but even so, some 50 years after the end of World War II the working hours of the Japanese are finally similar to those of workers in the West.

● What about holidays?

Under the revised Labor Standard Law of 1993, the following regulations concerning holidays were put into place:
—Workers must have at least one day off per week.
—After six months at the same company, workers with an attendance rate of 80% or more are entitled to ten days **paid leave**.
—After 18 months at the same company, paid holidays are increased by one day each year to a maximum percent of 20.

According to law, Japanese workers have more than 120 days off, including holidays and paid holidays. But Japan still has a long way to go before workers can enjoy month-long summer vacations like the workers in Germany, France, and several other countries who get 150 days a year off from work.

A unique factor is that Japanese white-collar workers, who tend to be loyal to their companies that promise lifetime employment, often think that taking long vacations would put a burden on their companies. But younger workers have fewer such concerns, and more and more companies are giving their workers longer vacations.

Q 日本人はどれくらいの収入を得ていますか?

　　労働省の調査によれば, 従業員30人以上の企業の, 1998年の1人当たりの月間給与総額は41万5675円です。これには**残業手当**や特別給与(ボーナス)を月にならしたものも入っています。

　　この賃金の数字を外国と比較してみますと, 日本を100とした場合, 日本より賃金が高いのはスイスだけで, 約120という指数になります。ドイツ, スウェーデンは約85, アメリカ, イギリスは65ぐらいです, 指数を見ただけでは, 日本人の労働者の賃金が恵まれているように見えますが, バブル経済がはじけた後, 土地の価格がかなり下がったとはいえ, それでも一般庶民が簡単に買える金額ではなく, また, 一般の商品の価格も外国に比べれば高めですから, 賃金が世界2位とはいえ, それが**生活の豊かさ**を証明するとはかぎりません。

Q 給料や地位はどうやって上がりますか?

Office workers

　　日本の企業の雇用形態は, 終身雇用, **年功序列**が主ですから, いったん採用されると, 賃金は**学歴**, 勤続年数に応じて上がっていくのが普通です。

　　しかし, 業務上の昇進は, 実力によって個々に差異がありますから, 年齢や勤続年数が同じでも, 賃金には違いが生じます。

　　しかし, **構造的な不況**で, 従来の年功序列型賃金制度では, 企業は持ちこたえることができないと言われ始めています。

● What is the average income in Japan?

According to a 1998 survey conducted by the Ministry of Labor, the average monthly salary of people working for companies with more than 30 employees is 415,675 yen, which includes **pay for overtime work** and bonuses.

When these wages are compared with those of other countries, with Japan indexed at 100, the only country higher is Switzerland at 120. Germany and Sweden are at about 85; and the United States and England are around 65. The figures appear to indicate that Japanese workers are blessed. After the bursting of the economic bubble, land prices have fallen considerably, but they are still high enough to make it extremely difficult for most people to buy a home. And since general prices are higher in Japan than elsewhere, the second highest wages in the world do not necessarily indicate an **abundant lifestyle**.

● How do employees in Japanese companies obtain promotions and pay increases?

Lifetime employment and **promotion by length of service** are the main features of the Japanese employment structure. Once someone has been employed, it is normal for their wages to rise in accordance with **qualifications** and length of service in the company.

However, because there are differences in the level of ability of employees, even among those of the same age or length of service, differences in wage levels do arise.

With the Japanese economy in a **structural depression**, the pressure is on companies to become more efficient, and some are unable to keep operating under the system whereby wages rise with length of service.

そこで，年功序列型の賃金制度の画一性を改めて，実力・成績にもとづく「**年俸制**」にする企業も，少しずつですが増えてきています。

年俸制をとっているのは，まだ，全企業のうち1割ぐらいですが，今後とも年俸制が多くなってくることは間違いありません。

Q 日本では単身赴任が多いのはなぜですか？

単身赴任と言われる転勤が多くなった理由として，次のことが挙げられます。

1つは，子供の教育のためです。子供を有名校に進学させたいと願っている家庭にとっては，子供を親の転勤につきあわせ，学校をかわらせることは，受験に不利になります。特に，子供が都会の**進学校**に通っている場合はそうです。

もう1つの理由は，交通の便の発達のおかげです。狭い日本ですから，これだけ空の便や新幹線が整備されますと，よほどの僻地でないかぎり，日本全国どこへ行くにもわずかの時間しかかかりません。週末に家族のもとに帰ってきて，月曜の朝早く赴任地に戻ることも可能になっているのです。

Q 日本人は名刺がないと仕事ができないのですか？

日本ではビジネスに**名刺**はつきものです。初対面の人とは名刺交換するのが習慣として定着しているので，名刺を持たずに**取引先**を訪問することはありません。

日本人の名前は，音が同じでも文字が異なる

Consequently, a small but increasing number of companies are introducing an **annual salary system** based on performance to replace the uniformity of wage structures based on length of employment.

At present, only 10% of companies are using the annual salary system, but there is no doubt that the percentage will increase over time.

● Why do Japanese employees often leave their families behind when they transfer to other towns?

This type of transfer, known as *tanshinfunin*, has become increasingly common in recent times for the following reasons:

Families must consider their children's education. For families who want to send their children to prestigious schools, making a job-motivated move can put the children at a disadvantage. This is particularly the case when the child attends a **school with a good academic reputation** in one of the major cities.

Transport is another reason for the increase in *tanshinfunin*. Japan is a relatively small country with a comprehensive network of air and rail links, and unless you are living somewhere very remote it takes only a short time to travel from one place to another. It is possible therefore to spend the weekend with your family and travel back to the work place early on Monday morning.

● Can't the Japanese do business without business cards?

In Japan, **business cards** are indispensable for business. It's a well-established custom to exchange these cards with people you meet for the first time. The Japanese never visit **clients** without bringing business cards.

Japanese names are often pronounced the same, but are

場合がよくあります。正確な名前を相手に伝えるためにも必要になっています。

　歴史的に見ると，古くは19世紀初期に使われていた和紙の名刺が残っていますが，これは氏名だけを手書きしたものでした。印刷した名刺は西洋から伝えられ，幕末開国のころ（1860年代）に外国人と接する役人が使ったのが始まりだったようです。

Ｑ ハンコは，いつ，どんなときに必要なのですか？

Personal seal

Registered seal

　ハンコ（判子＝印鑑）には**実印**と**認め印**の2種類があります。

　実印は，居住地の区市町村長に届け出をし印鑑登録をして，間違いなく本人の印鑑であることを証明できるようにしたものです。

　まず一般の会社内ではそれぞれの認め印を，自分の書いた書類に責任を持つという意味で押したり，他から回ってきた書類を承認したという意味で押したりします。会社員にとって，なくてはならないものです。

　また，契約書などに同意する意志を示すとき，**官公庁**に届け出をするとき，指定された配達物を受け取るときなどにも使います。配達物などは，最近は署名でも済むことが多くなりました。

　ふつう印鑑を使うときは認め印でいいのですが，重要な取引上の文書，特に金銭取引の契約などには実印を使うことが求められます。

Ｑ 日本では転職する人は多いですか？

　日本の会社の多くは，まだ，年功序列型で終身雇用です。ですから定年まで保障された会社

written differently. So these cards are also necessary to convey people's names precisely.

Historically, *washi* calling cards (some of which still exist) on which only the name of the person was hand-written, were used at the beginning of the 19th century. Printed calling cards were first introduced by the West. The card seems to have been initially used by Japanese officers who had to make contact with non-Japanese when the country opened its doors at the end of the Edo period.

● When and on what occasion are seals necessary?

There are two types of seals: **registered seals** and **personal seals**.

Registered seals must be registered at the ward, city, or village mayor's office where the bearer resides to identify that the seals actually belong to the person registered.

In most companies, businessmen stamp their seals on documents they've written to signify that they will be responsible for the contents, or to signify officially that they have taken a look at them. Thus, seals are necessary in business interactions.

Seals are also used to express agreement in contracts, to give notices to **government offices**, to receive designated deliveries, etc. These days, **signatures** are also acceptable for receiving deliveries.

For general use, personal seals are adequate, but registered seals are required for important business documents, particularly financial transaction contracts.

● Do many people switch companies?

Most companies still operate on a system of lifetime employment and promotion according to length of service, so people

から出ることは不安なことです。

　　転職しようとしても,「この人はなぜ前の会社をやめたのだろうか, なにか不都合なことがあったのでは……」などと, 疑われることも心配なのです。

　　仮に転職ができたとしても, 同じ賃金をもらうことができるかどうかも分かりません。日本のこれまでの労働環境では, 転職していこうという人が少なくならざるをえないのです。

　　しかし, 1991年以降のバブル経済の崩壊で, 業績の悪化した企業では, 人員の整理や縮小を目指して, 社員の中途退職を奨励する**退職金制度**を設けたり, 過剰な人材の配置転換を進めるといった**リストラ**の動きが活発になり, やむをえず**転職**に追い込まれる人が増えてきています。

　　一方, 若い人たちの間では, 会社に一生を捧げるという意識が薄れてきていることも事実で, また, **年俸制**なども導入されてきましたので, 自分の能力を生かすために積極的に転職に挑む人たちが多くなっています。

Q 日本の会社の定年は何歳ですか?

　　1985年の段階で, 60歳定年の制度をとる企業が, すでに50%を超えていました。それに拍車をかけるために, 1986年,「60歳定年制法」が施行されました。

　　従って, 現在, 多くの企業が**60歳定年**に移行しています。しかし, これまで60歳から支給されていた**老齢年金**は, 段階的に65歳に引き上げられていますので, 定年を62歳, あるいは65歳

are generally unwilling to leave an organization which offers the security of guaranteed employment until they retire.

Even if people want to change companies, they worry that prospective employers will wonder why they left their previous job and assume they did so under unpleasant circumstances.

Even supposing that a person does succeed in obtaining a position in a different company, he or she is not assured of receiving the same salary. The employment structure in Japan has until now made it difficult for many people to change jobs.

However, since the end of the economic bubble in 1991, many troubled companies are trying to reorganize and reduce their staff, and have started to set up **retirement funds** to encourage workers to leave the company before retirement age. Companies are now more actively pursuing **restructuring** with such measures as shifting of personnel, and so the number of people being forced into **career changes** is increasing.

Among the younger generation, however, the idea of dedicating oneself to a particular company for life is losing appeal, and as the **annual salary system** becomes more widespread, it is expected that more people will change jobs to make the most of their abilities.

● What is the retirement age in Japanese companies?

In 1985, 60 was the retirement age in over half of the companies, and to accelerate this trend the government introduced the Retirement-at-sixty Law in 1986.

Most companies therefore have moved to a system of **retirement at 60**. In the past, the age for receiving an **old-age pension** was 60, but this is being increased in stages to 65. And now there are growing calls to raise the retirement age to 62 or

にしてほしいという声も強まっています。仮に定年が延長されなくても，65歳まで働く場のある社会にしてほしいというのが，国民の願いです。

Q 働く女性と男性の割合はどれくらいですか？

Female office
workers

　1998年，企業に雇用された労働者の数は，男女あわせて5368万人です。そして，そのうち39%の2124万人が女性です。

　女性が携わっている仕事は，サービス業，卸売り・小売業，金融保険業，事務などが主ですが，サービス業では約3分の2は女性です。

　職場での男女の均等な機会と待遇の確保のために，1986年に「**男女雇用機会均等法**」が施行されました。これによって，職場への女性の進出も活発になり，男女の**賃金格差**も是正されてくるだろうと言われました。しかし，1992年からの**不況**のために，特に大学卒業の女性の就職難の時代が続きました。

　一方，パートタイム労働は毎年増え続け，1997年には日本の全雇用者のうち21.1%を占めていますが，そのうち約70%が女性です。1999年，男女雇用機会均等法は改正され，女性の**募集，採用，配置，昇進**についての取り扱いは，これまでの努力目標から禁止規定になりました。同時に，女性の深夜残業など，これまで女性を特別視して保護していた規定も廃止され，雇用の機会の上でも，実際の仕事の上でも男女が平等に扱われることが定められました。

Q 結婚しても働く女性は多いですか？

　結婚したことを理由に，女性に退職を求めたという時代は，日本でももう遠い過去のことにな

65. Even if the retirement age is not increased, most people want Japanese society to allow workers to continue working until 65.

● What proportion of the work force is female?

In 1998, the total number of people employed by businesses was 53,680,000. Of that number, 21,240,000 or 39% were women.

Women work mostly in the service industries, wholesale and retail sales, at financial institutions and insurance companies. In the service industries, they comprise two thirds of the employees.

The **Equal Employment Opportunity Law** was passed in 1986 to ensure that men and women received equal opportunities and working conditions. It was predicted that this law would increase female participation in the work force and correct the **imbalance of wages**. Unfortunately, since the Japanese economy took a **nosedive** in 1992, it continued to be difficult for women, particularly university graduates, to find employment.

Part-time employment, on the other hand, is increasing every year, constituting 21.1% of the work force in 1997, 70% of whom were women. In 1999, the Equal Employment Opportunity Law was revised to make it illegal to **recruit**, **hire**, **place**, and **promote** workers on the basis of sex, whereas before equality was only encouraged. At the same time, laws that separated out women, such as those that prevented women from working late hours, were done away with, providing legal equality in job opportunities and working conditions.

● Do many women work after they marry?

Even in Japan it has been many years since women were expected to quit their jobs upon marriage. A **maternity leave**

りました。**育児休暇**などの制度も確立されていますし，結婚して子供が出来ても，仕事を続ける人は多くなりました。

実際に，1997年の女子雇用者約2130万人のうち，57.3%が既婚者です。

25年前の1975年では，女子雇用者は，約1160万人でしたから，今や働く女性は2倍に増えたわけですが，当時でもそのうちの60%は既婚女性でした。

年金

Q 日本人はどんな年金に入っていますか?

1986年の法改正に基づくと，日本の**年金制度**は大きく次のように分けられます。

- 国民年金
- 厚生年金
- 共済年金

国民年金は，20歳以上の男女に義務づけられている年金です。自営業，主婦，学生，厚生年金に加入していない企業の従業員などが入ります。無職の人，外国人にも適用されます。

厚生年金は，**民間の企業**に勤める人のための年金です。

狭義では，共済年金は，**国家公務員，地方公務員**として勤める人のための年金です。勤労者，20歳以上の人は以上のどれかに加入することが原則です。

1995年現在，6995万3000人が，退職後にそ

system has been established, and the number of women continuing to work after having children has increased.

In fact, of the 21,300,000 working women in 1997, 57.3% were married.

In 1975, the number of women in employment was approximately 11,600,000, so the number of women working has virtually doubled in the last twenty-five years. Even back then though, 60% of those women were married.

Pensions

● **What kind of pensions are provided for the Japanese?**

Based on the revision of the Pension Law in 1986, the Japanese **pension system** consists of the following plans:

—National Pension
—Welfare Annuity
—Mutual Benefit Annuity

National Pension is mandatory for everybody aged 20 or over who is self-employed, whether housewives, students, or employees of non-member companies of the Welfare Annuity system. It also applies to unemployed people as well as foreigners.

The Welfare Annuity is a pension for people working for **private enterprises**.

In a narrow sense, the Mutual Benefit Annuity is designed for **national public servants** and **local public servants**. The working population and people aged 20 or older in Japan must join one of the above pension plans.

In 1995, 69,953,000 people were paying premiums for their

なえて年金を払っています。一方，年金をもらう
人は，2166万人です。

Q 年金はどれくらいもらえるのですか？

国民年金でもらう年金は「老齢基礎年金」とい
い，25年以上加入していれば，月額6万7017円
（1999年改正）を支給されます。

厚生年金でもらうのは「老齢厚生年金」といい，
40年の加入の男子で，同じく1999年の計算で，
平均して23万8150円です。

共済年金は，国家公務員，地方公務員，その
他の共済組合などによって，それぞれ違いがあ
りますが，厚生年金よりも支給月額が，1〜2割
多いようです。

日本の医療

Q 日本の医療施設は充実していますか？

日本の**医療**はその技術の上でも，施設の充実
度の上でも世界の上位にあると言われています
が，実際はどうでしょうか。人口1000人あたりの
医師の数，**病床**の数を各国と比べてみましょう。

国名	医師数	病床数
日本	1.8	16.2
ロシア	4.1	11.7
ベルギー	3.8	7.6
ドイツ	3.4	9.7
スイス	3.2	20.8
スウェーデン	3.1	6.3

pensions after retirement, whereas the number of people receiving pensions payments was 21,660,000.

● How much can one receive as pension money?

If you have participated in the **National Pension Plan** for more than 25 years, you will recieve 67,017 yen per month as "basic old-age pension" (the 1999 revision).

With the **Welfare Annuity plan**, an average male with more than 40 years of membership will get 238,150 yen per month, as "old-age pension."

The **Mutual Benefit Annuity** encompasses different plans depending on what mutual benefit association one belongs to, such as for national or local public servants, but recipients are likely to get 10 to 20% more than the monthly amount provided by the Welfare Annuity plan.

Health Care in Japan

● Are Japanese medical institutions fully equipped?

Japan's **healthcare system** is said to be one of the best in world in terms of skill and facilities, but what is the real situation? Let's compare the number of doctors and **hospital beds** per 1,000 people in various countries.

Country	Doctors	Hospital beds
Japan	1.8	16.2
Russia	4.1	11.7
Belgium	3.8	7.6
Germany	3.4	9.7
Switzerland	3.2	20.8
Sweden	3.1	6.3

アメリカ	2.5	4.1
オランダ	2.5	11.3

（世界銀行「世界開発指標」1999年版）

Medical treatment
and care of old
people

　上の表から見ると，他国に比べて医師の数は決して多いとは言えません。しかし，日本では，1000人あたり1.5人の医師の確保という目標が1983年には達成されていますので，今は医師が余っているとされています。実際には，日本の医院や病院はいつも混んでいて，時には何時間も待たされることがあるので，医者の数が少ないと感じている人も多いようです。

　施設の面では，ベッド数はスイスに次いで多く，インドやアフリカ諸国の1とか2という数に比べて，恵まれた医療環境だと言うことができます。

Q いちばん多い日本人の死亡原因は何ですか？

　人口10万当たりの主要な死因別の死亡者数を見てみましょう。

	1980年	1997年
悪性新生物（ガン）	139.2人	220.4人
心臓疾患	106.3人	112.2人
脳血管疾患	139.7人	111.0人
肺炎	28.4人	63.1人
事故	25.1人	31.1人
自殺	17.7人	18.8人
老衰	27.7人	17.2人

（厚生省「人口動態統計」）

　上の表で特徴的なことは，ガンによる**死亡率**がますます高くなっていることですが，同時に心

| United States | 2.5 | 4.1 |
| Netherlands | 2.5 | 11.3 |

(World Bank, World Development Index, 1999)

According to these figures, the number of doctors is not exceptionally high. However, Japan reached its goal of 1.5 doctors per 1,000 people in 1983, and so now it appears that there are too many doctors. In actuality, doctors' offices and hospitals in Japan are almost always crowded and the long waits make most people feel that there are certainly not enough doctors.

As for **facilities**, Japan has the second most hospital beds after Switzerland. Compared to India and African countries with one or two hospital beds per thousand people, Japan can be said to have good healthcare facilities.

● What is the most common cause of death in Japan?

You can find the answer in the following report, which shows the number and cause of deaths per 100,000 people.

	1980	1997
Cancer	139.2	220.4
Heart diseases	106.3	112.2
Cerebrovascular diseases	139.7	111.0
Pneumonia	33.8	63.1
Accidents	25.1	31.1
Suicide	17.7	18.8
Old age (natural causes)	27.7	17.2

(Minister of Health and Welfare, *Vital Statistics*)

The above chart indicates that the **mortality rate** from cancer, and also heart disease, pneumonia and bronchitis, is on the

臓疾患も肺炎・気管支炎による死亡も増えています。医学は進歩を続けているというのに，1997年の病気による死亡者は，1980年に比べて3割増という数字になっているのです。

Q 健康保険はだれでも加入することができますか？

官庁，公共機関，民間の事業体に雇われている人とその家族は，勤務先で強制的に健康保険組合に加入することになっています。**保険料**は基本的に，労働者側と使用者側がだいたい半分ずつ払い込みます。

一方，雇用者であるかどうかを問わず，誰でも入ることができるのが，全国の市町村が公営している**国民健康保険**と言われるものです。小規模の会社の雇用者，自営業者，仕事をしていない人，学生，外国人などが対象となっています。

1961年，健康保険組合に加入していない住民は，必ず国民保険に入るように強制されていて，これが日本の**社会保障制度**の基盤を作っています。

Q 介護保険とはどんな保険ですか？

世界一の高齢化社会である日本では，体が不自由になったお年寄りの介護が21世紀の大きな**問題**の一つです。個々の家庭の力だけでは，面倒をみることはとても不可能ですから，医療と同じように保険制度にして，国がお年寄りの介護サービスを提供しようというのが，この**介護保険制度**です。2000年4月から実施されています。

私たち被保険者が，毎月，保険料を**保険者**である市町村に支払うことで，介護サービス提供機関からサービスを受けることができるようにな

increase. Although medical advances are being made, the number of deaths from illnesses in 1997 was 30% higher than in 1980.

● Can anyone participate in the health insurance programs?

Upon joining an organization, the employees and the families of those employed by government offices, the private sector and public organizations automatically join the program. The employee and employer pay about 50% each of the **insurance premium**.

Anyone can join the **National Health Insurance** program operated by municipalities throughout the nation. Those insured include employees of small companies, self-employed people, unemployed people, students, and foreigners.

Since 1961, people who are not members of the Health Insurance Union have been required to join this program, which is the foundation of Japan's **social security system**.

● What is Long-Term Care Insurance?

With the oldest population in the world, Japan must decide how to care for its helpless elderly—one of the biggest **challenges** of the 21st century. It being nearly impossible for each individual family to take care of their elderly by themselves, **Long-Term Care Insurance** tries to provide healthcare services in the same way that the national insurance system provides medical care. The system became effective in April 2000.

Those being insured, the citizens, pay premiums to the **insurer**, the local government, making it possible for care facilities to provide services to those in need. The program is directed

りました。対象者は65歳以上の高齢者ですが，40歳から60歳までの間の介護を必要とする人も対象となります。

　介護を必要とした場合には，市町村に申し込むと調査が行われ，どの程度の介護を必要とするかの認定を受けてから，**介護サービス**が開始されます。

日本の宗教

Q 日本人にはどんな**宗教**がありますか？

　こんな数字があります。日本の**宗教法人**の報告に基づいた信者数の数字です。

神道系	1億455万人
仏教系	9511万人
キリスト教系	176万人
その他	1121万人

（文化庁編『宗教年鑑1998』）

　この数字を合計すると，なんと2億1263万人になってしまいます。これは各宗教団体が，亡くなったり脱会したりした人を信者数から外さないで報告しているからです。

　一人一人の日本人に「信じている宗教は？」と聞くと，キリスト教や新宗教の**信者**を除いて「ありません」と答える人が多いはずです。

　ところが，「あなたの家の宗派は？」と聞くと，「浄土宗です」とか，「日蓮宗です」という返事が返ってきます。つまり，それぞれの家が昔から**先祖を祀る**ところとして持っている寺が，その人の

to those 65 and older, but anybody between 40 and 60 who is in need of care may also be eligible.

When care is needed and a request is made to the local government, an investigation is conducted and, if the request is approved, the **care services** begin.

Religions in Japan

• What religions are there in Japan?

The following is the number of believers or followers of religions based on reports of Japanese **religious corporations**.

Shintoism	104.55 million
Buddhism	95.11 million
Christianity	1.76 million
Other religions	11.21 million

(Agency for Cultural Affairs, *Yearbook of Religions 1998*)

Strangely enough, these numbers, when added up, amount to 212.63 million, which is far greater than the Japanese population. It is partly because the religious corporations surveyed did not report the number of people who ceased to be followers.

When one asks the Japanese, "What's your religion?" many of them, excluding Christians and **followers** of new religions, will answer "I have no religion."

However, when asked "What is the religion of your family?" they might answer "Jōdo sect of Buddhism," or "Nichiren sect of Buddhism." That means the religion that each family has had since ancient times for the purpose of **worshipping**

宗教となっているのです。**信仰心**とは別問題な
のです。

Q 神道の神はいつ生まれたのですか？

Ise Shrine

　8世紀の初めに編集された「古事記」と「日本
書紀」に、神々の誕生の物語や神々の系譜が，
神話として描かれています。

　その神話によれば，最初の3神，天之御中主
神，高御産巣日神，神産巣日神がいたそうで，こ
の神は姿形がありませんでした。その後，伊邪
那岐命，伊邪那美命という男女の神が登場し，
この2神が産み落としたのが，日本の8つの島だ
というのです。これらの神々は日本民族の先祖
の象徴として崇拝の対象となっているものです。

　神道では，自然の事物の一つ一つに宿る精
霊が崇拝の対象となりますので，「八百万の神」
と言われるほどたくさんの神がいます。

Q 神道は日本の国教なのですか？

　神道は，日本固有の宗教です。仏教，儒教，
道教などの外来の教義の影響を受けながら宗
教として形成されていきます。

　そして，江戸時代には「古事記」「日本書紀」
に記録された神のみを忠実に信仰しようという
考えが現れます。この考えは神の子孫とされる
天皇を崇拝する思想と結びつき，朝廷に代わっ
て日本を支配していた江戸幕府を倒す運動に
発展しました。

　明治維新後，神道は国家の保護を受け，天皇
を神格化するなどして，国家神道となります。太
平洋戦争後は政教分離となり，神道は多くの宗
教の中の1つとなっています。

their ancestors has stayed with the household. Often it has little to do with one's **religious faith**.

● When were the gods of Shintoism born?

The *Kojiki* and the *Nihon shoki*, two chronicles written in the early eighth century, depict the ancient myths and history of Japan.

According to the chronicle myths, there existed the first three gods; Amenominakanushi-no-kami, Takamimusubi-no-kami, and Kamimusubi-no-kami were invisible. Later, a god couple, Izanagi-no-mikoto and Izanami-no-mikoto, produced the eight islands of Japan. These gods are objects of worship at shrines as symbols of ancestors.

All natural objects and phenomena are also worshipped and considered as having gods, so there are myriads of gods in **Shintoism**—as the phrase goes, *yaoyorozu-no-kami* (8 million gods).

● Is Shintoism Japan's national religion?

Shintoism is the indigenous religion of Japan. Influenced by Buddhism, Confucianism and **Taoism**, Shintoism later became ideologized.

In the Edo period, there was a view that encouraged the ancient faith in gods described in the *Kojiki* and the *Nihon shoki*. This view, associated with the worship of the emperor as a descendant of the gods, developed into a movement to over-throw the Edo feudal government.

After the **Meiji Restoration**, Shintoism was protected by the State and the emperor became deified. However, after World War II, the practice of religion was separated from the state, and Shintoism became just one of many religions in Japan.

Q 日本の仏教にはどんな宗派がありますか?

仏教は広くアジアで信仰されている宗教です。東南アジアでは「**小乗仏教**」と呼ばれ, 出家をして寺にこもり, **修行**をして, 自分の悟りを得ることを目的としています。

中国, 韓国を経て538年に日本に伝わった仏教は「**大乗仏教**」と呼ばれ, 人類の平等を説き, 広く大衆が救われるという考えに基づいています。

Nichiren

現在, 日本国内で活動している仏教の宗派には, 禅の3派を含めて次の13があります。

華厳宗, 法相宗, 律宗, 天台宗, 真言宗, 浄土宗, 浄土真宗, 時宗, 融通念仏宗, 日蓮宗, 臨済宗, 曹洞宗, 黄檗宗。

Q 「南無阿弥陀仏」「南無妙法蓮華経」とはどんな意味ですか?

「南無」というのは「神・仏などすぐれたものに服従し, 尊敬する」という意味です。ですから, 「南無阿弥陀仏」は「阿弥陀仏を敬い, その**教え**に従います」という意味で, 広く仏教の各**宗派**で唱えます。

一方, 「南無妙法蓮華経」は「妙法蓮華経に従い, その教えを守ります」という意味になり, こちらは日蓮宗で唱えます。

Q 禅とはどんなものですか?

仏教の派の1つである「禅」の目指すところは, 「心から**迷い**を無くして, 真理に到達するために瞑想をすること」です。そのために, 座って無心の気持ちで修行することを「座禅」と言います。

• What sects are there in Japanese Buddhism?

Buddhism is a religion widely followed in Asia. **Hinayana Buddhism**, which aims at attaining emancipation or self-enlightenment by becoming a priest and undergoing **austerities** in a temple, is the major religion in Southeast Asia.

The Buddhism which reached Japan in 538 via China and Korea is **Mahayana Buddhism**, based on the idea that people are equal and can be saved by faith in Buddha.

Currently, the number of Buddhist sects operating in Japan is 13, including three Zen sects: Kegon sect, Hossō sect, Ritsu sect, Tendai sect, Shingon sect, Jōdo sect, Jōdo Shin sect, Ji sect, Yūzū Nembutsu sect, Nichiren sect, Rinzai sect, Sōtō sect, and the Ōbaku sect.

• What do *"namu Amida butsu"* and *"namu myōhō renge kyō"* mean?

Namu means "to obey and worship a superior existence such as gods and the Buddha." Therefore, when one prays "*Namu Amida butsu*," one says "I worship Amida Buddha and follow his **doctrine**." This prayer is used in many **sects** of Buddhism.

On the other hand "*Namu myōhō renge kyō*" means "I obey *myōhō renge kyō* (the sutra), and observe its doctrine," which is used in the Nichiren sect.

• What is Zen?

The aim of the Zen sect, one of the denominations of Buddhism, is to meditate in order to eliminate **hesitation** or **delusion** and awaken to the truth. One of the practices used to acquire serenity of mind is *zazen*, which means to sit in silent meditation.

Zazen

禅は紀元前からインドにあったものですが，後に**達磨大師**を含めた僧によって広められました。達磨は9年間も座り続け修行をしたと伝えられています。12，13世紀に，日本の僧たちが中国で修行をして禅宗を日本に伝え，現在，臨済宗，曹洞宗，黄檗宗が続いています。

Q どんな時に寺に行きますか？

日本では人が亡くなりますと，ほとんど仏式で**葬儀**が行われます。そして，亡くなった人の遺骨は寺の墓に納めます。そのためにどこかの寺の**檀家**という，寺を支えるメンバーになっているはずです。

寺は本来，その地域に根ざしたもので，欧米のキリスト教会のような存在と言っていいでしょう。キリスト教の日曜礼拝のように，寺でも定期的な**説法会**が行われていたのです。

しかし，今ではこういう説法会に来る若い人は少なく，葬式の時以外には，めったに寺に行くことはありません。京都や奈良への観光旅行で有名な寺を訪ねる人は，数限りないのですが……

Q どんな時に神社に行きますか？

神社も，寺の檀家と同様に「**氏子**」というメンバーで支えられています。しかし，信仰で結ばれた関係というわけではなく，神社のある**地域の連帯**といった感じでつながっています。

私たちが神社に行くのは，まず，正月の**初詣**でです。その年の無事と多幸を祈ります。

結婚式は今でも神前が人気。神社に行かな

Zen existed in India before Christ, and it was later spread by priests including **Bodhidarma**, who is believed to have continued meditating in a sitting posture for nine years. After studying in China, Japanese priests introduced Zen to Japan in the 12th and 13th centuries. The Zen sects in Japan today are the Rinzai sect, Sōtō sect, and Ōbaku sect.

● On what occasions do people go to temples?

Most **funerals** in Japan are conducted in the Buddhist tradition and the dead are buried according to Buddhist rites. Remains of the dead after cremation are placed in a grave at a temple. Therefore, the family of someone who is buried at a temple becomes a supporting member called *danka*.

Originally a temple was deeply rooted in the community, and it was like a church in Christianity in the sense that regular **lecture meetings** for believers were held.

But very few young people now go to such events. Most people seldom go to temples except for funerals. However, temples in Kyōto and Nara, two representative ancient cities, are always filled with tourists.

● On what occasions do people go to Shintō shrines?

Just as temples have *danka* as supporters, shrines have *ujiko*, which are not necessarily united by faith, but by a sense of **community solidarity**.

Most Japanese go to shrines to offer their **first prayer of the year** on New Year's Day. They pray for happiness, peace and good health in the coming year.

For wedding ceremonies, Shintoism is among the first choices

Meiji Shrine

くても，式場に設けられた**神殿**の前で，結婚を誓います。

子供が生まれてから30日前後になると，「宮参り」といって，必ず神社にお参りします。

11月には，子供の成長を祝う「七五三」があり，3歳と7歳の女の子，3歳と5歳の男の子を着飾らせて神社に連れていきます。

そして，日本人の生活の中で大事な位置をしめる祭りは，神社の大事な行事です。私たちは何かを祝う気持ちの中で，神社を位置づけているようです。

Q 日本にはキリスト教徒はどれくらいいるんですか？

文化庁編「宗教年鑑」によりますと，1997年のキリスト教の各派の信徒の合計は約176万人でした。

キリスト教は1549年から，フランシスコ・ザビエルをはじめとするスペイン，ポルトガルのローマ・カトリック教，イエズス会の**宣教師**によって，日本に広められていきました。そして，わずかの期間に信徒を獲得し，1580年には，その数は12万になっています。

The Virgin Mary Kannon worshipped by hidden Christians （東京国立博物館）

しかし1640年，キリスト教は禁制となり，以後，1868年に明治維新で禁が解かれるまで，キリスト教徒たちは「隠れキリシタン」として生きていかざるを得なくなります。

太平洋戦争後の民主主義の時代になったとき，キリスト教の各派が日本に入り信者が急増しましたが，最近の信者数の伸びは少ないようです。

for couples. Many hotels and wedding ceremonial halls have **Shintō altars**, so couples do not have to go to a shrine to take their marriage vows.

When a couple has a baby, the baby is taken to a shrine around 30 days after his or her birth.

In November, on the occasion for celebrating *shichi-go-san* for girls at the ages of three and seven, and boys at three and five, children in their finest clothes are taken to a shrine.

Festivals, which play an important role in the lives of the Japanese as popular annual events, are also held at shrines. The Japanese consider shrines as places of celebration.

● How many Christians are there in Japan?

According to the *Yearbook of Religions* compiled by the Agency for Cultural Affairs, the total number of Christians of various sects in Japan was approximately 1.76 million in 1997.

Christianity was first introduced to Japan in 1549, and was propagated mainly by Spanish and Portuguese Catholic **missionaries** of the Society of Jesus including Francisco Xavier. In a short period of time Christianity acquired many believers, and their numbers reached 120,000 in 1580.

After 1640, when Christianity was banned, persecuted Christians had no choice but to live as *kakure kirishitan* (hidden Christians) until the Meiji Restoration lifted the ban in 1868.

After World War II, when democracy and related ways of thinking were first introduced, the number of Christians increased rapidly, but the speed of growth has slowed down in the past couple of decades.

Q 新宗教にはどんなものがありますか?

　　数多くの新宗教がありますが，今も活動を続けているいくつかを，誕生の**時代を追って**挙げてみましょう。

江戸幕府末期から明治時代にかけて
- 神道系＝天理教，黒住教，金光教など

明治の末期から太平洋戦争終結まで
- 神道系＝大本教，生長の家，世界救世教，PL教団など
- 仏教系＝創価教育学会（創価学会），霊友会，真如苑，立正佼成会など

戦後から2000年ごろまで
- 神道系＝天照皇大神宮教，世界真光文明教団など
- 仏教系＝阿含宗など
- その他＝幸福の科学，オウム真理教など

　　信者の総数は，各教団の発表によれば，日本の全人口の1割に達すると言われています。

　　その中で，1986年に麻原彰晃を教祖として生まれたオウム真理教は，自らの**世紀末思想**を正当化するために，1995年3月20日の朝，通勤時間で込み合う東京の地下鉄の駅に，猛毒のサリンをまくという事件を引き起こしました。**死者**11人，負傷者5000人という大惨事でした。

　　麻原彰晃をはじめ多数の信者が逮捕されて裁判を受けました。また，事件の再発が懸念されましたので，オウム真理教に**破壊活動防止法**の適用が検討されました。その適用は見送られましたが，引き続く彼らの宗教活動に対する国民の不安は強く，2000年1月に活動を規制する法の適用を受けて，日常の活動が**監視**されることになりました。

● What kind of new religions exist in Japan?

Countless religions have come and gone, but below are some of the existing religions **in chronological order** of establishment.

From the end of the Edo era to the Meiji era

- Shintoism—Tenrikyō, Kurozumikyō, Konkōkyō, etc.

From the end of the Meiji era to the end of the World War II

- Shintoism—Ōmotokyō, Seichō-no Ie, Sekai Kyūseikyō, Perfect Liberty Kyōdan, etc.
- Buddhism—Sōka Kyōiku Gakkai, Reiyūkai, Shinnyoen, Risshō Kōseikai, etc.

From 1945 to 2000

- Shintoism—Tenshōkōtaijingūkyō, Sekai Mahikari Bunmei Kyōdan, etc.
- Buddhism—Agonshū, etc.
- Others—Kōfuku-no Kagaku, Aum Shinrikyō, etc.

The total number of such new religious believers is said to be about 10% of the Japanese population.

One such religion, Aum, founded by Shoko Asahara in 1986, set loose poisonous sarin gas on Tokyo's subways on March 20, 1995 in order to justify their **end-of-the-world doctrine**. The result was 11 **fatalities** and 5,000 other victims.

Asahara Shokō and several followers were arrested and put on trial. Out of a fear of a reoccurrence, an **Anti-Subversive Activities Act** was considered but decided against. In response to the concerns of the public about the ongoing activities of the Aum religion, a law to restrict their activities was passed in January 2000, allowing the police to **monitor** their daily activities.

5

日本の文化

Japanese Culture

Kinkakuji ▶

現代の文化

Q 日本でノーベル賞をもらった人はどんな人ですか?

日本人で初めて**ノーベル賞を受賞**したのは湯川秀樹でした。1949年に「中間子理論の研究」で物理学賞を受賞し, 敗戦でうちひしがれていた日本人に明るい希望を与えました。

続いて1965年には朝永振一郎が, 1973年には江崎玲於奈が物理学賞を受賞し, 1981年には福井謙一が化学賞を, 1987年には利根川進が医学生理学賞を受賞して, 科学技術の優秀さを世界に示しました。

Ōe Kenzaburō,
Nobel laureate
in literature in 1994

科学技術以外では, 1974年に, 元首相の佐藤栄作が平和賞を受けています。

文学賞は, 1968年に川端康成が受賞しています。「雪国」「伊豆の踊り子」などの作者です。

Contemporary Culture

● Who are Japan's Nobel laureates?

Japan's first **Nobel laureate** was Yukawa Hideki. He received a Nobel prize in physics for his *Chūkanshi riron no kenkyū* (Study of Meson Theory) in 1949, giving hope to the Japanese people crushed by their defeat in the war.

Yukawa was followed by Tomonaga Shin'ichirō in 1965 and Esaki Reona in 1973, who were both awarded Nobel prizes in physics; and then Fukui Ken'ichi, who was awarded a Nobel prize in chemistry in 1981 and Tonegawa Susumu, who was awarded a Nobel prize in physiology and medicine in 1987, thus demonstrating to the rest of the world Japan's excellence in science and technology.

Outside the fields of science and technology, former Prime Minister Satō Eisaku received the Nobel Peace prize in 1974.

Kawabata Yasunari received the Nobel prize for literature in 1968; he was the author of such works as *Snow Country* and *The Izu Dancer*.

　そしていちばん最近では1994年に文学賞を受賞した大江健三郎です。「ヒロシマ・ノート」「万延元年のフットボール」などの作品があります。

Q 日本にはどれくらい新聞がありますか？

Japanese daily
newspapers

　日刊新聞が何点発行されていて，1,000人当たりどれくらいの部数発行されているのか，主要な国を比較してみましょう。

		紙数	1,000人当たり
日本	（1997年）	122	580部
アメリカ	（1996年）	1,520	212部
ドイツ	（1996年）	375	311部
イギリス	（1996年）	99	332部
フランス	（1996年）	117	218部
ロシア	（1996年）	285	105部

（ユネスコ「文化統計年鑑」1998年）

　日本の新聞発行の特徴は，巨大な部数を持つ**全国紙**と，各地域の新聞とが共存していることです。しかも，多くの新聞が朝刊と夕刊をセットにし，しかも，店頭売りだけではなく各家庭への配達制にしていることも他の国にない特徴です。

　また，都市の駅売りを中心に，多くのスポーツ新聞と，タブロイド版の夕刊紙が人気があります。

Q いちばん売れている新聞はどれですか？

　日刊新聞の朝刊の**発行部数**だけで比べると次のようになります。「日本新聞年鑑」（1998/99年）によると，読売新聞がいちばん部数が多くて，1021.6万部，続いて朝日新聞834.2万部，毎日新聞395.8万部です。

The most recent Nobel laureate is Ōe Kenzaburō, who received the Nobel prize in literature in 1994. Among his works are *Hiroshima Note* and *The Silent Cry*.

● How many newspapers are published in Japan?

The following is the number of daily newspapers being published and circulation per 1,000 people in Japan and other countries.

		No. of papers	per 1,000 people
Japan	(1997)	122	580
United States	(1996)	1,520	212
Germany	(1996)	375	311
United Kingdom	(1996)	99	332
France	(1996)	117	218
Russia	(1996)	285	105

(UNESCO, *Statistical Yearbook*, 1998)

A characteristic of Japanese newspaper publication is that **nationwide newspapers** and local newspapers coexist in each region, and that—in addition to sales in shops—almost all morning and evening newspapers are, as a set, delivered to homes and offices.

Sports newspapers and evening tabloid newspapers are quite popular and are mainly sold from kiosks at train and subway stations in urban areas.

● Which newspaper has the largest circulation?

When we compare the daily morning papers, *Yomiuri Shimbun* has the largest **circulation** with 10.216 million readers, followed by *Asahi Shimbun* (8.342 million) and *Mainichi Shimbun* (3.958 million), according to the *Japan Newspaper Yearbook* 1998/99.

　これを世界の新聞と比べてみましょう。

ロサンゼルス・タイムズ	105.0万部
ニューヨーク・タイムズ	107.5万部
ウォール・ストリート・ジャーナル	177.5万部
デイリー・ミラー	237.6万部
ル・モンド	36.9万部
ウェルト	30.4万部
人民日報	300.0万部

（「日本新聞年鑑」1998/99年）

　外国の新聞は朝刊専門紙か夕刊専門紙です
し，数字の多い少ないで新聞の人気を決める
こともできませんが，**各家庭への配達制度**に支え
られた日本の新聞の販売数字は，世界から見
ると驚異的です。

Q 日本にはどれくらいのテレビ局がありますか？

NHK, Nippon Hōsō
Kyōkai

　1997年の時点で，日本放送協会以外の**民間
放送会社**の数は127社です。1953年のテレビ放
送開始の時はわずかNHKのみ，しかも東京局
だけでした。
　現在次々と増えているのは放送衛星による衛
星放送局，通信衛星によるケーブルテレビ局で
す。
　日本では放送の**デジタル化**が進んでいます。
BS（放送衛星）放送は2000年12月にデジタル本
放送が開始され，地上波は，2003年には東京，
大阪，名古屋の三大都市圏で，2006年には全国
でデジタル放送が開始されます。
　放送のデジタル化によって，1台の受像機が放

Let's compare these figures with those of other newspapers of the world.

Los Angeles Times	1.050 million
New York Times	1.075 million
Wall Street Journal	1.775 million
Daily Mirror	2.376 million
Le Monde	0.369 million
Die Welt	0.304 million
People's Daily	3.000 million

(Japan Newspaper Yearbook, 1998/99)

Unlike Japanese papers, most of the above papers are either morning papers or evening papers, and it is hard to measure the popularity of newspapers only by circulation. But it is certain that the sales of Japanese newspapers, supported by their **home delivery systems**, are quite high compared to newspapers in other parts of the world.

● How many TV stations are there in Japan?

The number of **private TV stations** (excluding NHK) was 127 in 1997. When television broadcasting started in 1953, NHK, Nippon Hōsō Kyōkai, was the only station and Tōkyō was the only area where people could receive broadcasts.

There has been a rapid increase in the number of satellite broadcasting stations and cable TV stations using communications satellites.

The **digitization** of broadcasting in Japan is moving ahead. Digital satellite broadcasts are set to begin in December 2000, while terrestrial digital broadcasting will be introduced in the three major cities of Tōkyō, Ōsaka and Nagoya in 2003. The rest of the country will follow in 2006.

With digitization, one receiver can be used to pick up

送，通信，コンピューター使用できる時代がくることになりました。同時に，本格的な多チャンネルの時代を迎えることになり，海外メディアの日本進出の動きも加速され，放送局間の**生き残りをかけた競争**は激しくなると予想されます。

Q 日本ではどんなテレビ番組に人気が集まっていますか？

番組は，通例，3か月単位で変更されますから，**視聴率**の悪い番組は次々と消えていき，また新しい番組が誕生していきます。

1980年代まで人気があった歌謡番組は，1990年代に入ってからは少なくなりましたし，国民的番組とまで言われた，NHKの紅白歌合戦の人気はかなり落ちて，中止がうわさされるなど，全体の番組の人気の傾向には大きな変化が見られます。

その変化の中で，人気を保っている番組のパターンを挙げておきましょう。

・スポーツ中継
・ニュースショー／ワイドショー
・クイズ番組
・連続ドラマ

Q 日本人はどんな本や雑誌を読みますか？

Bookstore

日本人はいろんなタイプの本を貪欲に読みます。この日本人の読書好きな姿には次のような特徴があります。

1つは，週刊誌の人気があらゆる年齢の人に高いことです。政治・社会問題からヘアヌードやマンガ，**連載小説**などまで幅広く取り上げた，主に30代以上の男性向けのもの。次に芸能界の裏話や実用ページで売る女性週刊誌。いずれ

broadcasts, for communication, and as a computer. At the same time, the number of channels offered will increase dramatically, and as more foreign media corporations move into Japan, it is expected that a ferocious **battle to survive** will result.

● What kinds of TV programs are popular in Japan?

The TV program lineup changes every three months, and programs with lower **audience ratings** disappear as new programs appear one after another.

Programs featuring hit songs were popular until the 80s, but the number of such programs decreased in the 90s. Even the legendary annual all-star music program broadcast by NHK on New Year's Eve, the *Kōhaku Utagassen*, has lost much of its popularity. TV programming seems to be undergoing a major shift because of the changing needs of the viewers.

Under such circumstances, sports broadcasting, news shows, "wide shows" featuring news and gossip about celebrities, quiz shows, and serial dramas are maintaining their popularity.

● What kinds of books and magazines do Japanese read?

The Japanese are avid readers of various types of publications. Their reading trends are characterized as follows:

Weekly magazines are widely read by people of all ages. Magazines catering to men in their 30s, which deal with a wide range of topics such as politics and social problems, nude photos, comics and **serial novels** boast large circulations. Ladies' weekly magazines featuring gossip and scandal involving

も数十万部の売れ行きです。

そして、特に若い人たちに強い人気があるのがマンガ雑誌です。なかには毎週数百万部を売るものまであります。

多くのマンガは週刊あるいは月刊の雑誌に連載されて人気を得た後、単行本になってロングランで売れ続けています。

次に**文庫本**の人気です。価格が安く、また、通勤の混んだ電車の中でも読むことができる文庫は、今ではあらゆる分野の内容を網羅しており、日本人の読書には欠かせないスタイルの本となりました。

Q 日本で有名なマンガ家はだれですか?

Tezuka Osamu

数え切れないほどたくさんの優れた**マンガ家**がいますが、絶対に挙げなければならない2人を紹介します。

まず、手塚治虫(1928–1989)。

勇敢で心あたたかいロボット少年の活躍を描いた『鉄腕アトム』、ライオンの子が、森の指導者に育っていく姿を描いた『ジャングル大帝』など、数々の名作を描いています。日本のアニメーションの育ての親でもあります。

もう1人は長谷川町子(1920–1992)。3世代家族の日常の生活に繰り広げられる笑いを、嫁を中心に描いた**4コマ・マンガ**の『サザエさん』は、1946年の新聞連載開始以来、日本全国の子供から大人までの心をなごませてくれました。今でも、本が売れ、テレビのアニメ・マンガの人気番組です。

celebrities, and articles providing practical knowledge of daily life also sell several hundred thousand copies.

Magazines specializing in *manga*, Japanese-style sophisticated cartoons, are widely read by young people. Some sell several million copies every week.

Popular *manga* are turned into books after serialization in weekly or monthly magazines, most of which enjoy long-running popularity.

Pocket books, which are inexpensive and small enough to read in a crowded train, have become an integral part of the reading habits of the Japanese. Now virtually every genre of reading is available in this form.

● Who are the famous comic book artists in Japan?

Although it is almost impossible to count the number of gifted **comic book artists**, two are definitely deserving of mention.

First of all, there is Tezuka Osamu (1928–89).

He produced a number of famous works, including *Astro Boy*, a story about the adventures of a brave and kind-hearted robot boy, and *Jungle King*, a story about a lion who is groomed to become the leader of the forest. He is considered the father of Japanese animated film.

The other is Hasegawa Machiko (1920–1992). Her **four-frame comic strip**, *Sazaesan*, centers around a young wife and gives a comic look into the daily life of her three-generation family. Ever since it first appeared in the newspapers as a serialized comic strip, it has warmed the hearts of adults and children throughout Japan. Even today, the comic strip sells well in book form, and the TV animated program based on the strip is also very popular.

Q 日本のアニメーションの名作は何ですか?

The Princess
Mononoke
© 1997 NIBARIKI・TNDG

日本は世界最大のアニメーション生産国です。anime という言葉が英語として**定着している**ほどです。古くは手塚治虫の『鉄腕アトム』のテレビ用アニメーションが,アメリカで『アストロボーイ』として人気を博しました。

最近では『セーラームーン』というテレビ・アニメがアメリカでも大人気になりました。そのほか数多くのテレビ用アニメが輸出され,世界中で見られています。

また現代のアニメ作家としては宮崎駿（はやお）が傑出していて,『風の谷のナウシカ』や『となりのトトロ』など,発表する作品すべてが大ヒットとなっています。1997年に公開された『もののけ姫』は,**興行収入**186億円,観客動員数1360万人という日本映画史上最大のヒットとなりました。

Q 世界で活躍する日本の音楽家はだれですか?

Ozawa Seiji

戦後,多くの若い音楽家が,世界の**音楽コンクール**で入賞しており,世界を舞台に活躍しています。その最初の人がボストン交響楽団の**常任指揮者**（せいじ）の小沢征爾です。彼は2002年から,ウィーン国立歌劇場の音楽監督に就任することになりました。東洋人が**由緒正しい**世界最高レベルのヨーロッパの歌劇場の音楽監督になるのは,音楽史上,初めてのことです。

バイオリンでは,五嶋（ごとう）みどりがすでに一流の地位を築いています。演奏会で弦が切れても,コンサートマスターのバイオリンを借りて冷静に

• What are some famous Japanese animated films?

Japan is the world's largest producer of animated films. The Japanese word *anime* has even **gained currency** in English. Older works include Tezuka Osamu's animated film for TV, *Tetsuwan Atomu*, which gained popularity in the United States as *Astro Boy*.

More recently, *Sailor Moon* became very popular in the United States. There are numerous other animated films that have been exported and are being watched around the world.

Another outstanding contemporary animation artist is Miyazaki Hayao, whose works such as *Kaze no Tani no Naushika* (Nausicaä of the Valley of the Wind) and *Tonari no Totoro* (My Neighbor Totoro) have all become big hits. His *Princess Mononoke*, which came out in 1997, was the most successful Japanese movie ever. It was watched by 13.6 million people and generated **box-office returns** of 18.6 billion yen.

• Which Japanese musicians are active internationally?

In the postwar period, many young musicians have won awards at international **music competitions** and are active worldwide. The first of these internationally acclaimed musicians is Ozawa Seiji, **resident conductor** of the Boston Philharmonic Orchestra. In 2002 Ozawa will become musical director of the Vienna National Opera. This will be the first time in musical history that a person of Oriental extraction has achieved such a high-level position in the **tradition-bound** world of European opera.

Although she is still young, violinist Gotō Midori has already joined the top ranks of performers. An American textbook has even included an episode from one of Gotō's concerts, during

Nakamaru Michie

引き続けたというエピソードは，アメリカの教科書にも紹介されました。

ピアノではモーツァルトの**演奏**で世界的に有名になった内田光子がいます。

ソプラノでは中丸三千繪(みちえ)が，ヨーロッパで通用する**歌唱力**と舞台映えのする容姿を持っているといえるでしょう。

クラシック以外では，シンセサイザーを使った作曲，演奏をしている喜多郎と冨田勲，そして**アカデミー音楽賞**を受賞した坂本龍一が世界的に活躍しています。

Q 日本で人気のあるクラシック音楽は何ですか？

日本人の好みは世界とくらべてそんなに変わりませんが，日本で特別に人気のある2曲があります。1つはヴィヴァルディの「四季」で，とくにイ・ムジチ合奏団の**演奏**に人気があり，クラシック音楽の中で一番の売れ行きを保っています。

もう1つはベートーベンの**第9交響曲「合唱付き」**で，年末になると，この曲のコンサートがほうぼうで行われ，この合唱に参加することを楽しみにしているアマチュア歌手たちが数多くいます。ベートーベンの**第5交響曲**もポピュラーで，ジャジャジャジャーンという出だしを知らない人はいないと言っていいでしょう。

次いで人気があるのはショパン。そのロマンティックなメロディーは若い女性に強い人気がありますし，概して日本人はロマン主義派の音楽が好み，ということができます。

Q 今の若い日本人はどんな音楽が好きですか？

聴く，ということで言うならば，ロック，ヒップホッ

which she borrowed the concert master's violin when one of her strings suddenly snapped and coolly continued to play.

Pianist Uchida Mitsuko has become famous worldwide for her **performances** of Mozart.

Soprano Nakamaru Michie can best be described as having not just **singing talent** but also a striking stage presence which wins great respect in Europe.

Musicians outside of **classical music** who are active worldwide include Kitarō and Tomita Isao, both composers and performers of synthesizer music, and Sakamoto Ryūichi, who was awarded an **Academy Award for Best Soundtrack**.

● What kind of classical music is popular in Japan?

Although Japanese tastes are not so different from those of the rest of the world, there are two compositions that are especially popular among the Japanese. One is Vivaldi's *Four Seasons*, particularly the **rendition** by the I Musici Orchestra, which is the best-selling classical recording ever in Japan.

The other is Beethoven's ***Ninth Symphony* with chorus**. At the end of the year, concert performances of the Ninth are held everywhere, and many amateur singers look forward to singing in these choruses. Beethoven's ***Fifth*** is also popular, and it is not an exaggeration to say that everybody knows the "da-da-da-da" opening.

Next in popularity comes Chopin, who is a particular favorite with young women. It is fair to say that generally the Japanese like the music of the romantics best.

● What kind of music do today's young Japanese like?

For listening pleasure, young Japanese show interest in a

Matsutōya Yumi

プ, レゲエ, ユーロビート, ニューテクノなど, アメリカやイギリスのヒットチャートに入っているあらゆる音楽に, 若者たちは興味を示しています。

しかし, 自分たちで口ずさむことができるという点では, 日本のオリジナルのポピュラー音楽の方が人気です。ユーミン(松任谷由実), ミスター・チルドレン, その他, CDを出すたびに数十万枚を売る歌手やグループがいます。

ポピュラー音楽でCD売り上げの日本新記録は, 1999年の3月に発売された宇多田ヒカルのアルバム「First Love」(東芝EMI)です。わずか2か月で650万枚を突破しました。英語と日本語を無理なく交じり合わせた**歌詞**と, 若い世代の**気持ち**を反映させたサウンドが人気となったものです。

日本では, カラオケが隅々まで普及していて, ヒットした日本のポピュラー曲はすぐにカラオケに取り入れられますから, これも人気を支える大きな力になっています。

Q 「演歌」とはどんな歌ですか?

Misora Hibari

「演歌」は, 日本の**風土**と日本人の**情緒**に根ざした歌と言うことができます。

「演歌」という言葉は, 明治時代の中ごろから使われていましたが, 当時は, 思想を歌に託したもので, 演説に対して用いられた言葉でした。しかし1910年代になると, 次第に, 男女の心情, 人間の**悲喜こもごもの気持ち**を表現するようになりました。

そして, 1930年代になってレコードが普及すると共に, 広く大衆の心に浸透し, やがて美空ひばり(1937-89)をはじめとして多数の演歌歌手が

variety of music on the hit charts in the United States and the United Kingdom such as rock, hip hop, reggae, Eurobeat, and new techno pop.

However, when it comes to singing songs themselves, domestic Japanese pop music is more popular. Yuming (Matsu-tōya Yumi), Mister Children, and other singers and groups sell several hundred thousand copies of each CD they release.

Utada Hikaru's album First Love (Toshiba EMI) set a new sales record in the world of Japanese pop. Released in March 1999, it sold over 6.5 million copies in only two months, its popularity assured by easy interweaving of Japanese and English **lyrics**, and music that captured the **emotions** of the young generation perfectly.

In Japan, *karaoke* has spread to every corner, and popular hit songs immediately are turned into *karaoke* music, which greatly helps to sustain the popularity of the songs.

• What is *Enka*?

Enka can be summarized as a genre of song firmly rooted in the **landscape** of Japan and the **emotions** of the Japanese people.

The word *enka* was in use from the middle of the Meiji period, but at that time it denoted ideas put in the form of song, and was applied to public speeches. From the decade of 1910 onwards, however, it came to refer to songs that deal with love between men and women, and **mingled feelings of joy and sorrow**.

Then in the 1930s, as records grew more popular, *enka* became a part of the national consciousness. Numerous singers appeared—of whom Misora Hibari (1937–89) was the most

出現して，1960年代，70年代と，演歌の黄金時代が築かれていきました。

演歌の多くは，世の定めや世間によって引き裂かれた男と女を物語る悲しい詩と，**哀愁を誘う小節（こぶし）の利いたいた**メロディーを特徴としています。

今の若い人たちは演歌で歌われる古くさい世界に興味を抱かなくなってしまいましたが，少し年配の日本人にとっては，日本の歌と言えばやはり演歌。今でもカラオケで熱唱するオジサンが**後を断ちません**。

Q 世界的に有名な日本の美術家はだれですか？

Hirayama Ikuo

外国人の方々から見ると，たぶん，**北斎（ほくさい）**や**歌麿（うたまろ）・写楽（しゃらく）**という江戸時代の**浮世絵師**の名が出てくると思います。彼らの絵はゴッホやモネなど多くのヨーロッパの画家に影響を与えているのですから。

現在，世界的に人気のある日本画の画家としては，杉山寧，東山魁夷（ひがしやまかいい），高山辰雄，加山又造，平山郁夫などが挙げられますが，偶然にもみんな名前に『山』という字があるので「日本画の五山」といわれています。

Q 日本画は西洋の絵の手法とどう違いますか？

日本画という言葉は，明治以降，**洋画**，特に**油絵**が入ってきたことから言われるようになった言葉です。

一口に日本画といっても，実際は様々な**流儀**や**様式**があり，最近の日本画家には洋画とほと

famous—and the 60s and 70s were the golden age of *enka*.

The majority of *enka* songs are characterized by sad lyrics that tell of grim destiny or of lovers cruelly separated, and by melodies which make use of grace-notes in order to **evoke pathos**.

Young people have lost interest in the old world sung about in *enka* songs, but for older people *enka* is the most essential form of Japanese music. Even now **there is no shortage** of middle-aged men putting their heart and soul into singing *enka* at *karaoke*.

• Which Japanese artists are famous worldwide?

Names that probably come to mind for many foreigners are Edo period *ukiyo-e* **printmakers** such as Hokusai, Utamaro, and Sharaku. This may be because these artists have influenced many European artists such as van Gogh and Monet.

Presently, internationally popular *nihonga* (Japanese-style painting) artists include Sugiyama Yasushi, Higashiyama Kaii, Takayama Tatsuo, Kayama Matazō, and Hirayama Ikuo; each of these five coincidentally have the character for mountain (*yama*) in their names, and so are known as "The Five Mountains of Japanese Painting" (*Nihonga no gozan*).

• How is *nihonga* (Japanese-style painting) different in technique from Western-style painting?

The word *nihonga* came to be used after the introduction of **Western-style painting**, especially **oil paintings**, after the Meiji period.

The word *nihonga* actually comprises a variety of **schools** and **styles**. The styles of some recent *nihonga* artists are similar

んど変わらない画風の人もいます。

　日本画の絵の具は**岩絵の具**を用い，にかわを媒材にし，紙や絹に描きます。

　画材が異なるため，使う材料によって絵の具や墨のにじみを防ぐ方法，線の引き方，色彩のぼかし方などに伝統的な技法があり，かなりの修練が必要とされるという点が西洋の絵とは違います。

Q 代表的な日本の映画作家には，どんな人がいますか？

　太平洋戦争終結後，次々とアメリカ映画が日本に輸入され，**娯楽**としての映画の人気が高まりますが，日本の**映画作家**も活発に映画製作に乗り出し，優れた映画作家が続出しました。その中で，次の3人を代表として紹介しましょう。

Kurosawa Akira

　まず，黒沢明（1910-98）です。1951年，彼が監督した『羅生門』（1950）が，**ベネチア**国際映画祭でグランプリを受賞して，一躍，日本映画のレベルの高さを世界に示しました。彼はその後，『生きる』（1952年），『七人の侍』（1954年），など，次々と**名作**を生み出し，世界の映画人の尊敬を浴びる存在となりました。

　映画手法で世界の映画人に影響を与えたのが小津安二郎（1903-63）です。『晩春』（1949年），『東京物語』（1953年）など，普通の家庭の日常の生活感情を，低いカメラ位置のロングショットで静かに追った手法は今でも斬新です。

Kitano Takeshi

　1960年ごろから，テレビに押されて，映画の人気は次第に落ちてしまいますが，新しい映画作家はた次々と出てきており，その中で，現代を代表するのは北野武（1947- ）です。コメディ

to those of Western-style painters.

Nihonga uses **mineral-based pigments** with *nikawa* (hide or fishbone glue) as a medium on paper or silk.

There are traditional methods of blurring the colors, drawing lines, and preventing the blurring of ink or pigments that can vary with the type of materials used. These methods require extensive training, an aspect that differs from Western-style painting.

● Who are the main moviemakers of Japan?

After the end of World War II, American movies flowed into Japan and the popularity of movies as a **pastime** increased, but Japanese **moviemakers** also became active with the rise of a series of talented artists. Here we will look at three such moviemakers.

First is Kurosawa Akira (1910–1998). His 1950 *Rashōmon*, received the Grand Prize at the **Venice** International Film Festival in 1951, putting international focus on the high level of Japan's film industry. This was followed by *Ikiru* (1952, To Live), *Shichinin no Samurai* (1954, Seven Samurai), and other **acclaimed films** that made Kurosawa a respected film director around the world.

Then there is Ozu Yasujirō (1903–1963), whose directing technique also had an effect on moviemakers throughout the world. His low-camera angles and long shots that quietly revealed the emotions of typical family life in films such as *Banshun* (1953, Late Spring), and *Tōkyō Monogatari* (1953, Tōkyō Story) create a freshness that can be appreciated even today.

From around 1960, the popularity of movies has fallen with pressure from television, but new movie directors have continued to make their debuts one after another, including Kitano Takeshi (1947–), who well represents the moviemakers of

アンとして活躍する彼が監督・主演した
『HANA-BI』は，1997年，カンヌ国際映画祭でグ
ランプリを獲得しました。**少ない台詞**と**鋭い画面
の展開**が評判となりました。

日本の伝統的な文化

Q 短歌はなぜ日本人に愛されるのですか？

Ishikawa Takuboku

　短歌は7世紀の初めには完成された，日本独
自の詩の形式です。8世紀に**編纂された**「万葉
集」にその原型があります。

　5音，7音，5音，7音，7音の順に言葉をあて
はめ，自分の感情や季節の情景を表します。俳
句に必要な**季語**というものはありませんし，何を
表現するかは自由です。

　　東海の　小島の磯の　白砂に
　　我泣きぬれて　蟹とたわむる

　これは石川啄木（1886–1912）の歌です。声に
出して読んでみますと，5・7・5・7・7という音の
リズムが分かります。短歌の言葉の**響き**が，耳
に快く響くことも，日本人に長く愛し続けられて
いる理由の1つでもあります。

Q 俳句はどうやって作られていますか？

　俳句も**日本独自の定型詩**で，世界でいちばん
短い詩です。17世紀末にこの形ができ上がった
と言われ，江戸時代に盛んになり，芭蕉，蕪村

today. Kitano, also known as a comedian, directed and starred in HANA-BI, which won the Grand Prize at the Cannes International Film Festival in 1997. The movie's **sparse script** and **sharp screen development** won high praise.

Traditional Culture of Japan

• Why do the Japanese love *tanka*?

The *tanka* is a uniquely Japanese poetic form perfected in the beginning of the seventh century. Its original form can be seen in the *Manyōshū*, an anthology of poems **compiled** in the eighth century.

Words which express the poet's feelings or the seasonal conditions are set in a 5–7–5–7–7 syllabic structure. With no **"season words"** as required in *haiku*, *tanka* allows more freedom of subject matter.

> *Tōkai no / kojima no iso no / shirasuna ni*
>> (On the white sand of a rocky beach on a small island off the Tōkai coast)
>
> *Ware nakinurete / kani to tawamuru*
>> (Soaked in tears, I play with a crab)

This is a poem by Ishikawa Takuboku (1886–1912). If you read it aloud, you will hear the 5–7–5–7–7 rhythm. The pleasing **resonance** of the words is one of the reasons Japanese have long cherished the *tanka*.

• How are *haiku* composed?

Haiku is a **poetic form** also **unique to Japan** and is the shortest poetic form in the world. It is said that the *haiku* form was created in the 17th century and flourished in the Edo period, when master

Matsuo Bashō

という達人が現れました。

　俳句は日本語の5音、7音、5音の3つの句に言葉をあてはめて作ります。例を挙げましょう。

　　　古池や
　　　蛙飛び込む
　　　水の音

その語句の中に季節を表す言葉、「季語(きご)」と言われるものを必ず入れることが原則になっています。上の俳句では「蛙」が季節を表す言葉です。どんな語がどんな季節を表すかは、「歳時記(さいじき)」という本に書かれています。

Q 歌舞伎はいつごろ始まったのですか?

Okuni's *Nembutsu odori*

　1603年ごろに、出雲大社の巫女(みこ)と称する阿国(おくに)という女性が京都で演じた「念仏踊り」が初めであるとされています。

　しかし、1629年に女性が出演することが禁止され、男性だけで演ずるようになり、元禄期(1688–1704)に現在の歌舞伎のスタイルができ上がりました。

　明治になると西洋文化が急速に入ってきて、歌舞伎にもそういう新しさを取り入れようとしたことがあります。が、20世紀に入ってからは、古典劇としての伝統を守ることに方向が定まり、現在に至っています。

　有名な歌舞伎役者の**屋号**(やごう)(俳優の名)は、**血筋**で伝えられていくという保守的な慣習に守られた世界です。

Mie, a *Kabuki* performance

　東京に歌舞伎座という常設の劇場があり、1年中、歌舞伎を演じています。

poets such as Bashō and Buson emerged on the scene.

Haiku are composed of words accommodating a three-line, 5–7–5 Japanese syllabic structure. Here's an example:

Furuike ya	(An old pond)
kawazu tobikomu	(a frog jumps in)
mizu no oto	(sound of the water)

A basic rule holds that *haiku* must contain a *kigo*, or a word that expresses the season. In the above *haiku*, the frog is the seasonal word. *Saijiki* is a compendium of *kigo* which specify which words are associated with which season.

● When did *kabuki* originate?

Kabuki is believed to have originated around 1603, when a woman attendant from the Izumo Shrine named Okuni performed a dance called *Nembutsu odori*.

However, in 1629, women were banned from the stage, leaving only men to perform; and by the Genroku period (1688–1704), the current *kabuki* style was perfected.

With the Meiji period came a sudden influx of Western culture, and *kabuki* even attempted to incorporate some of these new influences. However, in the 20th century, the trend focused on preserving *kabuki* as a traditional theatrical form, a trend which continues to this day.

It is a world that preserves conservative traditions, such as the practice of passing down the **stage names** of famous *kabuki* actors according to **family lineage**.

In Tōkyō, a permanent *kabuki* theater called the Kabuki-za stages performances throughout the year.

Q 能の始まりはいつごろですか?

Nō

　能は，謡曲と言われる歌と舞いで表現されます。奈良時代に大陸から入ってきた，軽業・奇術・歌舞などの雑多な芸能である「散楽」の中の歌舞が，日本の文化の中で独自の発展を遂げたもので，鎌倉時代の後半ごろには能の原型ができています。

　1374年に将軍足利義満が，これを見て賞賛し，以後，彼の庇護を受けて発展します。そして，観阿弥と世阿弥の父子が，芸術的な詩劇としての能と，その理論を確立しました。

　現在，観世，宝生，金春，金剛，喜多の五つの流派があります。

Q 能と狂言はどんな関係ですか?

Kyōgen

　双生児の関係のようなものです。
　能のルーツと同じ「散楽」から生まれたこっけいな物真似が，時代を経てこっけいな対話式の喜劇となっていったのが「狂言」です。
　一方，真面目な，というとおかしいですが，謡いと舞いで表現する歌舞劇になったのが「能」です。
　現在，能の上演をする時には，たいてい能，狂言，能という順序で行われています。

Q 文楽の始まりはいつごろですか?

　文楽は，人が後ろから人形を操る日本特有の人形芝居です。浄瑠璃という音楽と語りに合わせて人形を動かします。1つの人形を3人が

• When did *nō* originate?

Nō theater is expressed through dance and music called *utai*. *Nō* is based on the song and dance taken from *sangaku*. *Sangaku* was a form of entertainment introduced from the continent during the Nara period and included acrobatics, magic, and song and dance. This song and dance developed in a uniquely Japanese way, and by the latter half of the Kamakura period, the stylistic features of the *nō* theater were completed.

In 1374 the shōgun, Ashikaga Yoshimitsu, watched a *nō* performance and was deeply impressed; after this, the *nō* theater advanced under his **patronage**. Kan'ami and his son Zeami developed the artistry of the *nō* theatrical form and established its **theoretical underpinnings**.

Today, there are five schools of *nō* theater: the Kanze, Hōshō, Komparu, Kongō, and Kita.

• What is the relationship between *nō* and *kyōgen*?

They are like twins.

A form of comic **imitations**, originating from *sangaku* which is also the origin of *nō*, developed over the years into a **farcical drama** based on comic dialogue which then became *kyōgen*.

On the other hand, it was the more serious **song-and-dance dramas** known as *utai* and *mai* which became the *nō* theater.

Today, stagings of *nō* usually present plays in the order of *nō*, *kyōgen* and *nō*.

• When did *bunraku* begin?

Bunraku is a form of **puppet theater** unique to Japan in which the puppets are manipulated from behind. They are manipulated in accordance with music and **chants** known as *jōruri*.

Bunraku

操ります。

　このスタイルは安土桃山時代の終わり，文禄・慶長（1592–1614）ごろにでき，江戸時代に入るとともに全国各地で興行されるようになりました。

　その後，17世紀終わりごろ，竹本義太夫によって人形を**操る技術**は高度になり，さらに物語もたくさん作られて完成の域に達していきます。

　文楽は東京なら国立劇場，大阪では国立文楽劇場で定期的に**公演**が開かれています。

Q 落語，講談，浪曲というのはどんな芸能ですか？

Hanashika,
Yanagiya Kosan
（撮影・横井洋司）

　落語は，江戸時代から行われていた芸で，落語家（あるいは噺家）と呼ばれる語り手が，1人だけで舞台の真ん中に置いた座布団に座って，ストーリーのある面白い話をします。

　落語家は座ったまま，声と**身振り**一つで，男にも女にも，子供にも年寄りにも，武士にも町人にもなります。使う**小道具**は扇子と手ぬぐいだけです。

　話の最後に「**落ち**」といって，客を笑わせる工夫があるのが，落語の特徴です。**だじゃれ**になっているものもあれば，意外な結末になっているもの，また，落語家のしぐさが「落ち」になっているもののあります。

　講談は，落語と同様に1人で，舞台の上で物語を語る芸です。台を前にして，張り扇子という扇子で台をたたいて調子を取りながら語ります。

　話の内容は，落語のようなこっけいなものではなく，戦争を材料とした事実や，**敵討ち**，あるいは**人情話**などが主です。

　講談を語る人を講釈師と言います。

Kōshakushi

One puppet requires the coordination of three people.

This form developed around the Bunroku and Keichō periods (1592–1614) at the end of the Azuchi-Momoyama period, and came to flourish in various regions beginning in the Edo period (1600–1868).

Around the end of the 17th century, Takemoto Gidayū perfected the **manipulation** of the puppets, while a great number of dramas were written which reached a new height of artistry.

Bunraku **performances** are regularly staged at the National Theater in Tōkyō and at the National Bunraku Theater in Ōsaka.

● What are *rakugo*, *kōdan*, and *rōkyoku*?

Rakugo, an art form originating in the Edo period, is performed by a *rakugoka* (sometimes called *hanashika*) who sits on a cushion (*zabuton*) in the middle of the stage and tells entertaining stories.

While remaining seated, the *rakugoka* uses voice and **gestures** to play men, women, children, the elderly, warriors and commoners. The only **props** are a fan and a handkerchief.

A characteristic of *rakugo* is the **punch line**, called the *ochi*. The *ochi* can consist of a **play on words**, a surprising ending, or even a simple gesture.

Kōdan, like *rakugo*, is spoken by a single artist on the stage. The performer sits behind a small table and then hits the table with a fan (*sensu*) for emphasis.

Unlike the humorous *rakugo*, *kōdan* focuses on historical wars, **revenge**, **human compassion** and so forth.

Those who perform *kōdan* are called *kōshakushi*.

　　浪曲は，ストーリーのある話を語ることは講談と同じですが，話に三味線の伴奏をつけて，歌うように語るのが特徴です。江戸時代に，**寺に属さない僧侶**が仏教の説話を，なかば踊りながら，早口に歌ってあるいたことが始まりと言われています。

　　落語，講談と同様，舞台の上で1人で演じることは同じですが，浪曲の場合は三味線伴奏者がつきます。

Q 日本女性は皆，茶道，生け花の心得があるのですか？

　　いいえ。第2次世界大戦の終わりまでは，**茶道も生け花も独身女性には欠かせないものでした**。当時は「嫁に行く」ことが唯一の生きる手段であった女性にとって，これらは**必須の教養課目**だったのです。この傾向は第2次世界大戦前まで続きましたが，戦後，女性が社会に進出するにつれて少なくなり，現在は興味のある人だけがやっています。

　　それまでは，茶道や生け花に携わっていたのはすべて男性でしたが，生け花は，家の中の装飾に必要になるということで，茶道よりも早く，江戸時代には武家の女性のたしなみとなっていました。茶道は，作法の修得や精神の修養に適しているということで，明治の中頃から，結婚前の女性の習い事として人気がでました。

Q 茶道というのは，ふつうにお茶を飲むのとどう違うのですか？

　　茶道は室町時代の僧，村田珠光（じゅこう）（1422–1502）によって創造され，それを完成し，現代に続く茶

Rōkyoku is the same as *kōdan* in that a story is told, but the story is accompanied by the three-stringed shamisen and relayed in a singsong voice. It is said that *kōshaku* got its start in the Edo period when **wandering Buddhist priests** would walk about and dance while using rapid talking to relay the teachings of Buddhism.

Like *rakugo* and *kōdan*, *rōkyoku* is performed by a single performer on the stage, but the performance also includes a shamisen player.

● Do all Japanese women know how to arrange flowers and perform at tea ceremonies?

No. Until the end of World War II both the **tea ceremony** and **flower arrangement** were **prerequisites** for marriage for single women. At that time, getting married was virtually the only option they had. However, as more and more women started playing an important role in the post-war society, this gradually changed, and currently both art forms are taken up only by people who are truly interested in them.

A long time ago only men were engaged in performing tea ceremonies and arranging flowers. As an essential skill to decorate homes, flower arrangement was widely practiced among women of the warrior class in the Edo period (1600–1868). The tea ceremony, which is considered to help one learn etiquette and develop mental strength, gained immense popularity in the middle of the Meiji period (1868–1912).

● How is the tea ceremony different from just drinking tea?

The tea ceremony was initiated by Murata Jukō (1422–1502), and perfected by Sen-no Rikyū (1522–1591), who exalted the

Tea ceremony

道の形にしたのが千利休(せんのりきゅう)(1522–1591)です。

　茶道では，抹茶という，**茶の葉を粉末にしたもの**を用います。火をおこして湯を沸かし，抹茶をかき混ぜて飲むまでに，点前(てまえ)とよばれる様々な所作があり，これをいかに美しく行うかが第1のポイントです。
　そして，第2のポイントは，茶会における主人(ホスト)と客(ゲスト)との**心の交流**です。主人は客をもてなすために，**茶道具**から**掛け軸**，花，花入れなどにいたるすべての取り合わせに気をつかいます。客も，その心配りを理解するためには洗練された教養と感覚を持っていなければなりません。

Q 生け花とはどんなものですか?

Flower arrangement

　形式化された生け花が始まったのは，室町時代からと言われています。それ以前には**供花**という，仏前に飾る生け花がありました。このため生け花には，神や仏の心を表すもの，あるいは宇宙の調和を表すものという観念があります。生け花の基本とは，いちばん上の花を「天」，下の花を「地」，中間を「人」とし，それらの調和を考えるというものです。
　しかし，戦後になってからは，草月流のように，花以外の素材も使って現代感覚を盛り込み，**造形芸術**を目指す流派も生まれてきました。

　現在，生け花には2000以上の流派があると言われています。池坊流(いけのぼう)，小原流(おはら)，草月流などが代表的な流派です。

everyday act of drinking tea to an integrated art form by styliz-
ing manners and etiquette.

Maccha, or **powdered tea leaves**, is used in the tea ceremony.
As one of the ceremony's most fundamental elements, the host
has to follow various rules in every procedure of tea making,
from making the fire, adding hot water to tea cups, stirring the
tea with a whisk until it gets foamy, to serving it.

Another important element is a **shared sense of communication** between the host and the guests throughout the ceremony.
The host, in order to entertain his or her guests, takes utmost care
in every step of the preparation process, such as in choosing
everything from **tea utensils** to a **hanging scroll**, flowers, a vase
and other amenities to go with the environment. The guests, in
return, are expected to express their understanding of the host's
consideration and gratitude toward the host's efforts.

● What is *ikebana*?

Ikebana, or Japanese traditional flower arrangement, was
first stylized in the Muromachi period (1333–1568). Prior to
that, people were in the habit of **offering arranged flowers to
Buddha**. The concept of *ikebana*, therefore, developed into one
that expresses something Buddhistic or divine. It also embraces
harmony with nature, symbolized by three well-balanced basic
sprays signifying *ten* (heaven / universe), *jin* (mankind) and *chi*
(earth).

Since World War II, however, modern schools of *ikebana*
such as the Sōgetsu school, which uses materials other than
flowers, have appeared in an attempt to present this traditional
flower arrangement as a kind of **formative art**.

There are about 2,000 *ikebana* schools at present, including
the Ikenobō school, Ohara school and Sōgetsu school.

Q 家元制度というのは何ですか？

茶道，華道，**香道**，音曲などの伝統的な芸の世界で，その流儀の正統的な技法を伝え，その流派を統率する人を家元と言います。家元は**世襲**によって引き継がれていくのが普通です。

家元は大変な**権力**を持っています。茶道，華道などを教えるためには，家元が発行した免許状が必要で，その免許状を発行する権利は家元が握っているからです。

免許は段階的になっており，上の段階の免許をもらう度に**免許料**を納めなければなりません。いちばん上の段階になると，何百万円も必要というケースもあります。

Q どんな時に筆で字を書きますか？

Writing with a brush

学校では**書道**の時間がありますが，私たちが実生活で**筆**を使う機会はほとんどなくなりました。今では，公的な文書でさえ筆で書いたものは受け付けてくれないのです。筆を使うことがあるとすれば，次のような機会でしょう。あらたまったパーティーや何かの会合で，自分の名前を書かなければならないとき，結婚や出産などのお祝いの**祝儀袋**や，お葬式の時の**不祝儀袋**に名前を書かねばならないときなどです。

しかし，それも筆でなければいけないわけではなく，**サインペン**などを用いることが多くなりました。

Q 盆栽はどうやって作りますか？

草木を小型の陶器などの容れ物に植えて，自

● What is the *iemoto* system?

In the world of traditional Japanese arts such as tea cere-mony, flower arrangement, **incense ceremony**, and traditional music, the *iemoto* is a person who consolidates his or her partic-ular school by transmitting the correct methods of that school. The rank of *iemoto* is usually passed on by **direct inheritance**.

The *iemoto* has great **authority**. Licenses issued by the *iemoto* are necessary in order to teach such arts as the tea cere-mony and flower arrangement and it is the *iemoto* who has the sole authority to grant these licenses.

Licenses are usually graded according to rank, and every time a higher rank is granted, a **licensing fee** must be paid. The highest ranks in some cases require a fee of several million yen.

● When do Japanese write with a brush?

Although **calligraphy** is taught in school, there are hardly any occasions in our lives today that require the use of the **brush**. Today, even for official purposes, writing with a brush is not accepted. Writing with a brush may be used for the following occasions: when writing your name at formal parties or meet-ings, when writing your name on special **envelopes for mone-tary gifts** given on celebratory occasions such as weddings or births, or on **envelopes for condolence money** given at funerals.

However, even these occasions do not necessarily require the use of a brush; more and more people now simply use a **felt-tip pen**.

● How are *bonsai* cultivated?

Bonsai is a **horticultural art** unique to Japan whereby

Bonsai

分の好みの形に育てていく日本特有の**園芸**です。

　育てる植物はいろいろですが，マツ，カエデ，ウメ，サツキなどが多いようです。

　適切な土を用意し，肥料を与え，時には**植え替え**をして，幹や枝に針金を巻いて姿を整えたり，**剪定**をしたりします。

　盆栽は1年，2年ではなかなかいい形には育ちません。何年も何十年もかけて育てていきます。

Q 日本の陶磁器は有名なのですか？

　奈良時代には中国から釉薬をかけて焼く方法が伝わりますが，この時代はまだ生活用具としての陶器でした。

　平安時代には生活用の陶磁器の**窯**と，高級な用途のための2種類の窯が誕生します。そして室町時代に茶の湯が流行すると，高級で，また**地方色が豊かな**陶磁器が製作されるようになります。

　江戸時代には**上絵つけ**が始まり，焼き物の主流となり，有田焼や九谷焼などの磁器が作られました。特に有田焼には，19世紀にオランダの東インド会社から大量の引き合いが来ており，世界の陶芸家に影響を与えています。

Q 日本の漆器はどこが優れていますか？

　陶磁器は海外でチャイナと呼ばれていますが，ジャパンと呼ばれているのは日本の**漆器**です。

grasses and trees are transplanted into small earthenware containers and are grown into desired shapes.

Although there are many different plant varieties, the pine, maple, plum, and azalea are particularly common.

Care for *bonsai* consists of selecting the appropriate type of soil, use of fertilizer, periodic **repotting**, wiring the branches or trunk to control the shape, and **pruning**.

A period of one or two years is not enough to allow *bonsai* to grow into the right shape. *Bonsai* takes many years and sometimes decades of nurturing.

● Are Japanese ceramics famous?

In the Nara period (710–794), the Chinese technique of glazing and firing was introduced to Japan, but only earthenware goods for daily use were made during this period.

The Heian period (794–1185) gave birth to two types of **kilns**: one appropriate for ceramics for daily use and the other designed for various high-grade applications. In the Muromachi period (1333–1568), the popularity of the tea ceremony gave rise to the production of high-grade ceramics **rich with regional variations**.

The use of **overglaze enamels** began in the Edo period (1600–1868), and they became standard for ceramics of the period, as with the Arita and Kutani porcelains that were being produced at the time. In particular, in the 19th century a great number of orders were received by the Dutch East India Company for Arita ware, and thus Arita ware came to exert influence on ceramic artists around the world.

● What is so prized about Japanese lacquerware?

Ceramics are known as "china" abroad, but "japan" is the term signifying Japanese **lacquerware**.

日本では縄文時代の前期の**発掘物**から，漆塗りの櫛やお盆が発見されています。日本書紀によれば，6世紀末に専門の漆器**職人**がいたことが書かれています。

漆器に用いる**ウルシ**は，世界各国で**樹液**の品質が違いますが，日本のウルシがもっとも品質がいいと言われています。

Q 日本の刀は世界の刀とどう違いますか？

日本刀は西洋の剣と比べて**柄**が長く，**刃**は片刃で反りがあり，その重さから言っても，基本的には両手で持つように作られています。ちゃんばら映画で，片手で振り回しているシーンがありますが，実戦ではそうはいかない重さです。

刀は軟鉄を心金に，鋼を皮金にして包む独特の鋳造法でつくられます。

刃の部分だけに焼き入れがなされるので刃に文様が現れ，鋼を鍛錬したことによる地肌の文様とともに固有の美しさが表れている，という点に特徴があります。

Q 人間国宝はどうやって決まるんですか？

伝統的な芸能の演技術や工芸の技術など，人や集団が技として受け継いでいるものを「**無形文化財**」と言います。

その中で特に重要な技を「重要無形文化財」といい，この技術を保持している人を，通称，**人**

In Japan, lacquered combs and trays were found among **unearthed goods** from the early Jōmon period. According to the *Nihon shoki*, there were **artisans** specializing in lacquerware at the end of the sixth century.

The **lacquer** used for lacquerware differs around the world according to the quality of **tree sap**, and Japanese lacquer is considered to be the highest in quality.

• How are Japanese swords different from other swords from around the world?

Compared to Western swords, Japanese swords have longer **hilts**, are curved on one side of the **blade**, and the weight of the swords is designed for double-handed manipulation. Although in *samurai* films, one may see a scene in which the sword is used with only one hand, in actual fighting the heavy weight of the sword would not allow this.

A unique forging technique is applied in the swordmaking. A layer of *kawagane* (skin steel) is welded on top of the *shingane* (inner steel), steel of a particularly pliant kind.

Since only the blade portion is tempered, it exhibits a temper pattern which, along with the blade's patterned texture resulting from the forging process of the steel, is a distinguishing feature of Japanese swords.

• How are Living National Treasures designated?

Performing techniques for traditional forms of entertainment and techniques for traditional crafts that have been handed down by individuals or groups are considered to be "**intangible assets**."

Those considered particularly important are deemed Important Intangible Assets, and persons who preserve these skills are

間国宝と称しています。これを指定するのは文
部大臣です。

　1999年4月現在，芸能関係47人，工芸技術関
係46人の人間国宝がいます。人間国宝には年
金200万円の**特別助成金**が国から与えられます。

commonly referred to as **Living National Treasures**. These designations are given by the Minister of Education, Culture and Science.

As of April 1999, there are 47 people involved in the arts and 46 craftspeople who are designated as Living National Treasures. They receive an annual **stipend** of 2 million yen from the government.

6

日本人の衣食住

Clothing, Cuisine and Housing in Japan

Ready-built houses ▶

日本人の衣生活

Q 日本人はいつから洋服を着るようになりましたか?

洋服が日本の実際の生活に取り入れられたのは明治になってからです。明治政府は軍装にヨーロッパの**軍服**を採用し, 役人, 郵便集配員や鉄道員にも洋服を着ることを定めました。近代国家の体制を早急に整えるために必要だと判断したのです。これによって, 一般人の間にも, 急速に洋服が普及しました。

しかし, 女性の洋装は, 一部の**上層社会**の婦人たちが, 1883年に出来た社交場の鹿鳴館に着て現れただけで, 大変高価ということもあり, また, 次第に高まる国粋主義の風潮とともに, 洋服は看護婦の制服だけに限られました。

女性にも洋服が見られるようになったのは, 女性がバスの**車掌**やタイピストなどの仕事に進出し始めた大正時代になってからのことです。

Clothing of the Japanese

● **When did the Japanese start wearing Western clothes?**

Western clothes were introduced in the Meiji period (1868–1912). The Meiji government adopted a European-style **military uniform** and decided that officials, mailmen and railroad workers should wear Western clothes because they felt that change was necessary for the Japanese government system to quickly transform itself into a modern state. This expedited the spread of Western clothes among ordinary people.

However, dresses, partly because they were very expensive, were worn only by women in **high society** at parties held at the Rokumeikan, a Western-style official party house built in 1883. As nationalism spread across the nation, Western clothes were limited to nurse uniforms.

It was in the Taishō period (1912–1926) that working women such as bus **conductors** and typists started wearing Western clothes on a daily basis.

Q どんな時に着物を着るんですか?

Young ladies in kimono at a Coming-of-Age ceremony

　年配の人や, 仕事の上で着物を着る必要がある人以外, ふだんに着物を着ている人はほとんどいなくなりました。

　せいぜい正月に, 年の初めの改まった気分を味わうために着物を着たり, 年明けの仕事始めの日に, 女性が着物で出勤する, といったところでしょうか。

　お宮参りや七五三のお祝いには, 子供に着せますが, 最近はドレスやスーツを着せることも多いようです。

　成人式, 結婚式, 卒業式や正式なパーティーなどの改まった席では女性が着物を着ることがあります。

　日本舞踊など, 日本の伝統の芸能を継いだり, 学んだりする人や, 料亭の仲居さんなどは和服を着ることが必要になります。

　木綿の浴衣は着物の一種で, 夏に着たり, 和風の旅館に泊まると寝巻きとして出してくれますが, 略式の着物ですから, 公式の場には出られません。

日本人の食生活

Q 日本人の平均的な食事はどんなものですか?

　日本人の食生活は**西洋化**が進んで大きく変わり, ずいぶんと多様になりました。いちばん大きい変化はパン食の取り入れです。朝食にはパンに簡単な卵料理, ミルク, そしてコーヒーや紅茶

● On what occasions do people wear *kimono*?

Very few people, except some elderly and those who wear them out of professional necessity, wear *kimono* daily.

On New Year's Day some men and women wear *kimono* to bask in the holiday mood, and some women wear them on the first working day of the year.

Babies are often dressed in *kimono* on their **first visit to a shrine**, and at the *shichi-go-san* festival, many children are dressed in *kimono*, although a growing number of parents choose Western clothes over *kimono* on this occasion.

Coming-of-Age Day, wedding ceremonies, graduation ceremonies and formal parties provide women opportunities to wear *kimono*.

People in the world of traditional arts such as Japanese dancers and workers at Japanese-style restaurants need to wear them more often than most people.

Yukata, which is made of cotton, is a kind of *kimono* worn in summer or as pajamas at Japanese-style inns. Since it is considered very casual, one is not supposed to wear it on formal occasions.

Culinary Life of the Japanese

● What is the typical diet of the Japanese?

Japanese eating habits have become quite diverse with all the changes of **Westernization**. One of the major changes is the introduction of bread. Many people now eat bread and eggs and drink coffee, tea or milk for breakfast.

School lunch

で食事をする人が多くなってきました。

　サラリーマンの昼食は，昔は**弁当**を持っていく人も多かったのですが，今では会社の近くの食堂で，洋風から和風まで……その日の好みで様々です。

　多くの小・中学校では**給食**があります。育ち盛りの子供たちのために栄養のバランスを考えた食事です。

　家に帰って食べる夕食もあれこれ取り混ぜたもので，和風，中華，洋風など**様々**ですが御飯に汁物，そして肉または魚，野菜などのおかず，というのが日本の食事の平均的な内容です。一般的に言って子供たちは，昔からの和食よりもハンバーグ，カレーライス，スパゲティなど洋風を好むので，家庭の食事の傾向は子供たちに引っ張られています。

Q 日本人は米を毎日食べますか？

Japanese food

　朝食にパン食が増えたり，昼食は麺類で済ます人も多いということは事実ですが，1日に1回は米を食べないと気が済まないという人が多いことも事実です。

　しかし，次の農林水産省「食糧需給表」の数字があります。日本人1人1日当たりの**米穀類**の供給量です。

	1960年	1980年	1997年
米	314.9g	216.3g	182.8g
小麦	70.6g	88.3g	88.9g

　上の表から，米を食べる量がずいぶんと少な

Decades ago, workers often took **packed lunches** to the office, but nowadays any kind of dish ranging from Western to Japanese is available in restaurants near office buildings.

Most elementary and junior high schools have **school lunch programs**, offering well-balanced meals specially designed for fast-growing children.

Dinners served at home are also **diverse**, including Japanese, Chinese and Western dishes. A typical dinner consists of rice, soup, and several dishes containing meat, fish, and vegetables. Generally speaking, children prefer Western food such as hamburgers, curry with rice, or spaghetti to traditional Japanese dishes, and in many families the meals are made according to the children's preferences.

● Is rice still the mainstay of the Japanese diet? Do people eat it every day?

It is true that many Japanese feel like eating rice at least once a day, although some have bread for breakfast and noodles for lunch.

The following *Table of Food Supply and Demand* from the Ministry of Agriculture, Forestry and Fisheries indicates the daily amount of **rice and flour** consumed per capita.

	1960	1980	1997
Rice	314.9 grams	216.3 grams	182.8 grams
Flour	70.6 grams	88.3 grams	88.9 grams

The above chart shows that while the level of rice con-

くなっていることがわかります。ところが，小麦の量はほとんど同じです。

　実は，日本人の食事は，米やパンなどの**炭水化物**よりも，肉や乳製品や果物にますます頼るようになってきているのです。

　調査によれば，1960年と1997年では，肉類は6倍，牛乳，**乳製品**は4倍，果実は2倍に増えています。

Ｑ 日本人がいちばん好きな食べ物は何ですか？

　日本人の**食生活**は多様になりましたので，何が一番人気かは明確ではありません。

　ただ，大衆的なレストランの調査で，いちばん注文が多いのは，ハンバーグ，カレーライス，スパゲティだそうで，一般の家庭でもこの3種が多いようです。

　外国の人から見ると，日本と言えば，寿司，てんぷら，すきやき……となるのでしょうが，そんなに毎日食べているわけではありません。

Ｑ 醬油はいつごろから日本で使われているのですか？

Shōyu

　文献に「しょうゆ」という言葉が登場するのは室町時代の中期，16世紀の終わりごろです。室町時代の終わりごろには，**醬油**は急速に人々の間で使われるようになります。

　しかし，すでに奈良時代以前から，醬油の原型と思われる醬というものがありました。この醬は，穀類や鳥や獣，魚肉，野菜，**海藻**などに塩を加えて発酵させたものです。醬油や**味噌**は，これから発展したものなのです。

　すでに江戸時代に，現在も使われている溜，

sumption has greatly decreased, that of flour has stayed almost the same.

In fact, the diet of the Japanese has become increasingly dependent on other ingredients such as meat, dairy products, and fruits rather than **carbohydrates** such as rice and bread.

A survey reveals that in 1997, people ate six times as much meat, four times as much milk and **dairy products**, and twice as much fruit as in 1960.

● What is the favorite food of the Japanese?

Because the Japanese **eating habits** have become diversified, it is hard to choose only one dish as their favorite food.

According to a survey conducted by a group of general-public restaurants, the most frequently ordered items are hamburges, curry and rice, and spaghetti. These three dishes are favorites at home as well.

In the eyes of foreigners, *sushi*, *tempura* and *sukiyaki* may be typical Japanese dishes, but the Japanese do not eat them every day.

● How long has *shōyu* (soy sauce) been used in Japan?

The first known descriptions of *shōyu*, or soy sauce, appeared in literature during the middle of the Muromachi period (1333–1568) and at the end of the 16th century when **soy sauce** became common among ordinary people.

However, the original form of soy sauce dates back to the pre-Nara period (710–794), when *hishio*, fermented sauce containing grain, meat, fish, vegetables, **seaweed** and so forth was used. Soy sauce as well as **soybean paste** (*miso*) developed from this sauce.

Different kinds of soy sauce used presently, such as *tamari*

濃口，薄口などの様々な醬油の種類が生まれています。

Q 味噌はいつごろから日本で使われているのですか？

味噌は奈良時代にその**前身**となるものがあったようです。平安時代にはすでに味噌を売る店があったということです。

味噌は，蒸した大豆に麹と塩を混ぜて発酵させたものですが，鎌倉時代に寺院などでも作られており，15–16世紀の戦国時代には，兵士たちの**食糧**として重用されていました。

一般庶民に普及したのは，醬油と同じく室町時代からです。

Q 豆腐が健康にいい，と言われるのはなぜですか？

豆腐には，大豆の**植物性たんぱく質**が豊富で，カルシウムやカリウムなどの無機質やビタミンBも含まれており，肉や牛乳からたんぱく質をとる場合に比べて**脂肪**が少なく，カロリーも抑えられるのです。

豆腐は中国で作られたのが最初で，奈良時代に日本に伝わっています。

味が**淡白**なので，**刻んだ長葱**や**擦りおろしたショウガ**のような薬味を添え，醬油をかけてそのまま食べたりしますが，**調理法**は数百種もあると言われています。

Q 正しい箸の持ち方は？

最近の若い人には正しい持ち方ができない人が大勢います。家庭の食事も洋風が多くなり，子供のころにフォークやスプーンなどに慣れてし

(thick sauce), *koikuchi* (dark sauce) and *usukuchi* (light sauce), were made during the Edo period (1600–1868).

● How long has *miso* (soybean paste) been used in Japan?

The **original form** of *miso*, or soybean paste, is said to have existed in the Nara period (710–794). In the Heian period (794–1185), there were already stores selling *miso*.

Miso is made from soybeans, which are steamed and mixed with salt and *kōji* (fermented rice, barley or beans). It was made at temples in the Kamakura period (1185–1333), and in the Age of Civil Wars in the 15th and 16th centuries, it was used in **rations** for soldiers.

It was in the Muromachi period (1333–1568) that *miso*, along with *shōyu*, became popular among the general public.

● Why is *tōfu* said to be a health food?

Tōfu, made from soybeans, is rich in **vegetable protein**, calcium, potassium and Vitamin B. It is considered healthy because it does not contain as much **fat** as meat or milk, and its calorie content is very low for the amount of protein it provides.

Tōfu was first made in China and introduced to Japan in the Nara period (710–794).

When eaten uncooked, since it is **light** in taste, it is often topped with spices such as finely **chopped green onions** and **grated ginger**, and soy sauce. It is said that there are several hundred **recipes** using *tōfu*.

● What is the proper way to hold chopsticks?

Many youngsters nowadays are not able to hold chopsticks properly. Perhaps the reason is that they are more accustomed to eating Western food with knife and fork.

How to hold
chopsticks

まったからでしょう。

　まず，2本を少し離して，平行に人指し指の根
元と親指ではさみ，上のほうの1本の中ほどを，
人指し指の先の腹，中指の先の背，そして親指
の先の腹ではさみます。下のほうの1本は，中ほ
どを中指の先の腹と薬指の先の背ではさみま
す。**てこ**のようにして動かすことができるのは上
のほうの箸だけです。

　箸でフォークのように食物を突き刺すこと，箸
の先をなめること，箸の先を楊枝代わりに使うな
どするのはマナー違反です。

Q 日本は魚が豊富ですが，和食では どんな料理法がありますか？

Hand-shaped sushi

Grilled fish

　新鮮な魚なら薄く切った刺身がいちばん，と
いう人が多いでしょう。**ワサビ**やショウガと醤油
をつけて食べます。

　生の魚は握り寿司にして食べる方法もありま
すが，寿司の握り方はけっこう訓練を要します
ので，自宅で作ることは比較的少ないようです。

　いちばん手軽で多いのは**塩焼き**です。塩をち
ょっと振りかけて焼きます。マグロなどの赤身の
魚を除き，どんな魚も塩焼きができます。

　醤油をベースにしたタレをつけるのが，照り焼
きです。醤油味か味噌味で煮ることもあります。
このような料理法には，サバなど，**油ののった魚**
が向いているようです。

　てんぷらにするとおいしいのは，小エビ，**クル
マエビ**，イカ，白身の魚などです。

　ムニエルにするなど，洋風の料理法も取り入

To hold chopsticks properly, start by separating the two chopsticks, then place them horizontally parallel to each other on the index finger and under the thumb. Put the middle of the upper chopstick between the finger pad of the index finger and the nail side of the middle finger. Place the thumb on top of the upper chopstick. Use the finger pad of the middle finger and the nail side of the ring finger to hold the middle of the lower chopstick. Using the principle of **leverage**, you only move the upper chopstick to pick up food.

It is considered ill-mannered to poke food with chopsticks, to lick the tips of the chopsticks, or to use chopsticks for picking your teeth!

● What type of cooking techniques are used to prepare fish commonly eaten in Japan?

If the fish is fresh enough, *sashimi*, or thinly sliced raw fish, is preferred by many people. It is eaten with **Japanese horse-radish**, ginger and soy sauce.

Raw fish is also eaten in the form of *sushi*, but since preparing *sushi* requires special skills, it is not often made at home.

The most frequently used cooking technique is **grilling with salt sprinkled on top of the fish**. Any fish except for red-meat fish such as tuna can be cooked this way.

Teriyaki is prepared by marinating fillets of fish in a soy-sauce-based sauce, and grilling while basting with the sauce. Sometimes fish is boiled over low heat using soy sauce or *miso*, soybean paste. **Fish that is heavily marbled** such as mackerel is suited for these cooking techniques.

Shrimp, **prawn**, squid and white-meat fish are eaten in tempura, or deep-fried.

Western techniques such as meunière have been adopted in

れられていますが，少なくとも魚に関しては，和食の伝統のほうが強いようです。

Q 日本酒はどうやって作りますか?

Sake

　米と米麹（こうじ）と水を原料として，発酵させて，濾したものが「清酒」です。

　まず米を精米して洗い，糠（ぬか）を取り除きます。適度な水を吸収させたあと，水をきり，蒸して麹と水を加え，約20日間をかけて発酵させます。

　それを圧搾機にかけて酒と酒粕（さけかす）に分離します。分離した酒を静かに置いておくと，清酒と滓（おり）に分離します。

　この清酒を濾過器（ろか）で濾して，香りと味を調え，加熱して**殺菌した**ものを6か月以上，20度以下で熟成します。その上でさらに調合・調整をして加熱殺菌してでき上がりです。

　後は瓶（びん）に詰めて出荷されます。

日本人の住生活

Q 日本の家の平均的な広さはどれくらいですか?

Apartment complexes

　1998年の住宅・土地統計調査によれば，日本の1住宅当たりの面積は，**1戸建て住宅**で約126m²です。共同住宅などを含めると，約93m²です。

　1人当たりの床面積に換算すると約25m²だそうです。しかし，これをアメリカの61m²や，イギリスの35m²という数字と比べると大変低い数字で，日本の住宅がかつて「ウサギ小屋」と呼ばれたのももっともです。

Japanese cuisine, but Japanese traditional cooking is still the most common as far as fish is concerned.

● How is *sake* or Japanese rice wine made?

Seishu, which means pure *sake*, is made from rice, rice-fermented *kōji*, and water.

First, the rice is washed to remove the **rice bran**. After letting the rice absorb water, it is drained, steamed, mixed with *kōji* and water, and then fermented for 20 days.

The ingredients are compressed by machine to separate them into *sake* and *sakekasu* (leavings). The *sake*, by letting it stand for a while, is separated into *seishu* and *ori* (dregs).

The *seishu* is filtered, and its flavor and taste are adjusted. **Disinfected** by heating, *seishu* is cured at a temperature lower than 20 degrees for more than six months. After that, final adjustments are made before it is re-disinfected by heating.

The *seishu* is then bottled and shipped.

Housing in Japan

● What is the average size of Japanese homes?

A 1993 residential land survey showed that the average size of an **independent house** is about 126 m². If condominiums and apartments are included, the average is 93 m².

The average area for one person is 25 m², which is much smaller than the 61 m² in the United States and the 35 m² in the United Kingdom. This is the reason why Japanese houses were once called "rabbit hutches."

しかし，これでも1960年代と比べれば2倍近くの面積になっていますが，これからは1戸建ての住宅を購入すること自体が難しくなっていますので，1人当たりの床面積の数字が増えることは期待できないようです。

Q 日本では家の値段はどれくらいしますか？

東京では，都心に出るのに1時間ぐらいの所に，100m²ぐらいの土地付きの1戸建てを買おうとすると，5000万から6000万円はかかるのです。80年代後半から90年代初期のバブル経済の後，土地の値段は下がりましたが，それでも**異常に高い**ものです。

1998年の全住宅数のうち，持ち家の比率は60.3％で，1993年より0.5％上がっています。しかし，売り出される家自体が少なく，都会では，価格，供給の両面で，家を買うことが困難な状態が続いています。

Q 東京の便利な所に部屋を借りると，
いくらぐらいかかりますか？

部屋の広さや所在地で随分違いますが，例えば，通勤時間30–40分以内で，ワンルームか1DKの1人用の住まいの場合，1か月の**家賃**は6万円くらいからです。

ちょっと広くて駅から近いと，8万円くらいにはなるでしょう。日当たりなど，環境の良さを加えたら10万円を超します。

バスルームがない古いタイプのアパートなら，上記の半分くらいの家賃です。

日本では，入居の際に家賃の4か月か5か月分のお金を支払わなくてはなりません。通例，敷

The area of 25 m² is twice as large as it was in the 1960s. But buying a house is only going to get more difficult, and so chances are slim that the space per person will greatly increase.

● How much does a typical house cost in Japan?

If you were to buy a house on a lot of 100 m² within one-hour commuting radius of Central Tōkyō, you would have to pay 50 to 60 million yen ($5–600,000). This figure is **prohibitive**, even after land prices plunged after the bubble economy in the late 80s and the early 90s.

The ratio of owner-occupied houses to the total number of houses was 60.3% in 1998, 0.5% higher than in 1993. However, houses for sale are scarce in urban areas, making buying a home difficult in terms of both price and availability.

● How much does it cost to rent an apartment in a convenient location in Tōkyō?

Depending on the size and location, the **rent** for a small studio or one-bedroom apartment for one person within a 30 to 40-minute commuting radius starts at 60,000 yen a month.

If the room is larger or closer to a train station, the rent will go up to 80,000 yen, and even 100,000 yen for a sunny room in a good environment.

Old apartments with no bath or shower can be rented for about half the above prices.

When renting an apartment, it is often necessary to pay four or five months' rent as deposit and key money. Usually, a two-

金と言われる**保証金**が家賃の2か月分，礼金と言われる**契約金**のようなものが1，2か月分，そして，**不動産屋**に1か月分くらいの**仲介手数料**を払います。

敷金はそこを出る時，部屋を元の状態に戻すクリーニング代を引かれて返金されます。

Q 寝る時，現代では畳の上の布団（ふとん）派とベッド派，どっちが多いですか？

ふとん派が**多数**を占めています。繊維メーカーのクラレが1997年に行った調査では，ベッドを使っている人の割合は25.1%でした。20年前はベッド派は6.8%でしたから，ベッド派が急速に伸びています。特に若い世代ほどベッドを使う比率が高くなっています。

日本でベッドが使用されたのは病院や軍隊が最初です。その後，ホテルの出現によってベッドがポピュラーになりました。

Q 日本のトイレは「座る」式，「しゃがむ」式，どっちが多いですか？

Squatting-style toilet

衛生陶器工業会によれば，1998年に出荷された**便器**のうち87%が洋式，つまり**「座る」式**です。これは新規に設置された便器の割合ですから，次第に「座る」式が多くなっていることは事実です。

「座る」式が増えた理由は，一つには大小兼用にできるので，スペースを節約できること。また，しゃがんで力むよりは楽なので，**お年寄り**には心配がないことなどです。しかし，座る式に慣れた子供たちのなかには，しゃがむ式では用をたせないという子供が増えているそうです。

month rent **deposit**, one to two months' rent for **key money**, and a one-month **broker fee** to the **realtor** are all necessary.

The **deposit** will be returned to the rentor when he or she moves out, minus the fee for cleaning up the room.

• Which is more popular in Japanese bedrooms, *futon* on *tatami* mats or Western beds?

Futon-users are in the **majority**. According to a 1997 survey conducted by Clare, a textile company, the proportion of people who slept in beds was 25.1%. Since 20 years ago the percentage of bed-users was only 6.8%, this represents a dramatic increase. Among young people the proportion of bed-users is particularly high.

In Japan, beds were first used in hospitals and by the military. They later became popular when Western-style hotels were built.

• Which type of toilet is the more common, the Western-style sit-down type or the traditional squatting type?

According to the Sanitary Ceramics Industry, 87% of the **toilet bowls** shipped in 1998 were Western-style, sit-down types. This figure reflects the number of newly installed toilets, which indicates that **sit-down types** are on the increase.

The increase in the sit-down toilet is due to their economy of space, since it makes urinals unnecessary. They are also easier to use because you don't have to squat, a feature particularly welcomed by **seniors**. The number of children so used to sit-down toilets that they feel unable to use squatting toilets is also increasing.

生活と習慣

Life and Customs

日本の祝休日・祭り

Q 日本にはどんな国民の休日がありますか?

　　　法律で定められている祝休日は，現在，15あります。その祝休日が日曜日と重なったときには，翌日の月曜日が休みになります。

元旦（がんたん）　　　　　　1月1日

　　　多くの会社が，年末から1月4日までを休みにします。

成人の日　　　　　　1月の第2月曜日

　　　前年の4月2日からその年の4月1日までに20歳に達したすべての青年たちを祝う日。

建国記念の日　　　　2月11日

　　　日本書紀で神武天皇（じんむ）が即位したと言われる日を**太陽暦**に換算した日。

Japanese Holidays and Festivals

• What are the national holidays in Japan?

There are 15 national holidays determined by law. When a holiday falls on a Sunday, the following Monday substitutes for the holiday.

New Year's Day   January 1

Many offices are closed from the last day of the year through January 4.

Coming-of-Age Day   Second Monday of January

A day to celebrate the coming of age of anyone who has turned 20 in the previous year.

National Foundation Day   February 11

The day of the first Emperor Jinmu's enthronement, as written in the *Nihon shoki*. The date is based on the **solar calendar**.

春分の日   3月21日ごろ

太陽が**春分点**を通過する日。自然をたたえ，生物をいつくしむ日。

緑の日   4月29日

昭和天皇の誕生日だった日。崩御（ほうぎょ）の後，日本の緑を守る日とされました。

憲法記念日   5月3日

1947年，日本国憲法が**施行**された日を記念する日。

国民の休日   5月4日

これは特別な祝日ではないのですが，3日と5日にはさまれているので作られた休日です。

子供の日   5月5日

子供の健康，幸福を願う日。昔は「端午（たんご）の節句」と言って，男の子の成長を祝う日でした。**鯉のぼり**を立てます。

海の日   7月20日

海の**恩恵**に感謝する日。

敬老の日   9月15日

年配の人たちに敬意を表する日。1966年に制定されました。

秋分の日   9月23日ごろ

太陽が**秋分点**を通過する日。祖先をうやま

Vernal Equinox Day   Around March 21

The day when the sun passes the **vernal equinox**. It is a day to celebrate nature and all living things.

Greenery Day   April 29

The late Emperor Shōwa's birthday. After his death, it was designated as a day for preserving Japan's greenery.

Constitution Day   May 3

A day to commemorate the **enactment** of the Constitution of Japan in 1947.

National Holiday   May 4

It was decided that this day should be a national holiday because it is between May 3, Constitution Day, and May 5, Children's Day.

Children's Day   May 5

A day to hope for the health and happiness of children. It used to be called *tango no sekku*, a day of celebration for boys only. **Carp-shaped streamers** are flown on this day.

Marine Day   July 20

A day to thank the sea for its **blessings**.

Respect-for-the-Aged Day   September 15

A day to show particular respect for the elderly, enacted in 1966.

Autumnal Equinox Day   Around September 23

The day when the sun passes the **autumnal equinox**. It is a

い，亡くなった人々をしのぶ日です。

体育の日　　　　　　　10月の第2月曜日

1964年の東京オリンピックの開会の日を**記念**して1966年に定められた日。健康を奨励する日です。

文化の日　　　　　　　11月3日

1946年，日本国憲法が公布された日を記念して定められたもので，日本の文化の振興を考える日とされています。

勤労感謝の日　　　　　11月23日

勤労に感謝をし，**収穫**を祝う日。昔は「新嘗祭」と言って，新しく収穫した穀物を神に捧げて感謝をした日から由来しています。

天皇誕生日　　　　　　12月23日

現在の天皇の誕生を祝う日。天皇が存命の間続けられます。

Q 正月には何をしますか？

Kadomatsu

1年の初めに当たる正月は，本来は収穫をつかさどる神や，一族を守る祖先の霊を迎える年中行事です。門松やしめ飾りは，その神を迎えるためのものです。丸いお餅を2つ重ねた鏡餅は神さまが食べる食べ物です。

正月の朝には一家が集まって，寿命を延ばすと言われている「お屠蘇」というお酒を飲んで，

day to remember the dead and to show respect to one's ancestors.

Health-Sports Day   Second Monday of October

Enacted in 1966 in **commemoration** of the opening of the 1964 Tōkyō Olympics, it is a day to promote health.

Culture Day   November 3

A day to promote the cultural prosperity of Japan, in commemoration of the day when the Constitution of Japan was promulgated in 1946.

Labor Thanksgiving Day   November 23

A day to appreciate labor and to celebrate a good **harvest**. It used to be called *niiname-sai*, when new crops were offered to the gods with gratitude.

The Emperor's Birthday   December 23

The current Emperor's birthday. It will continue to be celebrated as long as the Emperor is alive.

● **What do the Japanese do during the New Year holidays?**

January 1 is the start of the new year. It was originally celebrated annually to welcome the gods of harvest and the spirits of ancestors who protect their families. *Kadomatsu* (gate pines) and *shimekazari* (sacred rope), both decorations for the new year, are prepared to invite the gods of harvest, and *kagami-mochi*, two pieces of round rice cake, one on top of the other, are offered.

On the morning of New Year's Day, the whole family gathers to wish one another good health and to celebrate the coming

新年が来たことを祝い，お互いの健康を祈ります。そして，「お雑煮（ぞうに）」という，汁の中に餅を入れた料理を食べます。雑煮の作り方は地方によって様々です。雑煮も含めて，正月のために作った料理は「おせち」と呼ばれます。

年の初めには，日本人の多くが神社や寺へ出かけて，これからの1年を無事に過ごせるようにと，**神仏**に祈ります。これを「初詣（はつもうで）」と言います。特に元日，二日，三日は，東京の明治神宮や，鎌倉の鶴岡八幡宮（つるがおかはちまんぐう）などの有名な神社や寺は，百万人を越す人で一杯になります。

子供に「お年玉」，たいていはお金をあげますが，これは神様が「お前たちもがんばれ」と授けてくれるもの，というのが趣旨です。

Q 節分とは何ですか?

Bean-scattering
ceremony

立春の前の日に行われる行事です。立春は2月3日か4日です。家の戸を開け，「**鬼は外，福は内**」と叫びながら煎った大豆を投げ，悪鬼や悪運を家から追い払います。

そもそもは宮中で**大晦日**に行われたもので，悪鬼を追い払って新年を迎えたのです。この風習に，**田植え**の行事に豆を投げるという固有の民間の風習が重なりあって，今の形になったようです。

Q 桃の節句，雛祭り（ひな）とは何ですか?

3月3日に行われる，女の子の誕生を祝い，これからの幸せを願う祭りです。雛祭には，昔の衣装を着せた雛人形に桃の花をそえて飾って，白

of a new year by drinking a special kind of rice wine called *otoso* that is said to promote longevity. And they eat a special dish called *zōni*, which contains mochi rice cakes in a vegetable soup. There are several ways to prepare *zōni*, depending on the region. Dishes, including *zōni*, that are prepared for the New Year's holidays are collectively called *osechi*.

At the opening of the year, most Japanese visit Shinto shrines or Buddhist temples where they pray to the **deities** that they will live safely through the coming year. These New Year visits to shrines and temples are called *hatsumōde*. On New Year's Day and on January 2 and 3, certain famous sites such as Tōkyō's Meiji Shrine and Kamakura's Tsurugaoka Hachimangū shrine are filled with over a million visitors.

Children are given *otoshidama* (a New Year's present) by adults, in most cases money, as a gift from the gods to encourage children to do their best.

● What is *setsubun*?

Setsubun is held one day before the **first day of spring**, which is February 3 or 4. People open the doors of their houses and drive the demons, or bad luck, out of their homes by throwing soybeans and shouting "**Demons out! Good luck in!**"

It was started originally as an imperial event on **New Year's Eve** for the purpose of getting rid of demons to welcome in a happy New Year. Later it was incorporated with the indigenous custom of throwing soybeans at the time of **planting rice seedlings**, and it has thus evolved into its present form.

● What is *hinamatsuri*?

This is the girls' festival on March 3, when the birth of girls is celebrated and wishes are expressed for their future happiness. *Hinamatsuri* is the day on which *hina ningyō*, a set of

Hina ningyō

酒という米で作った甘い飲み物を供えます。

そもそもは，水辺で体を**清める**風習でしたが，代わりに紙人形を使うことになり，その後，江戸時代になって，その人形が「雛人形」として工夫されるようになりました。

Q お彼岸というのは何ですか？

仏教の行事ですが，日本だけに生まれた習慣です。**春分の日**の前後3日間を「春の彼岸」，**秋分の日**の前後3日間を「秋の彼岸」と言います。寒さ・暑さが切り替わる時です。祖先を供養する日で，墓参りに行き，花やお萩という食べ物を供えたりします。

Q お花見はいつから始まりましたか？

Cherry-blossom viewing

日本人の花と言えば，桜と言われるほどです。パッと咲いた花の下で，桜を見ながら飲み食いを楽しむという風習が庶民の間に行き渡ったのは，江戸時代になってからのようです。

東京の上野公園のような桜の名所がたくさんあり，そんな所では，朝早くから飲み食いの場所を確保しようとして争う光景も見られます。

Q 花祭りとは何をする祭りですか？

4月8日の**釈迦**の誕生を祝う日です。正式には「灌仏会」と言います。釈迦の誕生のときに，竜が天から舞い降りてきて**香水**を注いだ，という故事に基づいて，釈迦の像に甘茶を注ぎます。

dolls dressed in ancient costumes, are displayed together with peach blossoms as decoration. A sweet drink made from rice called *shirozake* is offered.

The original form of this custom was to **purify** oneself in water, but later paper dolls were used instead of people bathing themselves. In the Edo period (1600–1868), paper dolls became more sophisticated ones, now called *hina ningyō*.

● What is *higan*?

Higan is a Buddhist event peculiar to Japan. The three days before and after the **vernal equinox** are called spring *higan* and the three days before and after the **autumnal equinox** are called autumn *higan*. Both *higan* are times of seasonal change. On these occasions people visit their ancestors' graves and offer flowers and sweets called *ohagi*.

● When did the custom of flower viewing start?

The favorite flower of the Japanese is the cherry blossom. While viewing cherry blossoms in full bloom, people enjoy eating and drinking. It was in the Edo period (1600–1868) that this custom, called *hanami,* became popular.

There are many places known for their beautiful cherry blossoms including Ueno Park in Tōkyō, where people compete from early morning for spaces for their parties.

● What do people do in *hanamatsuri* (the Flower Festival)?

Hanamatsuri on April 8 is the festival to celebrate the birth of **Gautama Buddha**. Formally called *kanbutsu-e*, the festival is based on the episode of Buddha's birth in which a dragon flew down from heaven and poured **fragrant water**. People now pour *amacha*, or sweetened tea, onto the statue of Buddha.

Q 端午の節句とは何ですか？

Carp-shaped
streamers

　　5月5日の「子供の日」に昔から行われていた行事です。家の外に**鯉のぼり**を立て，**武者人形**を飾って，男の子のすこやかな成長を祝います。

　　この習慣は武家社会で発展したものですが，民間ではこの日に，女性が先に風呂に入るとか，男が食事を用意するなどの女性上位の習慣があり，昔は男の子の祭りというだけではありませんでした。

Q 七夕とはどんな日ですか？

Tanabata, the Star
Festival

　　7月7日の夜，**天の川**をはさんで牽牛星と織女星が年に1度会う，という伝説にちなんだ行事です。

　　中国から伝わったもので，日本の宮中に入り，次第に民衆の間に広まりました。**短冊**に願いを書いて，庭に立てた竹の枝に結びつけます。

Q 盆（盂蘭盆）とは何ですか？

　　盆は本来は旧暦の7月半ばに行われましたが，今は7月13〜16日，地方によっては8月13〜16日に行われます。

　　盆は家に帰ってくる祖先の霊を迎える仏教の行事です。13日に祖先の霊を迎え入れる火をたき，16日の夜にまた火をたいて，霊を**あの世**に送ります。

● What is *tango no sekku*?

This is an event handed down from ancient times which is held on May 5, Children's Day. People express the hope that each boy in the family will grow up healthy and strong by flying **carp-shaped streamers** outside the house and displaying a **warrior doll**.

This custom developed in the warrior class of society in the feudal era, but the event was also observed among civilians of the time in a different way. Women were made superior to men on that day; for example, women took a bath before men and men prepared meals for women.

● What does the *tanabata* festival celebrate?

Tanabata, the Star Festival, is an event based on a legend in which two lovers, Kengyū (the star Altair) and Shokujo (Vega), who were separated by the **Milky Way**, meet just once a year on the night of July 7.

Originally from China and modified into its Japanese form, the event spread from the imperial palace to ordinary people. Bamboo branches are set up in the garden and decorated with **strips of paper** on which people write their wishes.

● What is *Bon (Urabon)*?

Originally celebrated in mid-July according to the lunar calendar, *Bon*, the Festival of Souls, is now held from July 13 to 16, or from August 13 to 16, depending on the area.

This is a Buddhist festival in honor of the **spirits** of the dead who return to their families. On the first day, spirits of ancestors are welcomed by an open-air fire, and on the night of the last day another open-air fire is made to see them off to **the other world**.

Q 月見には何をしますか？

Moon viewing

　9月の中旬の満月を「中秋の名月」と呼びます。この月を観賞するのが月見です。もとは中国の風習でしたが，平安時代から日本でも行われるようになっています。

　団子を作り，畑の作物といっしょに供え，**ススキ**を飾って月を観賞します。月見の**供え物**は，盗んでもかまわない，という習慣の地方もあります。

Q 七五三とはどんな祝いごとですか？

Shichi-go-san

　親が子供の成長を祝う行事です。男の子は3歳と5歳，女の子は3歳と7歳になった年の11月15日に，氏神様に連れて行き，子供たちの将来を祈ります。

　男の子は羽織にはかま，女の子は着物に着飾って神社に行きます。最近はスーツやドレスなどを着ている子もいます。

Q 大晦日には何をしますか？

　正月を迎える大晦日は，**1年の区切りをつけ**，きたるべき年に備えるための重要な日です。昔は正月の準備も大変で，餅をついたり，正月の間の食事としてお節料理を用意したり，主婦は大忙しでした。しかし今は，できあいを買ってきて済ませるという家庭も多くなりました。

　大晦日の夜は，正月の準備を終え，一家が揃って食事をし，除夜の鐘を聞き，元日の朝まで起きていたのが普通でした。地方によっては，大晦日に寝ると**白髪になる**，と言い伝えられていたところもあります。

● What do people do on *tsukimi*?

Tsukimi, which means moon-gazing, is a custom to appreciate the mid-September **full moon**, called *chūshū no meigetsu*. Introduced from China, the custom spread through Japan in the Heian period (794–1192).

Dango, a kind of dumpling, together with crops from the fields, are offered to the moon and among **Japanese pampas grass** decorations, people sit and appreciate the beauty of the moon. In some regions people are allowed to steal the **offerings**.

● What does *shichi-go-san* celebrate?

This is an event in which parents celebrate their children's growth. On November 15, 3- and 5-year-old boys, and 3- and 7-year-old girls are taken to shrines where their parents pray for their future.

Boys often wear *haori*, or a half-coat, and *hakama*, or a divided skirt, and girls wear *kimono*. Nowadays, some children wear suits or dresses.

● What do people do on New Year's Eve?

New Year's Eve is an important day for **wrapping up the old year** and preparing for the coming year. Decades ago, preparations for the New Year kept people very busy making rice cakes and special New Year's dishes called *osechi*, but nowadays many households buy them at stores.

At that time it was customary for a family to have dinner together after they had finished preparing. They listened to *joya no kane*, or the watch-night bell tolling at midnight, and stayed awake till the morning of the new year. In some regions, there is a saying that **one's hair turns gray** if one sleeps on New Year's Eve.

Q 日本人にとって祭りとは何ですか?

　　語源の「マツ」には，見えないものが見えるところに来るのを歓待する，という意味があります。

　　つまり，日ごろ目には見えない神様が来てくれるわけで，その神様を歓待するのが祭りというわけです。日本各地に伝承されている祭りは，基本的に神々と人の交流という形で行われています。

　　ただし，無数の神様の中には病気や**自然災害**をもたらす神もあり，こうした**災厄の神を追放する**のも祭りです。

Q 日本の三大祭りと言われるものは何ですか?

Gion Festival

　　日本人は"3"という数字で物事を一くくりにするのが大好きです。しかし，祭りについて3つを挙げるとなると説が分かれます。

　　たとえば，東京の三社祭り，京都の祇園（ぎおん）祭り，大阪の天神祭りの3つという説，東京の山王（さんのう）祭り，京都の葵（あおい）祭り，大阪の天神祭りの3つという説などです。

　　また各地域ごとに，東北三大祭り(青森ねぶた祭り，秋田竿灯（かんとう）祭り，仙台の七夕祭り)とか，京都三大祭り(葵祭り，祇園祭り，時代祭り)などとも言ったりします。

• What is the significance of festivals for the Japanese?

Matsu, the original meaning of the word *matsuri* (festivals) in Japanese, means "to welcome the invisible to a place where they become visible."

In other words, gods, who are usually invisible, visit during festivals, and are welcomed by the people. Japanese festivals handed down from ancient times are basically celebrated to bring about communication between gods and people.

Among the myriads of gods, however, there are some that bring about diseases and **natural disasters**, so festivals are also intended to **ward off evil gods**.

• What are the three largest festivals in Japan?

The Japanese like to use the number three to summarize things, but as far as festivals are concerned, opinions are divided on which three to choose.

For instance, there is a view that the Sanja Festival in Tōkyō, the Gion Festival in Kyōto, and the Tenjin Festival in Ōsaka are the three largest festivals. But another view holds that the three largest festivals are the Sannō Festival in Tōkyō, the Aoi Festival in Kyōto, and the Tenjin Festival in Ōsaka.

Each region has its three largest festivals. In the Tōhoku region, the Nebuta Festival in Aomori, the Kantō Festival in Akita, and the Tanabata Festival in Sendai are said to be the three largest. In Kyōto there are the Aoi Festival, the Gion Festival, and the Jidai Festival.

日本の結婚

Q 日本ではどんな結婚式が一般的ですか?

Shintō-style wedding

　　日本の結婚式は神前結婚式が7割と言われています。次に多いのが,キリスト教式で,仏式で行われるのはまれです。いずれも信仰にはあまり関わりがないのが特徴です。

Bride in Japanese style

　　昔は,結婚式は嫁入り先の家で行ったものですが,明治時代になって,神社での結婚式が行われるようになりました。

　　教会での結婚式は信者に限るのが原則ですが,事前にオリエンテーションを受ければ式を挙げられる教会があります。

　　神社や教会に行かなくても,**神主**や**牧師**が出張してきて,ホテルや結婚式場に作られた祭壇の前でできます。

　　挙式のあとは記念撮影をして**披露宴**となります。披露宴は,お世話になっている人や親しい人たちを招いて,結婚したことをお披露目する祝宴です。

Q 結婚式にはいくらぐらいかかりますか?

　　三和銀行が1998年に行った調査によれば,挙式・披露宴にかかる平均費用は314万円。**新郎・新婦**や**仲人**を含めた出席者数の平均は80人なので,出席者1人当たり約4万円というのが1つの目安です。

　　結婚は,結婚する当人たちだけでなく,家と家の結びつきでもありますから,相手の家に対しても恥ずかしいことはできず,それなりの披露宴

Japanese Marriages

● **What is the most common kind of wedding ceremony in Japan?**

About 70% of Japanese weddings are conducted in Shintō style. The next most common are those conducted in Christian style, followed by Buddhist-style weddings. Most couples do not associate their chosen style of wedding with a religious faith.

In olden times the wedding ceremony was held in the husband's home. Ceremonies in shrines became common in the Meiji period (1868–1912).

Christian-style ceremonies in churches are usually open only to Christians, but recently some churches admit couples who have taken classes on Christianity.

Hotels and wedding halls have facilities for both Shintō-style and Christian-style ceremonies, where **Shintō priests** and **ministers** come to preside over the ceremonies.

After the ceremony, **commemorative photos** are taken and **wedding receptions** are held. A wedding reception is an event to make the couple's marriage public, to which friends and acquaintances are invited.

● **How much does it cost to hold a wedding?**

A 1998 survey by Sanwa Bank showed that the average cost of a wedding ceremony and reception is 3,140,000 yen, and the average number of people attending the reception including the **bride, bridegroom,** and **go-between,** is 80. That means it costs about 40,000 yen per person.

Marriage is considered to unite not only the couple, but also the families of the couple. Rather elaborate wedding receptions, called *hirōen,* are common. In their planning and execu-

が行われるのが普通です。

しかし，"自分たちらしさ"を出したユニークな結婚式をしたいという人が増えており，結婚式のスタイルも少しずつ変わってきました。

Q 日本人の結婚の平均年齢はいくつですか？

厚生省の人口動態統計によれば，1997年に結婚した男性の平均年齢は29.9歳，女性は27.6歳となっています。ただし，これは全婚姻の平均で，初婚だけに限ると男性は28.5歳，女性は26.6歳です。

15歳から29歳までの女性で結婚している人の割合は10％を切るという調査（読売新聞読者調査 1995年）もあります。

結婚する女性の平均年齢が25歳以下だったのは1970年代前半までで，男女ともに日本人の結婚年齢は高くなっており，結婚する年齢の幅も大きく広がってきました。

Q どれくらいの人が離婚していますか？

厚生省の人口動態統計によれば，1997年の離婚件数は約22万件。結婚したのは約77万5000件ですから，3.5組のうち1組は離婚したことになります。離婚したカップルの婚姻期間は平均9.9年です。

離婚件数は増加する一方で，「バツイチ」とか「成田離婚」，「熟年離婚」などという新しい言葉も生まれました。

バツイチは「離婚経験1回」という意味の言葉の短縮語です。しかし，特に揶揄（ひゆ）するような意

tion, pains are taken to look respectable in the eyes of the families of both marriage partners.

However, the style of weddings has gradually changed as more people express a desire to hold unique weddings suitable to themselves.

● What is the average age of marriage of the Japanese?

According to the 1997 *Vital Statistics* by the **Ministry of Health and Welfare**, the average age of marrige for men is 29.9 and 27.6 for women. These figures are the average for all marriages; for people who marry for the first time, the average is 28.5 years for men, and 26.6 for women.

A 1995 *Yomiuri Shimbun* readers' survey revealed that less than 10% of women between 15 and 29 were married.

Until the early 1970s, the average age of marriage for women was less than 25, but it is getting higher for both men and women, and people are getting married at a wider range of ages.

● What is the divorce rate?

Statistics compiled by the Ministry of Health and Welfare show that in 1997 the number of **divorces** was about 220,000 compared to 775,000 marriages, which means one in every 3.5 couples divorced. The average **duration of marriage** for the divorced couples was 9.9 years.

The number of divorces has increased greatly, and the trend gave birth to new words, such as *batsu-ichi* ("one-time cross mark"), *Narita rikon* (Narita divorce), and *jukunen rikon* (mature-age divorce).

Batsu-ichi refers to people who have divorced once, but it does not have much of a **derogatory connotation**. Some women

味合いはなく，「わたし，バツイチよ」と平気で口にする女性もいます。

　成田離婚は，**新婚旅行**から帰ってすぐに離婚すること。日本では新婚旅行に海外を選ぶ人が多いのですが，パッとのぼせて結婚したものの，新婚旅行中に興ざめとなり，成田空港に帰り着くころには離婚を決めているカップルもいるのだそうです。

　また，熟年離婚は長年連れ添った夫婦が離婚することを言います。長年，結婚生活に耐えて夫に尽くしてきた妻が自由になりたいと言い出すケースです。多くの場合，夫の**定年**などを機に，離婚をしたいと妻が言い出します。

Q 国際結婚する人は毎年どれくらいいますか？

　厚生省の人口動態統計によれば，1997年に結婚したカップルのうち，夫が日本人で妻が外国人というケースは2万900組，逆は7349組でした。

　日本人男性が外国の女性と結婚するケースは，この10年で約5倍に増えています。

　国別に見ると，妻が外国人の場合は中国が最も多くて全体の31.7％，次がフィリピンの28.9％，後はさまざまです。

　夫が外国人の場合，トップは韓国・北朝鮮（朝鮮民主主義人民共和国）の人で36.4％，ついで米国人の18.7％，中国人の11.3％となっています。

openly admit they are *batsu-ichi*.

Narita rikon means to divorce immediately after the couple have returned from their **honeymoon**. Many Japanese couples choose foreign countries as their honeymoon destination, but some of them find their feelings have cooled during the trip and decide to divorce by the time they arrive back at Narita Airport.

The word *jukunen rikon* is used when a couple who have been married for many years seek a divorce. Some cases of *jukunen rikon* involve wives who want to be liberated after enduring the marriage and devoting their lives to their husbands for a long time. Many such wives express their wish for divorce taking advantage of their husbands' **retirement**.

● How many international marriages are registered every year?

The Health and Welfare Ministry's *Vital Statistics* show that, among the couples who got married in 1997, the number of couples consisting of a Japanese husband and a foreign wife was 20,900, and the number of couples consisting of a foreign husband and a Japanese wife was 7,349.

The number of cases where Japanese men marry foreign women has increased by five times during the past ten years.

According to their nationalities, wives from China constitute 31.7% of foreign wives, while second place is held by wives from the Philippines (28.9%).

For foreign husbands, 36.4% are Koreans, 18.7% are Americans, and 11.3% are Chinese.

日本の葬式

Q どんな葬式をするのが普通ですか?

Incense offering

　特に信仰している宗教がなければ, 多くの場合, 日本の**葬式**は, 仏式で行われます。

　亡くなると, 普通は家で**通夜**を行います。通夜は, **遺族**や近親者がロウソクや**線香**を絶やさずに, 終夜, 遺体を守ることです。

　そして, 翌日以降に, 家か寺院, あるいは葬儀場で葬式を行います。葬式の段取りなどは, 予算や故人の希望に合わせて, **葬儀社**に任せて行うのが普通です。

　葬式は, 故人の成仏を祈る葬儀, 最後の別れを告げる告別式, と続きます。葬儀では遺体を納棺して**祭壇**に飾り, 僧侶の読経を聞いて親族とごく親しい人が焼香(抹香をたくこと)します。焼香の代わりに献花をする場合もあります。

　一般の会葬者は**告別式**で焼香します。告別式のあと, 通常は遺体を**火葬場**に運びます。

Q 葬式にはいくらぐらいかかりますか?

　全日本葬祭業共同組合連合会の調べ(1999年)によれば, 葬式にかかる総費用の全国平均額は229万円となっています。地域別にみると, 最も平均額の高い東北地方で, 271万円, 最も低い中国地方では153万円と, 地域により大きな差が見られます。

　費用の内訳を**全国平均**で見ると, 葬儀社へ

Funerals in Japan

• What is the most common type of funeral?

Most of the **funeral services** in Japan are administered according to Buddhist rites if the deceased is of no specific religion.

After a death, a **wake** is held usually at the home of the deceased. A wake is an occasion when the **surviving family** and close relatives keep a night watch over the corpse, while candles are lit and **incense sticks** are offered.

During one of the following days, a funeral is held either at the home, a temple or a funeral hall. Ordinarily a **funeral home** takes care of the funeral according to the family's budget and the wishes of the deceased.

A funeral consists of a service in which prayers for the deceased are offered and a farewell ceremony in which those in attendance part from the dead. In the funeral service, the coffin is placed on the **altar** and the priest chants a sutra while relatives and close friends offer incense. Sometimes flowers are offered in place of incense.

Those in attendance offer incense during the **farewell ceremony**, after which the corpse is carried to the **crematorium**.

• How much does a funeral cost?

A 1999 survey by the All Japan Funeral Services Cooperative Union shows that funerals cost an average of 2.29 million yen. There are large differences from one part of Japan to another. Funerals are on average the most expensive in the Tōhoku region (2.71 million yen) and the least expensive in the Chūgoku region (1.53 million yen).

Speaking of **national averages**, 57% of the money is paid to

の支払いが57％，参列者の飲食費が20％，寺院への支払いが22％となっています。

　葬儀には，個人にゆかりの友人，縁者，知人から**香典**が届きますので，葬儀の費用の一部に当てられますが，香典をくれた方には香典返しといって，お返しをしなければなりません。一般に香典で受け取った額の半分はお返しに使われます。

　なお，**お墓**にかかる費用は200万〜300万円，**仏壇**は20万〜50万円もかかります。遺族の負担は大変です！

Q 香典はいくら持っていくのが常識ですか？

Envelope for
funeral offering

　故人の立場やつきあいの程度にもよりますが，普通のつき合いの程度であれば5千円から1万円が一般的です。不祝儀袋に入れ，**地味な色の**ふくさ（のし袋を包む小さな布）や風呂敷に包んで，通夜や告別式に持参します。この場合，**新札**は避けます。

Q 日本では必ず火葬にするのですか？

　日本では**公衆衛生**上，地方自治体の**条例で土葬**を禁止しているところが大半です。イスラム教など，宗教上の理由で土葬を希望する場合は，許可される公営**墓地**もあります。

　日本で外国人が亡くなった場合は，身元が分かれば警察から大使館や関係者に連絡されます。関係者に遺体が引き取られれば，日本での**埋葬許可**を受けることもできますし，母国に遺体を移送することも可能です。

funeral service organizations, 22% goes to temples, and 20% to cover the expenses of food and drinks for those attending the ceremonies.

Friends, relatives and acquaintances of the deceased provide **monetary offerings** which can be appropriated for part of the funeral expenses, but the mourner has to return something to them as a token of gratitude. Usually, one-half of the amount of monetary offerings received is returned.

In addition, it costs 2 to 3 million yen to set up a **grave**, and a typical **Buddhist family altar** costs 200,000 to 500,000 yen. So the surviving family has to shoulder a large financial burden.

● How much money do people generally offer at funerals?

It all depends on how close one was to the deceased, but acquaintances generally give 5,000 to 10,000 yen enclosed in a special envelope and wrapped in a piece of cloth of **subdued color** at the wake or the farewell ceremony. **New bills** are avoided on this occasion.

● Do the Japanese always cremate the dead?

In Japan, most local governments have **ordinances** prohibiting **burial** for **public hygiene** reasons. Some **cemeteries** allow burial for believers of Islam and other religions.

A foreigner's death in Japan is reported by the police to the embassy and related people when he or she is identified. Once the surviving family receives the body, they can either request **burial permission** in Japan or have the body sent home.

遺体の引き取り手がない場合は，区市町村長が葬儀をして火葬などを行います。

日本人の余暇・娯楽

Q 日本人は余暇にはどんなことをして過ごしますか?

日本人が**余暇**に，どんなことを，1年間に何回ぐらい楽しんでいるか，というデータ(レジャー白書 '98)があります。

音楽観賞	70.4回
パソコン	59.3回
体操	54.0回
ジョギング・マラソン	44.6回
テレビゲーム	41.4回

以下，園芸・庭いじり，ビデオ鑑賞，**外食**，水泳，バー・スナック・パブ，ドライブ，釣り，カラオケ，宝くじ，映画と続きます。これは年齢と性別なしでまとめた数字で，日本の典型的な家族の余暇の過ごし方を表していると言えます。

金額の上で見ると，回数は3回ですが，やはり国内観光旅行がトップです。次いでパソコン，そして，バー・スナックなどでの遊興が続いています。しかし，全体的には，金のかかることは敬遠し，身近なところで安く楽しむという時代になってきました。

Q 子供たちの楽しみは何ですか?

次々に新しいソフトが出るテレビゲームが圧倒的に強いようです。学校が終わっても，塾に行ったり，宿題に追われる彼らには，外を出歩

In case there is no one to receive the body, the chief of the municipality takes care of the funeral.

Leisure Time and Recreation of the Japanese

● How do the Japanese spend their leisure time?

The *1998 Leisure White Paper* provides data on what Japanese do in their **leisure time** and the frequency over a year:

Listening to music	70.4 times
Using personal computer	59.3 times
Physical exercises	54.0 times
Jogging	44.6 times
Video games	41.4 times

Other activities include gardening, watching videos, **eating out**, swimming, going to bars, driving, fishing, *karaoke*, buying lottery cards, and watching movies, in descending order of popularity. This survey did not consider age and sex and shows how a typical Japanese family spends its leisure time.

In terms of money spent, domestic trips rank first, although only an average of three trips are made in a year, followed by using personal computers and drinking in bars. Inexpensive forms of recreation available to anyone are becoming more and more popular these days.

● What do children enjoy doing?

An overwhelmingly popular recreation among children is video games, for which new software packages are issued one after another. Many children do not have much time to play,

Comic magazines

くひまはありません。**親の目をかすめて**取り組む
テレビゲームが，いちばんのスリルでしょう。

それにマンガです。週刊誌，月刊誌の連載物
を読むのを，彼らは絶対に欠かしません。

日本では，テレビゲームやマンガは子供たちだ
けの楽しみではありません。20代，30代まで幅広
い層が楽しんでおり，通勤途中の若い**サラリー
マン**がよく電車の中でマンガを読んでいます。

ちなみに，日本PTA全国協議会が1997年に
行った調査によれば，学習塾に通っている子供
の割合が，小学6年生で43%，中学3年生で
64%だそうで，遊ぶひまがないのがかわいそう
です。

Q お父さんたちの楽しみは何ですか？

Golf practice range

働き過ぎの日本のお父さんたちには，同僚と
の仕事帰りの一杯が楽しみ，という人が，まだま
だたくさんいます。そして，休みの日にはゴルフ，
何もしないときは**昼寝**……という人も多いでしょ
う。

しかし，世の中全体としては，週休2日となり，
労働時間が短縮されてきて，余暇が多くなってき
ましたので，余暇の時間を**自己の啓発**，健康づく
りのための活動，また，ボランティア活動などに
使いたいという人たちがどんどん増えています。

Q パチンコはいつごろ日本に
誕生したのですか？

パチンコの**原型**は1920年代にアメリカから伝
わったコリントゲームです。これが，1925年に改

especially outside after school because of *juku*, or cram school, and homework. It is a thrill for children to play video games **without their parents' knowledge**.

Reading *manga* (comic books) is another pastime the majority of children enjoy. They always look forward to reading serialized *manga* in weekly and monthly magazines.

In Japan, video games and *manga* are more than just entertainment for children. Large numbers of people in their 20s and 30s also enjoy them. Young **company employees** often read *manga* on trains as they commute.

A 1997 survey by the National Congress of Parents and Teachers Association of Japan found that the proportion of children going to extracurricular cram schools (*juku*) was 43% for sixth grade pupils and 64% for ninth grade pupils. It is indeed a pity that they don't have more time to play.

● What do men enjoy?

Many Japanese men, who are often described as **workaholics**, find their pleasure in having a drink with their colleagues after work. On holidays some play golf and others just relax and **take a nap**.

With the overall trend of having more leisure time because of two-day weekends and fewer working hours, more and more people want to make the most of their free time by getting involved in **self-improvement**, health activities, and volunteer activities.

● When was *pachinko*, or the vertical pinball game, born in Japan?

The **original form** of *pachinko* is the Corinthian game introduced from the United States in the 1920s. The game was mod-

良され，大人のための遊びになります。そして戦後，たくさんの台を並べ，**景品**を付けたことにより一気に人気が出ました。

玉をはじく方式も，指ではじく方式から**電動式**になり，今では，玉の出る確率はコンピュータで制御されています。

中央に示された絵や数字が一致すると，大当たりで多数の玉が出るようにし，ギャンブル的な性格を強くしたこと，景品を裏で現金に代える組織があることなどが，パチンコの人気を急激に上げたと言われます。

1995年にはパチンコ産業の売上高は26兆3420億円に達して，自動車産業をしのぐほどに成長しました。しかしこの年を境に売上高は減少に転じて，98年には20兆9600億と，2割あまりも少なくなりました。

それだけに客を引き寄せるための競争も激しく，近頃では**店構え**をおしゃれにし，景品に**ブランド品**を置く，**飲み物のサービス**を始めるなど，お客の獲得にむけた努力に必死です。

Q 囲碁の魅力はどこにありますか？

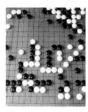

Go

囲碁は古く中国に発したゲームです。ルールは単純ですが，なかなか奥行きが深いのです。

碁盤の目は縦横それぞれ19の線の，361の交点で示されます。2人のプレーヤーが，この361箇所に交互に白と黒の石を置いて，相手よりも多い地を確保する勝負です。ゲームによって石の置き方は千差万別で，あっという間に**大逆転**されることもあります。

ified into *pachinko* in 1925, and after World War II, it instantly gained immense popularity by offering **prizes**.

In the course of development, the manually-operated system of striking balls was improved to **electrically-powered systems**, and now the ball distribution is controlled by computers.

Some of the reasons why *pachinko* has become so popular are that it has stimulated the taste for gambling characteristics with features such as slot machines, and also that there are underground organizations which provide services to exchange prizes for cash.

In 1995 the *pachinko* industry took in over 26 trillion yen, putting it ahead of even the automobile industry in terms of money spent. Compared to this peak year, *pachinko* parlor income dropped by about 20% as of 1998, when it totaled only about 21 trillion yen.

As competition for customers stiffens, some *pachinko* parlors in recent years have become quite fashionable in **decor**, and offer **brand-name products** as prizes and even **free beverages** to win customers.

● What is appealing about *go*?

Go originally developed in ancient times in China. Though its rules are simple, *go* provides a more sophisticated pleasure.

It is played by two players on a square board with 19 vertical lines, 19 horizontal lines, and 361 intersections. The two players alternately place stones of their color, either black or white, and compete in taking stones by surrounding as much territory as possible. The player with the most territory is the winner. There are literally thousands of different tactics in the game, and there is always the possibility of a **dramatic comeback**.

Q 将棋の魅力はどこにありますか？

Shōgi

将棋のルーツはインドにあり，それが西洋に伝わったものがチェス，日本に伝わったものが将棋です。それぞれ動き方の決まった駒を動かして**相手の陣**を攻め，王将を捕らえます。

ですから駒の働きやルールはチェスと大変よく似ていますが，日本の将棋の特徴は取った相手の駒を自分の駒として再度使用できることです。このためチェスではよく起こる「**引き分け**」がほとんどなく，白熱した戦いになります。

Q どれぐらいの人が海外旅行に行っていますか？

Crowded Narita Airport

1990年に1000万人を突破した海外渡航者数は，**湾岸戦争**のあった1991年を除いて増え続けており，1997年には1680万人を記録しました。

渡航者のもっとも多い国は，アメリカ合衆国です。アメリカだけで全渡航者数の3分の1を占め，特にハワイには**根強い人気**があります。

ついで韓国，中国，香港，台湾，オーストラリアが続きます。

近隣の国々に渡航者が多いのは，航空券や滞在費が安く，**時差**が少ないことなどが挙げられますが，これまでアメリカやヨーロッパに向けられていた興味がアジアに向けられるようになってきたからと言うこともできます。

近年では若者を中心に日程を自由に決められる格安航空券の人気も高く，世界中で日本人

● What is interesting about *shōgi*?

The game originated in India and became chess in the West and *shōgi* in Japan. By moving the various *shōgi* pieces, each of which has its own rules of advance, a player seeks to attack his **opponent's camp** (*jin*) and ultimately to capture its king piece (*ōshō*).

Therefore, the movement of pieces and rules are similar to those of chess, but one characteristic peculiar to *shōgi* is that a player can reuse captured pieces as his or her own. This rule of *shōgi* often generates exciting moments toward the end, with fewer **tied games** than chess.

● How many people travel outside Japan?

The number of Japanese who travel abroad in a given year passed the 10 million mark in 1990. Except for 1991, which was the year of the **Gulf War**, this number has continued to grow each year, reaching 16.8 million in 1997.

The largest number of travelers, about one third of the total, go to the United States—Hawaii, in particular, has a **deep-rooted popularity**.

Following the United States, overseas destinations are South Korea, the People's Republic of China, Hong Kong, Taiwan, and Australia, in that order.

Among the reasons many travelers go to nearby countries is the fact that air tickets and living expenses are relatively cheap, and also the fact that "**jet lag**" is less of a problem because of the closeness of time zones. It can be said that much of the interest in foreign travel that used to be directed toward America and Europe is now directed toward Asia.

Especially popular among young people in recent years are inexpensive air tickets that allow for flexibility in the setting of

バックパッカーの姿が見受けられるようになって
きました。

日本のスポーツ

Q 日本人が自分で楽しむスポーツは何が人気ですか?

ボウリング, 器具を使わない体操, ジョギング, プールでの水泳などが, 日常の健康のために人気のあるスポーツです。テニスも**幅広い年齢**の人が楽しんでいます。

野球は昔は**空き地**でよく行われていましたが, 今は空き地もなく, やりたくてもできなくなりました。若い人に人気があるサッカーやバスケットも, 特に都会ではプレーを楽しむ場所が十分にないのが現状です。そこで室内の限られたスペースでも楽しめるスポーツも多く行われています。幅広い年代で楽しまれる**卓球**やボウリングなどがその**代表格**といえるでしょう。

また, 高齢者では**日本で生まれた**ゲートボールという競技に人気があります。

5人ずつの2つのチームがT字型のスティックでボールを打ち, 3つのゲートを通過させる競技で, 運動量は少ないものの, **チームワークのかけひき**に面白味があります。

Gate ball (croquet)

ゴルフは, 日本にはゴルフ場は多いものの, **プレー代**が高く, 気軽には楽しむことができません。ビジネスの延長の「社用ゴルフ」は, **不景気**で**激減**だそうです。

冬になると, かなり多くの人たちがスキーを楽しみます。スノーボードの人気が出てから, スキ

schedules. So it is now quite common to find Japanese back-packers in almost any part of the world.

Sports in Japan

● What kinds of sports do the Japanese participate in?

For daily exercises for health, bowling, body exercise, jogging, and swimming are popular. Tennis is also very popular with people in a **wide range of age groups**.

Decades ago people used to play baseball in **vacant lots**, but now it has become almost impossible to do so because there are not many vacant lots left. Young people love soccer and basketball, but in urban areas it is very hard to find enough space to play. So it is also common to find sports that can be enjoyed inside in a limited space. **Prime examples** are **table tennis** and bowling, both of which are popular among people of many different age groups.

Popular among older people is the game of gate ball (croquet), which was **invented in Japan**.

Players divide into two teams of five persons each and try to hit a ball through a series of three gates using **T-shaped** sticks. The game requires relatively little body movement and is interesting because of its **teamwork-related strategies**.

Although there are numerous golf courses in Japan, the **green fees** are so prohibitive that not everyone can enjoy this sport. The number of opportunities to play golf at the company's expense **plunged** because of the **economic recession**.

Skiing is the favorite sport of the Japanese in winter. The skiing population in this snowy country has increased as snow-

ーに行く人の数はぐんと増えたようです。日本は雪が多い国なのです。

Q 観戦するスポーツは何が人気ですか？

Baseball game

Soccer game

実際に競技場に**観客**が押し掛けるスポーツとしては，まずはプロ野球，そして，特に若い人が多いのはJリーグのサッカー，ラグビー，バレーボールです。ラグビーは中高年齢の人にも人気があります。バレーボールには，**熱狂的**な若い女性のファンが目立ちます。

テレビ観戦では，プロ野球，そして大相撲が肩を並べます。次にJリーグのサッカーとプロゴルフのコンペが続きます。

春と夏の2回ある**高校野球大会**が始まると，日本全国が出身県からの出場校を応援して沸き立ちます。高校生の野球で，**これだけ騒ぎ立てる**日本の姿は，外国人には**異様に見える**そうですね。

Q 相撲は昔から日本の国技だったのですか？

Sumō match © JAMP

昔，相撲は**五穀豊穣**（ごこくほうじょう）を占ったり，**神意**をうかがう**神事**でした。史実に記録されている最初の相撲は642年のことで，その後，9世紀初めには宮廷の**儀式**になっていたのです。

12世紀以降，武士が政治の実権をにぎるようになると，相撲は，戦場での実戦的な**武術**としての性格を持つようになりました。しかし，江戸時代になると，神社の祭礼などにおける**興行**として行われるようになり，次第に見世物的になっていきました。

この相撲を，**国技**と呼ぶようになったのは明治時代末の20世紀初めからです。国家主義のもと

boarding has become quite popular.

● What sports are popular as spectator sports?

Professional baseball always attracts a large number of **spectators**. Japan League professional soccer, rugby, and volleyball have a lot of young fans, while rugby is popular also with middle-aged people. Young girls make up the greater part of **enthusiastic** volleyball fans.

TV viewers love broadcasts of baseball games and *sumō* wrestling bouts. Broadcasts of Japan League soccer games and professional golf tournaments also have high audience ratings.

When the **National Senior High School Baseball Championships** held in spring and summer begin, the whole nation cheers the team that represents their prefecture. The fact that people **make such a fuss** over high school baseball games might **seem odd** to some foreigners.

● Has *sumō* been the national sport from ancient times?

Sumō in ancient times was a **sacred event** to foretell an **abundant harvest** and to predict the **will of the gods**. The oldest bout of *sumō* recorded in history was in 642 A.D., and it was adopted as a court **ritual** in the early ninth century.

After the 12th century, when warriors began holding real power in politics, *sumō* acquired the characteristic of a practical **martial art** to be used in the battlefield. In the Edo period (1600–1868) *sumō* bouts began to be performed as part of **shows** in festivities at shrines.

It was not until the end of the Meiji period (1868–1912), or the early 20th century, that *sumō* was mentioned as the **national**

に天皇の神格化が進み，それと共に，元は宮廷の儀式であった相撲が国技化されていき，現在に至っています。

Q 相撲の世界はどんな世界ですか？

相撲の勝負は，相手を土俵から押し出すか，相手の体のどこかを地に着けさせれば勝ちになります。

Sumō stable

力士になるには，約50ある**相撲部屋**のどれか一つに所属しなければなりません。衣食住のすべてを部屋が面倒を見てくれ，強い力士になるべく養成されていきます。**親方**の家族以外はすべて男の世界です。

力士は，その実力によっていくつものランクにわけられています。最下位は序ノ口といい，ここからスタートし，序二段，三段目，幕下，十両，前頭と上がります。その上が小結，関脇，大関で，最高位が横綱です。

十両以上になると関取と呼ばれ，日本相撲協会から月給が出ますが，幕下以下には場所の成績に応じて与えられるわずかな**奨励金**だけです。

Q 柔道はいつごろ日本で生まれましたか？

柔道は1882年嘉納治五郎（1860 – 1938）によって創始されました。

柔道の技の源は柔術に求められます。柔術は，武士が**戦場**で敵と戦うときのさまざまな技から発展したものです。

嘉納治五郎もこの柔術を習得しますが，そのうちに，単に勝つための柔術に満足することができず，体を鍛え，精神を修養することを目的

sport for the first time. As the emperor was deified under nationalism, *sumō,* originally a court ritual, was given national sport status.

● What is the world of the *sumō* wrestler like?

The winner in *sumō* is decided when the opponent is forced out of the ring (*dohyō*) or when any part of his body touches the ground.

In order to become a *sumō* wrestler, one has to belong to one of the approximately 50 **sumō stables**. The stables take care of every aspect of the newcomers' lives including food, clothing, and housing, while training them to be strong wrestlers. It is a man's world except for the family of the **stable master**.

Wrestlers are ranked according to their ability. The lowest rank is called *jonokuchi*, which is the starting point. There are nine other ranks such as *jonidan*, *sandanme*, *makushita*, *jūryō*, *maegashira*, *komusubi*, *sekiwake* and *ōzeki*. In the top rank are the *yokozuna*, or grand champions.

Wrestlers above the rank of *jūryō* are called *sekitori* and receive monthly salaries from the Japan Sumo Association. What the other wrestlers get is a small **incentive** depending on their record in tournaments.

● When was *jūdō* established?

Jūdō was established in 1882 by Kanō Jigorō (1860 – 1938).

The origin of the techniques of *jūdō* can be found in *jūjutsu*, which developed from warrior fighting techniques on the **battlefield**.

Kanō, who had mastered *jūjutsu*, was not satisfied with fighting just for the pupose of winning, and created *jūdō* which aims for both physical and mental strength.

Jūdō

にした柔道を創り出します。

　1882年，東京の永昌寺に最初に講道館を開いたときは，畳数12畳の道場，門人はわずか9人だったといいます。それが今はオリンピック種目にもなりました。

　競技の国際化が進んだ結果，1997年にパリで開かれた国際柔道連盟の総会では，**カラー柔道着**の導入が決められました。これは伝統的な白い柔道着にこだわる日本の反対を押し切っての決定でした。1998年にミンスクで行われたワールドカップ柔道からは，実際に**国際大会**での着用が始まっています。

Q スポーツになった**日本古来の武道**には
　どんなものがありますか？

Kendō

　代表的なものを挙げましょう。**武具を使わない**ものとしては，柔術から発展した柔道。そして，中国から伝来して沖縄で発展した空手があります。

　剣道は武士の剣術から生まれてきたものです。練習に**竹刀**〈しない〉を用い，**面**や**胴当て**などを用いるようになったのは江戸時代からで，このスタイルで競技を行います。

　弓道〈きゅうどう〉も，その起源は昔に遡りますが，弓道という名前が使われるようになったのは，20世紀になってからです。弓道の競技には，近い距離の的を座って射るものと，遠い距離の的を立てて射るものの2つがあります。

Kyūdo

　日本の武道から発生したスポーツの共通した特徴は，**礼儀**，**精神性**を重視するところにあります。

In 1882, Kanō opened the Kōdōkan in the Eishōji Temple in Tōkyō, with only nine students in a 12 *tatami*-mat room as a practice gym. *Jūdō* is now a world sport and an Olympic event.

As a sign of the way *jūdō* competitions have become internationalized, it was decided at the general meeting of the International Jūdō Federation held in Paris in 1997 to introduce **colored *jūdō* uniforms**. This was decided in spite of objections from the All-Japan Jūdō Federation, which is strongly attached to the traditional white *jūdō* uniforms. Starting with the 1998 Hyundai World Cup for Men and Women in Minsk, Belarus, colored *jūdō* uniforms were worn for the first time at an **international competition**.

● What kind of traditional martial arts of Japan are practiced as sports?

Among traditional Japanese martial arts which are practiced as sports today, *jūdō* and *karate* are ones in which no **weapons** are used. *Jūdō* developed from *jūjutsu*, and *karate* was introduced from China and developed in Okinawa.

Kendō, a kind of fencing, was born from the martial arts of warriors. *Shinai*, or **bamboo swords**, together with *men* (**face masks**) and *dō-ate* (**body protectors**) began to be used in the Edo period (1600–1868).

Kyūdō, or Japanese archery, acquired its name in the 20th century, although its origin dates back to ancient times. Two different kinds of shooting ranges, a shorter one in which competitors shoot at a target while sitting, and a longer one in which competitors shoot standing, are used in *kyūdō* matches.

One feature of sports derived from Japanese martial arts is that they emphasize **courtesy** and **mental discipline**.

Q 日本のプロ野球のチームはいくつありますか?

セントラルリーグとパシフィックリーグに, それぞれに6チーム, 計12チームがあります。

それぞれのチームには**二軍**があります。チームを東西に分けて, イースタンリーグ, ウエスタンリーグというリーグ戦をしています。

Nomo Hideo

本場のアメリカから, 野球が日本に入ってきたのは1931年のことで, 1934年に初めて, 今の読売巨人軍ジャイアンツである「大日本東京野球倶楽部」が設立されました。そして, 1936年, 全7チームで, 全日本職業野球連盟が発足しました。現在の2リーグ制になったのは, 1949年からです。

1995年, 野茂英雄が華々しくアメリカの**大リーグ**に登場し, 1年目に大成功したことにより, 日本のプロ野球も注目を集めました。その後, 何人もがアメリカの大リーグに入り活躍しています。

Q プロサッカーはどんな状況ですか?

日本のプロのサッカー・リーグをJリーグと言います。Japan Professional Football League の愛称です。

1993年に開幕したのですが, この時は, 10チームでした。以後, 年々チームが増えて, 1999年にはJ1 (ディビジョン1), J2 (ディビジョン2)の二部制が導入されました。それぞれ16チーム, 10チームで構成され, シーズンの最終成績をもとにJ1の下位2チームとJ2の上位2チームが入れ替わるという仕組みです。

3月から11月までがシーズンで, 毎週, 水曜

● How many professional baseball teams are there in Japan?

There are 12 teams in total, six in the Central League and six in the Pacific League.

The 12 teams have **farm teams**, which comprise the Eastern League and the Western League.

Baseball was introduced from the United States to Japan in 1931, and the Dai-Nihon Tōkyō Yakyū Club, the forerunner of the present Yomiuri Giants, was founded in 1934. The Japan Professional Baseball League was launched in 1936 with seven teams, and the two-league system was introduced in 1949.

In 1995, Japanese pitcher Nomo Hideo made his debut in the **Major League** in the United States and had a successful first year, which created awareness about Japanese professional baseball. Following Nomo, several other Japanese players have also become active in the American major leagues.

● What is professional soccer like in Japan?

The Japanese professional soccer league is called J. League, an abbreviation for the Japan Professional Football League.

Since the league was launched with ten teams in 1993, the number of teams has increased every year. In 1999, a two-tier system was launched, comprising J1 (Division 1) and J2 (Division 2), made up of 16 teams and 10 teams, respectively. On the basis of scores accumulated at the end of each season, the bottom two teams of J1 and the top two teams of J2 mutually exchange division memberships.

The soccer season is from March to November. Games are

Nakata Hidetoshi

日と土曜日を中心に試合が行われています。

　日本のサッカーも年々実力をつけて，1998年の**ワールドカップ**では本戦への出場を果たしましたし，中田英寿選手など，イタリアの有名チームで活躍するプレーヤーも生まれています。

　また，2002年のワールドカップは日韓の共同開催です。

日常の生活・習慣

Ｑ 年賀状を平均して1人何通くらい出していますか？

New Year's card

　郵政省が発売した2000年用**年賀はがき**の枚数を単純に人口で割ると1人当たり約33枚になるそうです。

　外国人の目には，なぜ正月にこんなに沢山の挨拶状を出さなければならないのか，不思議なのだそうですが，クリスマス・カードと同じと思ってもらえばいいでしょう。

　日本人にとっては，正月は大事な1年の**節目**です。その節目の時に，いつもお世話になっている人には，改めて**お礼**を言い，日ごろご無沙汰している人には，お元気ですかと相手の消息を聞き，こちらの消息を伝えるという，人と人の交流を保つために，日本では大事な習慣になっているのです。

　年賀状は12月20日までにポストに投函すると，日本全国どこでも元旦（1月1日）に配達してくれます。

played on Wednesdays and Saturdays through the season.

Japanese soccer teams have improved over the years, and a national team was finally able to qualify in the **World Cup soccer championship** games in 1998. Nakata Hidetoshi and other Japanese players have become key players on well-known Italian soccer teams.

In addition, the 2002 World Cup soccer championship is to be hosted jointly by Japan and South Korea.

Daily Life in Japan

● On the average, how many New Year's cards does a person send?

About 33 per person. That is the number attained by dividing the number of 2000 **New Year's cards** the **Ministry of Posts and Telecommunications** sold by the total population.

Foreign people might wonder why the Japanese send so many cards at New Year's, but those cards are similar to Christmas cards for the Japanese.

The New Year holidays are very important for the Japanese as a **transition period** to a new year. They use this occasion to express **gratitude** to people who have in some way helped them and to send greetings to those they rarely see, informing them of how they are doing. So it is an important custom for keeping in touch and maintaining friendships.

If cards are mailed by December 20, they will be delivered on January 1 anywhere in Japan.

Q 初詣でのご利益は何ですか?

The first visit of
the year to a shrine

　一般には，年の初めに神社で1年の無事と平安を祈願するのが初詣です。なかでも，松の内と言われる1月7日までに**七福神**（恵比寿，大黒天，毘沙門天，弁財天，布袋，福禄寿，寿老人をそれぞれお祀りしている神社）のすべてに詣でると，7種の幸福，つまり，商売繁盛，財運，戦勝運，知恵，徳望，長寿，福徳が得られるとされています。

　また，受験生やその家族が学問の神様に志望校合格を祈願したり，独身者が縁結びの神様に良縁を祈願するなど，身近で切実な**ご利益**を期待して参拝する人もいます。

Q お中元，お歳暮は，だれに何のために 贈るのですか?

Chūgen

　いずれも，日ごろお世話になっている人にお礼として贈ります。恩師，仲人，会社の上司，取引先，**習い事の先生**，親戚，離れて暮らしている両親，などです。

　お中元はもともと7月15日を指す言葉だったので，7月上旬から15日ごろまでに贈るのが適当です。

　お歳暮は，12月上旬から20日頃までに届けます。年に1度のお礼，ということであれば，お歳暮だけでもいいのです。

Q 正しいおじぎの仕方はどうするのですか?

　相手と一定の距離をおいて向かい合い，互いに上体を曲げて頭を下げるのが基本です。

• What is the benefit of visiting shrines over the New Year holidays?

Generally speaking, people visit shrines at the beginning of the year to pray for safety and peace throughout the year. Particularly it is said that if they visit the shrines of the **Seven Lucky Gods** (Ebisu, Daikokuten, Bishamonten, Benzaiten, Hotei, Fukurokuju, Jurōjin) by January 7 during the period called *matsunouchi*, they will achieve seven happinesses: business prosperity, financial gain, victory, wisdom, virtue, longevity, and good luck.

Also, some people pay visits in the hope of obtaining more direct and necessary **benefits**, such as students preparing for entrance examinations, and their families, who pray that they pass the exams, or singles who hope to find **good partner**s.

• To whom and for what reason are summer and winter gifts given?

Both are gifts to those who have taken care of the sender and are given to express gratitude to teachers, go-betweens, company supervisors, business clients, **tutors**, relatives, faraway parents, and others.

Chūgen, the word for **summer gifts**, literally means July 15, so it is appropriate to send them around the first part of July to about the 15th.

Winter gifts should be delivered between early December and December 20. When expressing gratitude once a year, the winter gift is sufficient.

• What is the correct way of bowing?

The basic way is to lower the head by bending the upper body, standing face to face with the person you're bowing to,

Bowing

頭の下げ方は，相手との関係や，その場の状況によって異なります。

女性の場合，手に何も持っていないときには，両手を重ねるように体の前で合わせておじぎをするのが普通です。

椅子に座っているときは，椅子から立ち上がって行います。また，座布団を敷いて座っている場合には，座布団から降りて行います。そのとき，体の前で畳や床に軽く両手をつきます。

また，おじぎだけですませないで，その場に応じた**挨拶の言葉**を交わすことが必要であることは，握手の場合と同じです。

Q 日本人は握手は嫌いなのですか？

欧米人の到来とともに，この握手という挨拶に日本人は出会ったわけですが，挨拶の仕方に身分の上下でさまざまな格式がある日本では，そう簡単に，異国の人の手を握るわけにはいかなかったでしょう。

しかも，日本の**封建社会**では，男女が同席をすることも，親しく言葉を交わすこともいけないとされ，まして手を握り合うことなどもってのほかとされてきましたから，女性とも握手をするなどということが，挨拶としてなじまなかったことは当然です。

現在では，欧米人と接する機会が多いビジネスマンたちは，堂々と握手をするようになりました。しかし，ふだんの生活の中で日本人同士が握手をすることは，まだまだ多いとは言えません。

leaving a certain distance in between. The degree to which one lowers one's head differs according to the relationship with the person and the situation.

Women usually put their hands one on top of the other in front of the body, and bow in this way if they are not holding anything in their hands.

If they're sitting in a chair, they stand up to bow. If they're sitting on a *zabuton*, or cushion, they move from it to bow and put both hands lightly on the *tatami* mat or on the floor in front of them when bowing.

It is also necessary to exchange appropriate **greetings** when bowing, as well as when shaking hands.

● Do Japanese dislike shaking hands?

The custom of shaking hands came to Japan from the West. At that time, it was not so easy for Japanese to shake hands with foreigners, as they had been accustomed to traditional hierarchical forms of greetings according to class.

Additionally, under the Japanese **feudal system**, men and women had been prohibited from attending the same functions or exchanging greetings in a friendly manner, so shaking hands was inconceivable. It was natural, therefore, that shaking hands with women was not easily accepted as a greeting in those days.

At present, Japanese businessmen who have many occasions to meet Westerners shake hands comfortably. However, Japanese do not shake hands frequently in daily life.

Q 挨拶のキスをすることはありますか?

　　　浮世絵の**春画**にはよく見られるように, 性愛の表現としてのキスは昔からあって,「口吸い」と呼んでいました。性愛の行為としては, 民族を問わず, 人間としてごく自然な行為なのでしょう。

　　　しかし, 挨拶のキスとなると, 握手以上に日本人には抵抗があります。テレビで, ロシア人が男性同士でもくちびるを合わせて挨拶をしたりしているのを見ますと, 日本人は唖然とします。

　　　様々なキスの習慣については外国映画で見慣れましたから, ほっぺにチュッ, という程度は, 日本人も抵抗がなくなっていますが, 自分の方から顔を寄せてくる日本人はいないと思ってください。

Q じゃんけんはどうやるのですか?

Gū

　　　じゃんけんは, 勝ち負けを決めるため用いられます。

　　　普通は片手で行い, 拳を握ったグー(石), 手のひらを開いたパー(紙), 人差し指と中指, または親指と人差し指を開いたチョキ(ハサミ)の

Choki

いずれかを「じゃんけんぽん」という掛け声とともに, 相手に見えるように出します。

Pā

　　　グーはチョキに, チョキはパーに, パーはグーに勝ちます。皆が同じものを出したりして勝負がつかなかった場合は,「あいこでしょ」と言いながらやり直します。

Q 日本人の名前には意味があるんですか?

　　　江戸時代まで, **姓(苗字)**を持つことは武士階級の**特権**でした。つまり, 庶民は弥吉とか, 梅と

● Do Japanese kiss when greeting?

As seen in the *shun-ga* (**erotic picture**), Japanese historically kissed as an expression of sexual love, which was called *kuchisui*, or "lip sucking." Kissing is a natural and universal way of expressing human sexual love.

However, Japanese are reluctant to kiss as a greeting, and prefer to shake hands. For example, a TV scene where Russian men are seen kissing on the lips as a greeting is shocking to them.

Japanese have become more accustomed to various ways of kissing through foreign movies, so they might not be surprised to be kissed lightly on the cheek as a greeting, but it's unlikely that a Japanese would go up to someone for a "greeting" kiss.

● How do you play *janken* (scissors, paper, stone)?

Janken is played to determine who wins and who loses.

It is usually played with one hand to make one of three signs at the call "*jan-ken-pon*": *Gū* (stone) is shown with the hand in a fist, *pā* (paper) is shown with the hand open wide, and *choki* (scissors) is shown with the forefinger and middle finger open, or the thumb and forefinger open.

Gū wins over *choki*, *choki* wins over *pā*, and *pā* wins over *gū*. If the players show the same sign and can't decide who wins, they repeat the motion with the call *aiko-de-sho*, which means "tie."

● Do Japanese names have meaning?

Until the Edo period (1600–1868), having a **surname** was a **privilege** given exclusively to the warrior class. Common peo-

かいう名前だけだったのです。

　ところが，明治維新の後，1875年に，全国民は必ず苗字を持つように，という法令が出されました。そこで有名な**武家**や**貴族**の名前を無断借用したり，漁師だからと魚の名前をつけたりした人もいたといいます。

　姓は，地名から由来したものが圧倒的に多いようです。また，職業によってよくみられる姓もあり，例えば，鈴木，小野は神職が多いとされています。大陸から帰化した人たちの姓などもあります。秦，宗などです。

　日本で多い名前のベスト10は，統計によって多少違いますが，佐藤，鈴木，高橋，伊藤，渡辺，斎藤，田中，小林，佐々木，山本で，佐藤さん，鈴木さんは全国で200万人ずつくらいいるそうです。

Q 日本人はどんな花や植物が好きですか？

　こんなデータがあります。1998年に日本で卸売りされた花の本数の概算です。第1位は**キク**で20億本，第2位はカーネーションで6億本，第3位はバラで4億5000万本，第4位はユリで2億本です。

　キクの使用量が多いのは，法事などで仏前に捧げる花はキクが主体だからです。カーネーションは，母の日に母親にあげるという習慣があり，このためにも消費量が多いのです。

　しかし，**いろんな**層の人たちの好みとしては，バラ，ユリなどを挙げる人が多いようです。

　それから，忘れてならない花は桜です。春になると，日本人の多くは，桜の花を求めて野山

ple only had a first name, such as Yakichi or Ume.

However, in 1875 the Meiji government enacted a law requiring all citizens to have surnames. Some borrowed names of famous **warriors** or **aristocrats**, and others used the names of fish because they were fishermen.

A great majority of family names are derived from place names. Some names represent occupations. For example, Suzuki and Ono are common for people with ancestors engaged in jobs related to shrines. Hata and Sō are names of people from the Asian continent who were nationalized as Japanese citizens.

The ten most common Japanese names in descending order are Satō, Suzuki, Takahashi, Itō, Watanabe, Saitō, Tanaka, Kobayashi, Sasaki, and Yamamoto. There are about 2 million Satōs and 2 million Suzukis in Japan.

● What kinds of plants are popular with Japanese?

According to a rough calculation of the total number of flowers sold domestically by flower wholesalers in 1998, **chrysanthemums** were ranked at the top with sales of 2 billion, carnations took second place with 600 million, roses took the third place with 450 million, and lilies came in fourth place with 200 million.

One of the reasons why the figure for chrysanthemums is so high is that they are often used as offerings before the graves of the deceased in Buddhist rites. Carnations are popular flowers on Mother's Day.

Roses and lilies are generally liked by people of **all walks of life**.

When one talks about flowers the Japanese enjoy, one cannot forget cherry blossoms. In spring, people go out to moun-

や公園にくり出します。そして，桜の花の下で宴会を開きます。この「花見」という言葉の花は，何の花と言わないでも，桜の花をさしているくらいです。

Q 日本人はどんな動物が好きですか？

身近の動物としてなら，やはり，イヌとネコということになるでしょう。ペットフード工業会の調査によれば，1998年に，日本では，イヌが990万匹，ネコは610万匹ほどが飼われています。

今は生息数が少なくなってしまいましたが，日本人にはキツネとタヌキもなじみのある動物でした。昔は，変身して人をだますと言われ，たくさんの伝説や昔話に登場しています。

Raccoon dog

Q 松，竹，梅，鶴，亀がめでたいと言われる理由は何ですか？

松，竹，梅を**めでたいもの**とする考えは，もともとは中国のものでした。

中国では，冬の厳しい寒さにも負けずに葉の緑を保つ松，竹と，春に他のものに先がけて花を開く梅を，**高潔・節操・清純**のシンボルとしてとらえたのです。この考え方が日本に入ってきたのは，8世紀の奈良時代だと言われています。

また，鶴は優雅な姿をしていること，亀は寿命が長いことから，**おめでたい生き物**とされるのです。「鶴は千年，亀は万年」というたとえがあります。

Cranes

tains and parks to see cherry blossoms and have parties under cherry trees. Whenever one goes "**flower viewing**," one does not need to mention which flower will be viewed.

● What kind of animals are popular in Japan?

As for **domesticated animals**, dogs and cats are undoubtedly the most popular. According to a 1998 survey by the Pet Food Manufacturers Association there are 9.9 million dogs and 6.1 million cats in Japanese homes.

In legends and fairy tales, foxes and *tanuki* (a type of raccoon) have long been familiar to the Japanese. In olden times, these animals were believed to trick people by disguising themselves. Today the numbers of both these wild animals are dwindling.

● Why do the Japanese believe that pine trees, bamboos, plum trees, cranes, and tortoises are symbols of happiness and good luck?

The idea of cherishing pine trees, bamboos and plum trees as **symbols of happiness and good luck** originally came from China.

Pine trees and bamboos maintain their green leaves even in the severest cold of winter, and plum blossoms bloom long before spring starts. Therefore, the Chinese regarded them as symbols of **nobleness**, **integrity**, and **purity**. The Japanese imported this idea from China in the Nara period, around the eighth century.

Cranes and tortoises are considered **blessed animals** because the former have graceful figures and the latter live a long time. There is a saying that goes "Cranes live for a thousand years, and tortoises for ten thousand years."

Q 日本人に人気のある占いは何ですか？

Fortune teller

　昔からあるのは，暦法(れきほう)と**おみくじ**です。暦法は暮らしの**行動基準**やその日の吉凶などを記したカレンダーの一種，おみくじは神仏に祈願して吉凶を占うくじです。

　また，名前に使われる文字の**画数**から，その人の人生，性格，職業，対人関係などを占う姓名判断も古くから行われています。生まれてきた子供が運勢に恵まれるよう，つける名前の画数を気にする親は今も多く，そのための本も多く売られています。

　よく話題になるのは**星座占い**と**血液型占い**の2つです。特に星座占いは女性に人気です。最近では，東西南北を基準にした方角で占う**風水**が，ちょっとしたブームになっています。

　血液型占いとは，血液型によって人の性格は，異なっており，そこから人と人との相性や運勢を占う，というものですが，実は日本だけの人気のようです。血液型は遺伝しますが，それが性格を左右するかどうか，医学的にはまったく証明されていません。

Q 十二支とは何ですか？

　時刻や方角を12に分けて，それぞれに動物の名前をあてたものです。すべての時間は12を単位として移り変わるとした古代中国の考えか

• What forms of fortune-telling are popular among the Japanese?

Traditional fortune-telling is done using a special calendar and **written oracles**. The calendar indicates the **norms** for living and the fortune of the day. Written oracles are fortunes which people draw, praying to the gods or to Buddha for good luck.

From ancient times, there has been a type of divination known as *seimei handan*, which purports to give information about a person's life, character, occupation, personal relations, etc., based on the **number of strokes** in the Chinese characters that form the person's name. Even today there are many parents who pay attention to the number of strokes in the names they give to their children to improve the chances of good fortune. Many books are sold on the subject.

Also, two kinds of fortune-telling which have become popular topics of conversation these days are **horoscopes** and **fortune-telling by blood type**. Horoscopes are particularly popular among women. Recently, *feng shui* (wind and water), which tells fortunes based on direction, has become very popular.

Fortune-telling by blood type is based on the assumption that people have different characters according to their blood type. Some blood types reportedly harmonize well with others and bring good luck. This style of fortune-telling seems to be popular only in Japan. Blood type is inherited, but whether it can help categorize or define people's characters cannot be proved medically.

• What are the twelve zodiac signs?

The signs come from dividing time and direction into 12 blocks, each being given the name of an animal based on the ancient Chinese concept that time moves based on these 12

らきており，日本では12年を一回りとして各年に動物をあてたものが一般によく知られています。

　　12の動物というのは順番に子(ネズミ)，丑(牛)，寅(虎)，卯(兎)，辰(竜)，巳(蛇)，午(馬)，未(羊)，申(猿)，酉(鳥)，戌(犬)，亥(猪)です。生まれた年の動物によって，その人の**性格**や**運勢**が決まると言われています。ちなみに，2000年は辰，つまり竜の年です。

Q 「仏滅」とか「友引」というのは
何ですか?

　　これは『六曜』というものからきており，先勝・友引・先負・仏滅・大安・赤口という6種類の運勢が，毎日順番に現れてくるという，江戸時代からの信仰です。そもそもは中国から来た**歴法**です。

　　それぞれに幸運，不運がついていて，例えば仏滅は最悪の日なので，この日に結婚式を行うことは嫌われます。幸運な日とされる大安と比べると，結婚式の数は3分の1くらいになってしまいます。

　　また友引は良くも悪くもない日ですが，文字通り「友達を引っぱってしまう」というので，この日に葬式をすることは嫌われます。もちろん**科学的な根拠**はないのですが，この**俗信**は現代でも**根強い力**を持っています。

Q 日本伝承の妖怪には
どんなものがいますか?

　　愉快な妖怪が多数いますが，代表選手としていくつかを紹介するに止めます。

　　まず「河童」です。4，5歳の子供ぐらいの大

units. In Japan, most people are familiar with this 12-year cycle and the series of 12 animals, one allotted to each year.

The 12 animals are: mouse, cow, tiger, rabbit, dragon, snake, horse, sheep, monkey, bird, dog, and boar, each determining the **character** and **destiny** of a person born in that year. For example, the year 2000 is the year of the dragon.

● What are *butsumetsu* (Buddha's death) and *tomobiki* (trail days)?

These days originated from the *rokuyō* (six days) cycle, a concept from the Edo period (1603–1868) in which six different fortunes succeed each other in this order: *Senshō*, *Tomobiki*, *Sempu*, *Butsumetsu*, *Taian*, and *Shakku*. This is a kind of **fortune-telling calendar** which came from China.

Each day has its advantages and disadvantages, but *butsumetsu* is considered the worst day, so people avoid holding weddings on that day. The number of weddings on *butsumetsu* is about a third of those held on the good luck day of *taian*.

Tomobiki is neither a good nor a bad day, but it literally means "pull away friends," so people do not like to have funerals on this day. There are no **scientific grounds** for these **folk beliefs**, but they have a **deep-rooted influence**, even today.

● What ghosts or spirits are common in Japanese folklore?

There are many comical and mischievous spirits. Here are a few:

The first is a *kappa*, or water sprite, which is as tall as a

きさで，背中に**甲羅**があり，頭に水が入った皿があり，手足に**ひれ**があります。水陸両棲です。

「鬼」は身長が2.5m以上もあり，体の色は赤，青，黒などがあります。頭には2本の**角**があり，好きな食べ物は人間！

「天狗」は長い鼻を持ち，顔は真っ赤です。<ruby>山伏<rt>やまぶし</rt></ruby>の姿をして高い**下駄**をはいています。子供をさらって行きます。

「一つ目小僧」は，文字通り顔の真ん中に大きな目が1つ。悪い**いたずら**はしません。

「海坊主」はぬるぬるした大きい頭を持ち，海の中から顔を出します。**船員**たちは海坊主を見ても，知らん顔をしなければなりません。そうしないと，船を沈められてしまいます。

「雪女」は，雪の夜に白い着物を着て現れる雪の精です。

日本の妖怪たち
Japanese ghosts or spirits

天狗
Tengu

一つ目小僧
Hitotsume-kozō

鬼
Oni

four- or five-year-old child. It has a **shell** on its back, a dish with water on top of its head, and **fins** on its hands and feet. It lives both on land and in water.

Oni, or demons, are taller than 2.5 meters (8.2 feet) and their bodies are red, blue or black. They have two **horns** protruding from their heads. Their favorite food is human beings!

A *tengu*, or goblin, has a long nose and a very red face. It wears the costume of a *yamabushi*, or **mountain priest**, and tall *geta* (**wooden clogs**). It kidnaps children.

A *hitotsume-kozō*, a one-eyed goblin, literally has a large eye in the center of its face and does not play **tricks**.

An *umi-bōzu*, a sea goblin, has a big, slimy head which sticks out from the sea. **A ship's crew** should ignore it if they find it in the sea. If they do not, it will sink the ship.

A *yuki-onna*, or snow woman, is a snow spirit who appears in a white *kimono* **on snowy nights**.

河童
Kappa

海坊主
Umi-bōzu

雪女
Yuki-onna

索引
INDEX

日本語索引 • JAPANESE INDEX

英語索引 • ENGLISH INDEX

増補改訂第 2 版
英語で話す「日本」Q&A
Talking About Japan *Updated* Q&A

2000年 6 月 9 日　第 1 刷発行

編　著　　講談社インターナショナル株式会社
　　　　　株式会社　翻訳情報センター

発行者　　野間佐和子

発行所　　講談社インターナショナル株式会社
　　　　　〒112-8652　東京都文京区音羽 1-17-14
　　　　　電話：03-3944-6493（編集部）
　　　　　　　　03-3944-6492（業務部・営業部）

印刷所　　大日本印刷株式会社

製本所　　大日本印刷株式会社

落丁本、乱丁本は、講談社インターナショナル業務部宛にお送りください。送料小
社負担にてお取替えいたします。なお、この本についてのお問い合わせは、編集
部宛にお願いいたします。本書の無断複写（コピー）は著作権法上での例外を除き、
禁じられています。

定価はカバーに表示してあります。

ISBN4-7700-2568-8

対訳 英語で話す日本経済 Q & A
A Bilingual Guide to the Japanese Economy

NHK国際放送局経済プロジェクト・大和総研経済調査部 編　　　ISBN 4-7700-1942-4
46判（128 x 188 mm）仮製　368ページ

NHK国際放送で好評を得た番組が本になりました。クイズと会話形式で楽しく読んでいくうちに、日本経済の仕組が分かり、同時に英語にも強くなっていきます。日本語と英語の対応がひと目で分かる編集上の工夫もいっぱい。

対訳 おくのほそ道
The Narrow Road to Oku

松尾芭蕉 著　ドナルド・キーン 訳　宮田雅之 切り絵　　　ISBN 4-7700-2028-7
A5判変型（140 x 226 mm）仮製 188ページ（カラー口絵41点）

古典文学の最高峰のひとつ「おくのほそ道」を、ドナルド・キーンが新訳しました。画家、宮田雅之が精魂を込めた切り絵の魅力とあいまって、この名作に新しい生命が吹き込まれた、必読の1冊です。

対訳 竹取物語
The Tale of the Bamboo Cutter

川端康成 現代語訳　ドナルド・キーン 英訳　宮田雅之 切り絵　　ISBN 4-7700-2329-4
A5判変型　横長（226 x 148 mm）仮製　箱入り　180ページ　（カラー口絵16点）

ノーベル賞作家の現代語訳と傑出した芸術家の作品、そして日本文学の研究に一生を捧げたジャパノロジストの翻訳が合体した、大人のための「竹取物語」。

バイリンガル とってもかんたんマイレシピ
Stone Soup : Easy Japanese Home Cooking

渡辺節子 著　　B5判変型（189 x 257 mm）仮製　256ページ　ISBN 4-7700-2061-9

手軽な日本の家庭料理、わが家の味160品目の作り方を英語と日本語で紹介したクッキングブック。作り方や調理器具などのイラスト付き、カロリー計算・調理時間もひと目で分かります。

対訳 日本事典
The Kodansha Bilingual Encyclopedia of Japan

講談社インターナショナル 編　　　　　　　　　　　ISBN 4-7700-2130-5
B5判（182 x 257 mm）　　上製　箱入り　944ページ（カラー口絵16ページ）

「日本」を国際的な視点で理解できる幅広い知識と、実用的な英語が身につきます。ビジネス、海外駐在、留学、ホームステイなど、さまざまな国際交流の場で、幅広くご活用いただけます。

- 現代の政治制度、最新の経済情報を豊富に記載し、日本を総合的に理解できる。
- 分野別の構成により、テーマに沿って自然に読み進むことができる。
- 豊富なイラストと図版を収録し、完全対訳のレイアウトと欄外のキーワードで、重要単語や表現の日英相互参照に便利。
- 日本国憲法、重要な国際条約、年表をいずれも日英併記で巻末に収録。
- 英語からも日本語（ローマ字）からも引けるインデックスつき。

内容構成：地理／歴史／政治／経済／社会／文化／生活

講談社バイリンガル・ブックス

英語で読んでも面白い！

- 楽しく読めて自然に英語が身に付く日英対訳表記
- 実用から娯楽まで読者の興味に応える多彩なテーマ
- 重要単語、表現法が一目で分かる段落対応レイアウト

46判変型 (113 x 188 mm) 仮製

講談社バイリンガル・ブックス （オン・カセット/オンCD） 英語で聞いても面白い！

 印のタイトルは、英文テキスト部分を録音したカセット・テープが、また 印のタイトルは英文テキスト部分を録音したCDが発売されています。本との併用により聞く力・話す力を高め、実用的な英語が身につく格好のリスニング教材です。

講談社バイリンガル・コミックス

吹き出しのセリフは英語、コマの外にオリジナル版の日本語を添えた画期的なレイアウトで、原作のもつ雰囲気と面白さはそのまま。楽しく読みながら英語の勉強になる!

46判変型 (113 x 188 mm) 仮製

元気いっぱい、さくらちゃんです。
英語でもおもろいで〜

バイリンガル版
カードキャプターさくら
Cardcaptor Sakura

CLAMP 著

第 1 巻　　　192ページ　　　ISBN 4-7700-2644-7

国内にとどまらず海外でも大人気の「金田一君」

バイリンガル版
金田一少年の事件簿
The New Kindaichi Files

金成陽三郎 原作　　さとうふみや 漫画

第 1 巻	オペラ座館殺人事件		
	192ページ	ISBN 4-7700-2599-8	
第 2 巻	異人館村殺人事件		
	192ページ	ISBN 4-7700-2600-5	
第 3 巻	雪夜叉伝説殺人事件		
	176ページ	ISBN 4-7700-2601-3	
第 4 巻	雪夜叉伝説殺人事件・解決編		
	160ページ	ISBN 4-7700-2669-2	

ドラマ、アニメ、映画と絶好調の「鬼塚先生」

バイリンガル版
GTO
Great Teacher Onizuka

藤沢とおる 著

第 1 巻　　　192ページ　　　ISBN 4-7700-2602-1
第 2 巻　　　192ページ　　　ISBN 4-7700-2603-X
第 3 巻　　　192ページ　　　ISBN 4-7700-2604-8

講談社バイリンガル・コミックス

恋も仕事も絶好調！
ムリなく楽しく英語が話せる

バイリンガル版
部長 島耕作
Division Chief Kosaku Shima

弘兼憲史 著

| 第 1 巻 | 176ページ | ISBN 4-7700-2633-1 |
| 第 2 巻 | 128ページ | ISBN 4-7700-2634-X |

アラ、こんなに楽しくて、ごめんあそばせ。英語で笑う

対訳 サザエさん（全12巻）
The Wonderful World of Sazae-san

長谷川町子 著　ジュールス・ヤング 訳

第 1 巻	170ページ	ISBN 4-7700-2075-9
第 2 巻	168ページ	ISBN 4-7700-2093-7
第 3 巻	198ページ	ISBN 4-7700-2094-5
第 4 巻	164ページ	ISBN 4-7700-2149-6
第 5 巻	176ページ	ISBN 4-7700-2150-X
第 6 巻	160ページ	ISBN 4-7700-2151-8
第 7 巻	168ページ	ISBN 4-7700-2152-6
第 8 巻	168ページ	ISBN 4-7700-2153-4
第 9 巻	172ページ	ISBN 4-7700-2154-2
第10巻	172ページ	ISBN 4-7700-2155-0
第11巻	176ページ	ISBN 4-7700-2156-9
第12巻	168ページ	ISBN 4-7700-2157-7
化粧箱入り全12巻セット		ISBN 4-7700-2435-5

英語でOLしてみない !?

対訳 OL進化論
Survival in the Office

秋月 りす 著

第 1 巻	144ページ	ISBN 4-7700-2390-1
第 2 巻	144ページ	ISBN 4-7700-2501-7
第 3 巻	144ページ	ISBN 4-7700-2502-5
第 4 巻	144ページ	ISBN 4-7700-2695-1

英文書がスラスラ読める「ルビ訳」

The word *rubi* in the phrase "*rubi* translation" is derived from the name of a precious stone, the ruby. European type sizes were formerly assigned such fanciful names, and "ruby" indicated the small size of 5.5 points. In this series, difficult English words are glossed in *rubi* so that readers can fully enjoy the book without continual reference to a dictionary.

「ルビ訳」とは？ 「わかりにくい単語・イディオム・言い回しには、ルビ（ふりがな）のように訳がつく」——これが「ルビ訳」です。疑問をその場で解決し、最後までどんどん読み進むことができます。必要なとき以外は本文に集中できるよう、実物では「ルビ訳」の部分が薄いグリーンで印刷されています。

- 文脈がつかみやすく、「飛ばし読み」「中断・再開」してもストーリーが追えます。
- 自分なりの訳が組みたてられ、読解力がつきます。
- 基本的に辞書は不要。短時間で読み終えることができます。

46判変型（113 x 188 mm）仮製

講談社ルビー・ブックス

シャーロック・ホームズ全集
（全14巻）

コナン・ドイル 著

小林 司・東山あかね 作品解説

実用英語の総合シリーズ

- 旅行・留学からビジネスまで、コミュニケーションの現場で役立つ「実用性」
- ニューヨーク、ロンドンの各拠点での、ネイティブ チェックにより保証される「信頼性」
- 英語の主要ジャンルを網羅し、目的に応じた本選びができる「総合性」

46判変型 (113 x 188 mm) 仮製

8 マナー違反の英会話　英語にだって「敬語」があります

ジェームス・M・バーダマン、森本豊富 共著　　　208ページ　ISBN 4-7700-2520-3

英語にだって「敬語」はあります。「アメリカ人はフランクで開放的」と言われていますが、お互いを傷つけないように非常に気配りをしています。しかし親しい仲間うちで丁寧な英語表現ばかりを使っていては、打ち解けられません。英語にだってTPOがあります。

9 英語で「四字熟語」365　英語にするとこんなにカンタン！

松野守峰、N・ミナイ 共著　　　272ページ　ISBN 4-7700-2466-5

四字熟語をマスターし、その英語表現によってボキャブラリーも急増する一石二鳥のおトクな1冊！　日常よく使われる365の四字熟語を「努力・忍耐」「チームワーク」「苦境」「性格」「能力」「友情」「恋愛」「宿命」などの意味別に分類し、英語にしました。

10 「英語モード」で英会話　これがネイティブの発想法

脇山 怜、佐野キム・マリー 共著　　　224ページ　ISBN 4-7700-2522-X

日本では、へりくだって相手を持ち上げることが処世術。しかし、「未経験で何もわかりませんがよろしく」のつもりで "I am inexperienced and I don't know anything." なんて英語圏で言えば、それはマイナスイメージ。英語でコミュニケーションをするときは、日本語から英語へ「モード」のスイッチを切り替えましょう。

11 英語で読む「科学ニュース」　話題の知識を英語でGet！

松野守峰 著　　　208ページ　ISBN 4-7700-2456-8

科学に関する知識とことばが同時に身につく、画期的な英語実用書！「ネット恐怖症族」「スマート・マウスパッド」から「デザイナー・ドラッグ」「DNAによる全人類の祖先解明」まで、いま話題の科学情報が英語でスラスラ読めるようになります。

12 CDブック 英会話・ぜったい・音読　頭の中に英語回路を作る本

國弘正雄 編　千田潤一 トレーニング指導　　　144ページ CD(40分)付　ISBN 4-7700-2459-2

英語を身につけるには、英語の基礎回路を作ることが先決です。英語を身体で覚える…、それには、何と言っても音読です。本書には、中学3年生用の英語教科書から、成人の英語トレーニングに適した12レッスンを厳選して収録しました。だまされたと思って、まずは3ヵ月続けてみてください。確かな身体の変化にきっと驚かれることでしょう。

13 英語のサインを読む　アメリカ生活情報早わかりマニュアル

清地恵美子 著　　　240ページ　ISBN 4-7700-2519-X

広告や看板の読み方がわかると、アメリカの英語と暮らしが見えてきます。「スーパーのチラシに$2.99Lb.とあるけど」、「コインランドリーを使いたいのだけれど」。本書では自動販売機の使い方、案内板や利用説明書の読み方など、生活情報入手のコツを紹介します。

14 産直！ ビジネス英語　NY発、朝から夜までの英会話

藤松忠夫 著　　　224ページ　ISBN 4-7700-2458-4

英語がベラベラしゃべれるだけでは、NYでビジネスは出来ません。会議を司会する、人事考課の評定を部下に納得させる、ビジネスランチを成功させる、効果的に情報を入手するなど……。これらが英語でちゃんと出来て、あなたは初めて一人前です。それには、アメリカ人の常識・習慣・考え方を知ったうえで適切な英語表現を身につけることが欠かせません。

15 A or B？ ネイティブ英語　日本人の勘違い150パターン

ジェームス・M・バーダマン 著　　　192ページ　ISBN 4-7700-2708-7

日本人英語には共通の「アキレス腱」があります。アメリカ人の筆者が、身近でもっとも頻繁に見聞きする、日本人英語の間違い・勘違いを約150例、一挙にまとめて解説しました。間違いを指摘し、背景を解説するだけでなく、実践的な例文・関連表現も盛り込みましたので、日本人共通の弱点を克服できます。

あなたの英語が変わる
講談社パワー・イングリッシュ

これを英語で言えますか？

学校で教えてくれない身近な英単語

四捨五入する	round off
5^2	five squared
モーニングコール	wake-up call
ホチキス	stapler
改札口	ticket gate
昇進	promotion
協調介入	coordinated intervention
貸し渋り	credit crunch
介護保険	nursing care insurance
花粉症	hay fever
朝飯前だよ	That's a piece of cake!

講談社インターナショナル 編
232ページ
ISBN 4-7700-2132-1

日本人英語の盲点になっている英単語に、78のジャンルから迫ります。読んでみれば、「なーんだ、こんなやさしい単語だったのか」、「そうか、こう言えば良かったのか」と思いあたる単語や表現がいっぱいです。雑学も満載しましたので、忘れていた単語が生き返ってくるだけでなく、覚えたことが記憶に残ります。弱点克服のボキャビルに最適です。